The British Pop Music Film

The British Pop Music Film

The Beatles and Beyond

Stephen Glynn

First published 2013 by
PALGRAVE MACMILLAN

Palgrave Macmillan in the UK is an imprint of Macmillan Publishers Limited, registered in England, company number 785998, of Houndmills, Basingstoke, Hampshire RG21 6XS.

Palgrave Macmillan in the US is a division of St Martin's Press LLC, 175 Fifth Avenue, New York, NY 10010.

Palgrave Macmillan is the global academic imprint of the above companies and has companies and representatives throughout the world.

Palgrave® and Macmillan® are registered trademarks in the United States, the United Kingdom, Europe and other countries.

ISBN 978-0-230-39222-9

This book is printed on paper suitable for recycling and made from fully managed and sustained forest sources. Logging, pulping and manufacturing processes are expected to conform to the environmental regulations of the country of origin.

A catalogue record for this book is available from the British Library.

A catalog record for this book is available from the Library of Congress.

Typeset by MPS Limited, Chennai, India.

Contents

List of Illustrations

Acknowledgements

I am grateful to my editors at Palgrave, Felicity Plester and Catherine Mitchell, for their patience and wise counsel on this commission, and to Professor Steve Chibnall at DMU for his sensible advice and, not least, for letting me loose on his treasured collection of *Kinematograph Weekly*. The sections presented here on the Beatles amend and update work published elsewhere and I am grateful to I.B. Tauris, *The Journal of Popular British Cinema* and WVT for permission to rework this material.

I am (perhaps) fortunate in having a brother as a film/media academic: for Basil's example and innumerable leads I am deeply appreciative, as I am to my parents for their constant support. Above all I would like to thank Sarah and Roz, who have never watched (and I am sure never will watch) a Tommy Steele or Cliff Richard movie, yet who have encouraged/endured me throughout the years of talking about and finally working on this book. I dedicate this volume to them.

1
Introduction: Genre, Academia and the British Pop Music Film

Generic focus

Roughly halfway through Terence Fisher's *Kill Me Tomorrow* (1957), a low-budget Renown film shot in London and starring Pat O'Brien as a reporter needing cash to fund his son's eye operation, the hero discusses with the leader of a diamond-smuggling racket how much they would pay him to take the blame for a murder he saw them commit. This key scene, where morality cedes to money, is set in a dimly lit coffee bar, already a short-hand site for youthful anomie, deviancy and promiscuity. The nefariousness of the setting is underlined by the presence of a singer-guitarist: as the plot negotiates its major development, the camera diverts our attention onto Britain's first rock'n'roll star, Tommy Steele, singing snatches of 'Rebel Rock' to a young and enthusiastic audience. While O'Brien exchanges his good name for the sake of his son's health, Tommy is engendering teenage obstruction and ingratitude. 'Are you ready, rebel?' he sings, before presenting his strategy of non-cooperation: 'If they're gonna ask you nice, / Make them have to ask you twice. / Have a heart of ice / When you're at home.' The first film appearance of a British Rocker is simultaneously the focus for teenage energy and the voice of anti-parental rebellion. This fresh if uneasy relationship between the cinema and the teenager that Fisher's February release narratively illustrates had, on a broader scale, already been musically brokered with the January announcement that Steele would star imminently in a semi-biographical feature film.[1] The British pop music film was about to be born.

Kill Me Tomorrow is remembered, if at all, for Steele's brief screen debut,[2] but the cinematic sub-genre that it heralded is the focus of this study. The film's yoking of an ageing American star with an emergent indigenous crowd-puller carries both economic and ideological import and enacts in microcosm many of the competing factors that would shape the British pop music film genre. Indeed, this initial employment of British rock'n'roll mirrors the tensions that have historically existed in British cinema, between trying to emulate increasingly dominant American cultural forms and to build on declining indigenous traditions of popular culture. These tensions are inevitably translated into production and marketing strategies, but also inform generic development, which this study will trace. It therefore involves a *diachronic* investigation of generic roots and industrial interpenetration, especially the relationship to the American film musical and the developing pop music industry, and analyses the production ideology and working practices of filmmakers. A survey of the critical and popular reception of key pop music films, and how this fed into the success of associated musical product, is surrounded by a close analysis of the films themselves from both contextual and textual viewpoints. This *synchronic* textual approach will focus on the films' visual style and their narrative ideologies including, where appropriate, the construction of a national variant on the musical genre. This is necessarily informed by the contextual approach, since any analysis of popular music's visual grammar must be sensitive to the economic, institutional and social factors that shape its development as a cultural form. Indeed, particular to this sub-genre is the *necessity* of immediacy, with many judging the music and its stars an ephemeral phenomenon needing instant exploitation. In brief, this genre study will illustrate the institutional relationships between film and popular music and the manner in which the visual representations of pop have been inserted into a matrix of economic, socio-cultural and aesthetic ideologies.

Genre terminology and empirical parameters

This study is purposefully named 'The British Pop Music Film' since 'pop' is understood as more broadly inclusive of the competing musical styles encountered from 1956 onwards *and*, although the terms rock'n'roll, rock, prog, punk, reggae and hip hop can be used in an oppositional, even antagonistic sense, 'pop' indicates the dominant direction that these styles inevitably take.[3] The British 'pop music' film's life-span is roughly concurrent with what Arthur Marwick has termed 'the long sixties'.[4] For Marwick 'some time between the early fifties and the early seventies a "cultural revolution" took place in Britain' resulting in the creation of distinctive cultural artefacts including 'pop music (above all)'.[5] Marwick points out the binary oppositions with which the new music was involved: 'The central feature, undoubtedly, of the cultural revolution was the transformation of the popular music scene ... It sprang out of the separate culture of youth, yet it depended upon the spending power of the affluent teenager. It expressed protest against established society and the organised music industry, yet it became a massive commercial enterprise. It was genuinely innovative musically, yet it spawned a mass of repetitive trivia.'[6] Throughout the 'long sixties' a further duality saw youth both celebrated as the harbingers to an exciting and prosperous future and/or condemned as exemplifying a new moral and cultural bankruptcy. They are key motifs around which dominant interpretations of social change were formulated, and British pop music films work within the dynamic of these twin tropes, the thesis, antithesis and final synthesis of what Dick Hebdige has termed 'youth-as-fun' and 'youth-as-trouble'.[7]

Attempts to define a generic taxonomy are notoriously difficult. Christine Gledhill notes that there are no 'rigid rules of inclusion and exclusion' and that genres 'are not discrete systems, consisting of a fixed number of listable items'.[8] A flexible model notwithstanding, empirical assumptions need to operate and this study addresses a comparatively narrow range of films in which British 'pop' musicians star and in which their music features diegetically:[9] these *pre-existent* pop stars will be seen to offer both an ideological reading to the viewer and an economic spin-off to the industry. As such, this study will not explore pop music's contribution to mainstream film scoring: therefore while John Barry's appearance and performance in *Beat Girl* (1959) will be analysed, his work for Bond movies will not and, while their music contributes significantly to the feel of their respective film vehicles, Traffic do not appear in *Here We Go Round the Mulberry Bush* (Clive Donner, 1967), nor do Manfred Mann in *Poor Cow* (Ken Loach, 1967): their music is not a vehicle to enhance the musicians' iconic status, nor does it make a direct narrative contribution to the film. David Bowie's 'straight' acting roles either side of *Absolute Beginners* (1986), as in *The Man Who Fell to Earth* (Nicolas Roeg, 1976) and *Basquiat* (Julian Schnabel, 1996), are omitted since Bowie does not sing in the course of these films – hence they cannot be categorised as pop music films. In addition, this study has limited its scope to fictional and narrative films, partly because documentaries – such as concert films aka 'rockumentaries' – necessitate a different set of generic criteria already rehearsed elsewhere,[10] but mainly, agreeing with the editors of *Celluloid Jukebox*, because of a 'belief in pop itself as a form of fiction making'.[11]

The intended advantage of this precise categorisation and systematic approach is to avoid the overriding weakness in film genre study, notable from André Bazin and Robert Warshow's pioneering essays on the western and gangster film respectively,[12] which is termed by Barry Langford as 'endemic critical selectivity'.[13] Conversely, a cursory glance at the music film output of Elvis Presley[14] illustrates Steve Neale's claim that many films demonstrate a degree of 'overlap' between genres.[15] For Andrew Caine 'the pop film constitutes the definitive hybrid form of production'[16] and several of the musical films under discussion here could also be classified as British examples of the biopic, the social-problem film, exploitation cinema, comedies, the faux documentary, even a gangster film. It is for this reason that the term 'pop music film' is employed in this study rather than the generically 'purer' term 'musical'.

Genre and the problems of definition

Genre remains a troublesome constant in film studies. Is it a theoretical concept of analysis or a function of industry and market forces? Does it work to ease or restrict the changes in national cultural forms? Is it best assessed as a product or a process? Rick Altman explains genre as a polyvalent concept: it acts as a blueprint, 'a formula that precedes, programmes and patterns industry production'; as a structure, 'the formal framework on which individual films are founded'; as a label, 'the name of a category central to the decisions and communications of distributors and exhibitors'; and as a contract, 'the viewing position required by each genre film of its audience'.[17] Steve Neale concurs, seeing genres as a kind of 'systematised articulation' that 'are not to be seen as forms of textual codifications, but as systems of orientations, expectations and conventions that circulate between industry, text and subject'.[18] This study will replicate this tripartite structure for its case studies, investigating production histories (including marketing), the film texts and their consumption.

The latter category extends beyond Neale's industrial emphasis to recognise how critics, spectators and cultist fans, alongside production publicists, contribute to the 'intertextual relay' in which any film is embedded and its genre status established.[19] Generic marketing can thus be categorised as 'all the different discourses of hype that surround the launching of a film product onto the market, while consumption refers not just to audience practices but also to practices of critics and reviewers'.[20] While it will collate trade and national press reviews to demonstrate the 'parental' culture's critical reaction to 'youthful' pop music films, this study will not elaborate the role of taste formations among critics and audiences since this area has been explored in detail by Andrew Caine's *Interpreting Rock Movies*, using the critical framework of Pierre Bourdieu's *Distinction*.[21] I follow Caine in defining the genre as housing films that 'all starred figures who were primarily pop artists rather than actors'[22] but believe that extensive/exclusive scrutiny of these intertextual relays can lead genre criticism away from the film text itself, which this study sees as central to its dual investigation of the genre's formal and socio-historical import.

Genre and life-cycles

Literary theorist Franco Moretti offers a beneficial metaphor for genres when he calls them 'Janus-like creatures, with one face turned towards history and the other to form'.[23] Commenting on Moretti, Andrew Dix advocates that genre critics should 'turn cubist themselves, looking both at sets of formal conventions that define different film-types and at what these conventions signify historically'.[24] Formal conventions and historical significance constitute the twin concerns of this study. Dix understands that his elaboration of this metaphor introduces 'a false dichotomy between form and history' since formal or internal elements of a genre are not separate from historical processes but are imbued with them: genre criticism, he concludes, should be 'historicist through and through'.[25] While genres were traditionally seen as fixed forms, media theory increasingly regards them as dynamic in form and function. For David Buckingham 'genre is not ... simply "given" by the culture: rather it is in a constant process of negotiation and change'.[26] A tripartite schema to describe this process has proven very popular in genre studies. For Thomas Schatz a genre's three stages are 'experimental' before it has a recognisable self-identity, 'classical' when its conventions are stable and most coherent, and 'formalist' when its original purpose has been outlived and its conventions are openly quoted, even parodied.[27] Richard Dyer proposes a comparable directory of 'primitive', 'mature' and 'decadent' phases, though his labels could be said to add an air of moral judgement to Schatz's aesthetic-based terminology. 'The first shows the genre in embryonic form, the second the full realisation of its expressive potential and the third a reflective self-consciousness about the genre itself.'[28] It has proven an enduring concept: Jane Feuer,[29] John G. Cawelti,[30] and Brian Taves[31] all discuss how genres develop, become articulate and self-conscious until, predictable and worn-out, they self-destruct. There is, of course, a danger in this model sketching a single line of development, not allowing for deviant films 'mature' before their time or still 'primitive' when the genre has moved on. Nonetheless, this 'biological' model of a generic life-cycle is a paradigm highly pertinent to the pop music film which, perhaps more than other genres, has to be sensitive to and is susceptible to cyclical trends, being deeply rooted within a distinct cultural timeframe. Over a dozen years the British pop music film allows us to see the unfolding of the full life-cycle of a distinct sub-genre, beginning with the uncertain steps to ape or shape existing codes and conventions (1956–64), followed by the establishment of a more expressive, culturally varied format, one inclusive of a critical self-questioning (1964–67), and finally its deconstruction, a changing of its orientation from a narcissistic over-the-counter 'gospel of happiness'[32] to a politicised tract with counter-cultural aspirations (1967–70). Employing Dyer's terminology, this study will structure the British pop music film into 'primitive', 'mature' and 'decadent' phases. Thereafter, the genre shows occasional spasms of resuscitation, a lengthy if intermittent 'afterlife' that repeatedly investigates its previous incarnations. This will be explored as a fourth historical or revisionist phase, a component of the latterly labelled 'youth heritage' cinema.[33]

Whatever model is employed, the history of a genre must take into account broader historical processes since its dynamics are socially overwritten. For Terry Threadgold a genre's evolution is never 'the simple reproduction of a formalistic model, but always the performance of a politically and historically significant and constrained social process'.[34] Many commentators see mass media genres as recording and 'reflecting' or constructing and 're-presenting' values dominant at the time of their production and dissemination. John Fiske, for example, contends that generic conventions 'embody the crucial ideological concerns of the time in which they are popular'.[35] There is a further double danger here, both of reductionism, an avoidance of complexity within a set of films to make them fit into an overall social pattern, and of exaggeration, a facile, quasi-automatic correlation of generic changes with larger socio-cultural shifts. The difficulty with the simple assertion of a genre's ready capacity for historical revelation is that textual as well as contextual issues need to be taken into account. A pioneering generic analysis such as Will Wright's *Six Guns and Society* effectively demonstrated that the changes undergone by a genre 'reflected' social change and audience expectations, but it omitted any investigation of the relationship with other media.[36] Since genres are far from stable entities and are always in a state of relative transformation with the production of new films, we need, as noted by John Hartley, 'to understand genre as a property of the relations between texts'.[37] Genre is a complicated concept, for this intertextuality functions not just *within* the film canon. Film itself is rarely generically pure, an evident point if, as Susan Hayward notes, we consider the medium's heritage which is derivative of other forms of entertainment (vaudeville, music hall, theatre, photography, the novel, etc.).[38] Steve Neale contends that film constantly refers to itself as a cross-media generic formation[39] and this will be explored for the British pop music film which is composed of several intertexts that rework, extend and transform its codifying norms. Hayward also reminds us that genres act as vehicles for stars: they are the iconographic site in which the star can display the body or have it displayed.[40] This study has decided to focus on the cinematic casting of 'pre-existent' rock'n'roll stars since they illustrate how, from the inception of this new musical form, careers and star personas were strengthened through cross-media alliances of records, radio, press, television *and film*, a strategy indicative of the expanding synergistic rapport within the British and increasingly global entertainment industries. Thus the 'primitive' phase has Cliff Richard at its core, the 'mature phase' centres on the Beatles, while the 'decadent' phase belatedly brings the Rolling Stones to the cinema screen. These are very different pop stars, bringing an associative 'baggage' to the part they played and so, in addition to the capital importance of pop performers on celluloid, I explore their emblematic value, the way they signify, sometimes unwittingly, as what Christine Gledhill terms 'condensers of moral, social and ideological values'.[41]

Genre and academia

The critical reservations of the national and trade press to early British pop music films – for Margaret Hinxman *Beat Girl* was a reminder of 'how ghastly British films can be'[42] – was long mirrored by academic rejection. An indication of the enduring neglect of pop music films by film historians is shown by the fact that almost all books on pop and film emerge from fan culture before academia. These books can be placed in two camps. First are the celebratory, anecdotal works on specific stars or films, such as Roy Carr's colourful production history, *Beatles at the Movies: Scenes from a Career*.[43] Then come the concise critical compilations, list books with plot summaries and quality ratings, such as Marshall Crenshaw's *Hollywood Rock*.[44] Even the first fully academic study, K.J. Donnelly's 2001 *Pop Music in British Cinema*, is encyclopaedic before analytical, dominated by lists of films and musicians. Though it provides a highly knowledgeable decade-by-decade overview, a contemporary review complained that 'surely there's more to say about the contribution of *A Hard Day's Night* et al. than a few paragraphs'.[45]

How to explain this critical neglect? Overall, it has been part of the academic avoidance given to the British musical *tout court* – until 2007 the previous full treatment of the home-grown genre had been John Huntley's (less than laudatory) *British Film Music* of 1947. Also, and paradoxically, the pop music sub-genre initially suffered for the absence of a strong, imposing director – an auteur. At the time that most pop music films were being made, emergent film studies championed the work of directors with an identifiable style and content before 'mere' genre films: the early cinematic efforts of British pop stars with their formulaic plots and narrow characterisation were pointedly dismissed as valueless examples of filmmaking by numbers. Even the subsequent critical attention given to directors ranging from John Boorman to Michael Winner (sic) has largely bypassed their 'pop apprenticeship' pieces. Then, when British film criticism eventually turned its attention to genre, it long preferred the twin bastions of cultural integrity, 'realism' and 'quality', and as, through the sixties, seventies and most of the eighties, orthodox film criticism fought shy of the fantastic and the frugal, one can understand why pop music films with their song and dance sections and their cheap production values were excluded from the canon of critical respectability. Since the late 1980s, however, film historians have been increasingly willing to engage with films marginalised by the dominant realist discourse, termed by Julian Petley the 'lost continent' of British cinema.[46] Several critically despised but commercially successful genres benefited from this new revisionism as the nineties and noughties brought forth studies on Gainsborough costume melodramas, Hammer horror, British Crime, Science Fiction and Comedy cinema,[47] leaving Petley's continent now fully 'found'/(over?) excavated – bar one uncharted country, the British musical.

Then, after waiting for 60 years, two full-length academic studies, like *Summer Holiday* buses, come along at once. The year 2007 saw the publication of John Mundy's *The British Musical Film* and K.J. Donnelly's *British Film Music and Film Musicals*, volumes that complement the aims of this third, more narrowly focused study. To reapply Moretti's Janus model, Mundy faces towards the socio-historical, exploring the genre above and beyond escapist entertainment, while Donnelly's orientation is musicological, examining the articulation of music within the visual and narrative components of cinema. Mundy usefully demonstrates how the British musical model, embedded in home-grown traditions such as music hall, has articulated a national identity inflected with both class and regional differences, and emphasises, as this study will, that 'audiences were always positioned within multimedia entertainment landscapes, including film, radio, sheet music, live variety, records and television'.[48] His criticism features a number of readings that cogently tie film narratives to their contemporary social and political contexts, openly or allegorically: readings that support this study's approach towards the music film as ideologically inflected and a source of more than just utopian compensation. Reviewers, though, noted the absence of 'fresh information that might have been provided by archival sources, or a thorough reading of the cinema trade magazines'.[49] This study will explore archival press, trade and censorship sources in establishing production and reception contexts. Donnelly's work is a less unified coverage of the broader field of British film scores and film musicals. A collection of essays ranging from the use of music in Gainsborough melodramas to *Absolute Beginners* (1986) and prefaced by brief histories of soundtracks and musicals, the book persuasively demonstrates the international impact of British film composers. Its attention to the musical numbers themselves, the defining formal feature of the genre after all, is matched in the textual detail of this study.

This genre study is itself written by a Janus-like creature, a film historian *and* a fan of popular music. The historian seeks to contribute to the nascent cultural rehabilitation of the genre; the fan hopes to convey the fun, skill and occasional embarrassment experienced in viewing these films, recognising that the majority's primary function was, and must remain, foot-tapping fun and entertainment.

2
The Primitive Pop Music Film: Coffee Bars, Cosh Boys and Cliff

Introduction: evasions and imitations

The neglect afforded to the pop music film by historians was for a long time shared by the film industry itself. When rock'n'roll began to assail the minds and bodies of American youth in the winter of 1954–55, Hollywood paid it scant attention. It was difficult to judge whether this new craze had any staying power, and months producing a product already past its sell-by date was indefensibly bad (show) business. Thus, while teenagers went wild in down-town dance halls, their elders in the movie industry were happy to stick with Crosby, Sinatra and Armstrong and the commercial certainties of *High Society* (Charles Walters, 1956).

Though unsure about their music, American cinema had not fought shy of teenage emotion. Most surveys claim that the first film to pave the way for the eventual accommodation of rock music was Laslo Benedek's *The Wild One* (1953), starring (a 31-year-old) Marlon Brando as the leader of a gang of bikers.[1] However, while Brando's leather-jacketed fighter provides an appealing nihilistic stance (famously answering 'What are you rebelling against, Johnny?' with 'What have you got?'), in America it precedes the existence of rock and post-dates it in Britain where the film was banned for 14 years. The harbinger is more properly Nicholas Ray's *Rebel Without a Cause* (1955), a more attainable and sympathetic treatment of teenage rebellion with James Dean's moody introspection re-presenting and in the process reinforcing the growing frustration of young (white) Americans with the values incorporated by parental authority. While Dean's death that same year gave the young their first (and enduring) visual symbol of group identity, their musical rallying point would be concurrently provided by Richard Brooks' *Blackboard Jungle* (1955). Ostensibly a standard Hollywood piece in its

10

portrayal of a single sympathetic adult (teacher Glenn Ford) bridging the gap between socially deprived, violent youth and uncomprehending authority, Brooks' film attracted teenagers by the thousand with its last-minute use over the opening and closing credits of 'Rock Around the Clock', then a minor hit by a little-known dance band called Bill Haley and the Comets. Artistically defensible as an expression of independence by and for inarticulate youngsters, this ploy resulted in two countervailing trends: both film and soundtrack garnered huge economic returns from its teen fan base but also, and in spite of the film refraining from making any such connection, a direct link was established in the minds of the moral majority between rock'n'roll and teenage violence.

Therefore, the film industry suddenly had a tempting economic incentive to incorporate rock'n'roll in its movies, but the inevitable backlash of religious and community leaders towards the 'satanic' music that was perverting the decency of the young provided a strong ideological (and economic) counter-balance. With powerful enemies to answer to, and therefore money to lose, the major studios prevaricated. Small independent producers with less at stake rushed to fill the void. The first such player was Sam Katzman, a long-serving B-movie producer for the mini-major Columbia. His gamble in signing up Haley for a low-budget exploitation movie paid off handsomely as the inevitably titled *Rock Around the Clock* (1956) proved that, irrespective of a tame storyline, the excitement of rock'n'roll music could attract its own cinema audience. Katzman's instant follow-up, *Don't Knock the Rock* (1956), again directed by Fred F. Sears, again brought in the punters and proved beyond doubt the commercial viability of rock'n'roll cinema. With Twentieth Century Fox successfully testing out Elvis Presley in its period potboiler *Love Me Tender* (Robert D. Webb, 1956) – the film recouped its production costs after just three days on release – the celluloid rock conveyor belt was up and running. It was time for Britain to try out 'rocksploitation'.

British cinema of the 1950s has recently been reappraised as transitional, representing cultural changes through what Sue Harper and Vincent Porter term 'residual' and 'emergent' film types, 'old and new ways of presenting the world and pleasing audiences'.[2] Nonetheless, with its *perceived* diet of war films and Noman Wisdom comedies, mainstream British cinema in the 1950s was, as Jeffrey Richards notes, 'in ethos and outlook, in technique and approach ... essentially conservative, middle class and backward-looking'.[3] Thus in 1956 it had little inclination to concern itself with rock'n'roll, a loud, vulgar and American phenomenon, everything that was anathema to the indigenous film industry. Worst of all, its small but passionate audience would undoubtedly consider any British response an anaemic imitation of the American original.

Again ideology and economics created a climate of caution: more than in the States rock'n'roll was seen as threatening to the status quo. Following lengthy debates within the BBFC (British Board of Film Censors), *The Blackboard Jungle* had been released in Britain in September 1955, with 20 minor cuts and an 'X' certificate barring it to its depicted audience. Katzman's spin-off, however, was made available to British youth and almost straight from its UK premiere at the London Pavilion on 10 July 1956 *Rock Around the Clock* occasioned wild behaviour amongst audiences, with dancing in the aisles and cinema seats torn out. Anthony Bicat illustrated the collapse of Western civilisation: 'In Manchester ... "Rhythm-crazed" youngsters, after they had seen the film, held up traffic for half an hour and trampled in the flower beds of the municipal gardens.' More worryingly for the film industry, though, 'in Blackburn the Watch Committee banned the film':[4] there was a strong likelihood that local authorities would exercise their prerogative and prohibit further examples of celluloid rock. Even though the film's success led to Haley simultaneously occupying five places in the top 30 that September, rock'n'roll was just too hot to handle and so, again echoing the American scenario, the elders of the UK film industry stayed with Eric Portman, Celia Johnson and Janette Scott in *The Good Companions* (J. Lee Thompson, 1956).

However, two events in February 1957 – one could term them 'residual' and 'emergent' – removed both these early prejudices about home-grown rock and prompted the first rush of British pop music films. A UK tour by Bill Haley and the Comets, hastily arranged to cash in further on the film's success, proved a grave tactical error, the reality of Haley's chubby features, tartan suits and basic dance moves deeply disappointing his initially ecstatic fans. As Nik Cohn explained, 'Instead of a space age rocker, all arrogant and mean and huge, he turned out to be a back-dated vaudeville act.'[5] Suddenly home-grown rockers did not seem quite so anaemic. Conversely, and though eventually key to the demise of the pop music film, television now prompted its creation. The appearance on the BBC on Saturday 16 February of *Six-Five Special*, a show highlighting the more controlled, positive energy of live acts and jiving audiences, seemed to signal a national acceptance of the new music and its fan base. That its proposed six-week run lasted two years would confirm the new music's longevity.

The major studios were still wary, though, and their initial responses can again be categorised as both 'residual' and 'emergent'. The safest approach was to bypass altogether the Young Turks of rock'n'roll and showcase existing stars. In the stagnant waters of 1955 Frankie Vaughan had appeared to signal the new musical direction with his confident stage manner and loyal female following. These qualities made him seem an equally bankable cinema star for ABPC (Associated British Picture Corporation), and in the latter half of the fifties he appeared in four Herbert Wilcox films. He first starred in *These Dangerous Years* (1957) as a rough and ready Liverpool teenage Ted who wins a singing contest just after receiving his call-up papers and eventually finds moral decency in the strict codes of the Army. Then came *The Lady is a Square* (1959) where Anna Neagle's benefactress of classical music is shocked to discover her butler moonlighting as a pop star – though one that settles discord and reveals true judgement by appending a Handel oratorio to his lucrative crooning. A swift retread for Rank, *The Heart of a Man* (1959), saw Vaughan win a rags-to-riches challenge by becoming a chart-topping pop singer.

However, though diegetically growing in singing stardom, Vaughan's increasingly stiff acting style also revealed the difficulties for film companies in knowing which performers would best transfer their talents to the big screen. Thus, the second approach was to tackle the problem the other way round, to take a trusted actor and turn him into a new pop star. Common enough today, this was the approach taken by Warwick Films who employed Anthony Newley as rock idol Jeep Jackson in John Gilling's *Idle on Parade* (1959), a clear exploitation of Elvis' recent call-up to the US Army, and a deeply consensual film in its message that square-bashing is a more (morally) rewarding occupation than guitar bashing. The film's success launched Newley on a pop career, with Jeep's song 'I've Waited So Long' reaching number three in the British charts and the soundtrack EP simultaneously hitting the top 20. Six top ten hits, including two number ones, followed in the next two years, fostering further film ventures such as Ken Hughes' musical-comedy *Jazz Boat* (1959).

A third approach, initially more risky, to take 'real' rock'n'roll stars and – to varying degrees – trust them in a film vehicle showcasing their music, would again echo the American scenario in giving smaller independent producers the chance to move in for a potentially quick killing. First into the spotlights, camera and action was *Rock You Sinners* (1957), one of director Denis Kavanagh's numerous assignments for E.J. Fancey Productions. The title promised transgression, but in truth the film was far closer to jazz than emergent rock'n'roll, its off-beat drumming and screaming saxophone evident from the opening credits. A concerted attempt to exploit the new sound, but lacking any genuine empathy or musical youth, the film's most successful segments featured Tony Crombie, an established jazz drummer who, seeing what Bill Haley was doing, and earning, had brazenly followed suit with his newly formed band, the Rockets. Crombie's 'Teach You to Rock' is regarded as Britain's first rock'n'roll record, entering the *NME* chart on 20 October 1956, one week before 'Rock with the Caveman' by Tommy Steele. Even so, Crombie hardly fitted the film's billing as a 'best-selling artist', though his musical sequences, shot in a rough quasi-documentary style, provide clear socio-cultural evidence of energetic dance halls on the cusp of rock'n'roll. Far less successful is the perfunctory plot, where a plum-voiced London radio disc jockey (Philip Gilbert) 'discovers' rock'n'roll and puts together a show for a national television programme while his girlfriend misconstrues his purely business coffee bar discussions with singer Joan Scott. Though accorded a positive and patriotic review in the trade press: 'unpretentious as it is, the film clearly proves that the Americans have no monopoly on rock'n'roll fare. It should have no difficulty in winning the plaudits of non-squares,'[6] *Rock You Sinners* disappeared almost immediately. It only returned to public attention over 50 years later to feature in Matthew Sweet's *British B-movies: Truly Madly Cheaply* where it was held up to ridicule for its formal qualities – it is 'put together with stunning ineptitude' – but lauded for its unwitting historical testimony – 'in some ways it's a better insight into 1950s Britain than a newsreel'.[7] Thus it is an apt opening film for exegesis since such Janus-faced critique will be at the heart of this investigation. However, *Rock You Sinners* failed to impress the non-squares as it is an ersatz and imitative venture, an opportunistic 'grafting' of musicians from a different musical idiom. Nor can it ultimately claim pioneer status. Though the first produced – filming was completed on 13 February – Fancey's Small Films lacked an equal alacrity for distribution and exhibition which delayed release until 14 July, allowing Steele to even the score by entering the cinemas a fortnight earlier as the star of the first *publicly exhibited* British pop music film. This and later 'pop star discovery' narratives feature the environment synonymous with early British rock, a cradle now for positive energy and youthful optimism, the London coffee bar.

Coffee bar pop idols

The pioneer pop music film – *The Tommy Steele Story* (1957)

For George Melly 'The rise of Tommy Steele in the middle 50s is the first British pop event.'[8] Equally, the British pop music film begins on

30 May 1957 with the release of *The Tommy Steele Story*, produced by the middle-ranking Anglo-Amalgamated. Eschewing youthful vigour behind the camera, directing duties were given to 48-year-old documentary filmmaker Gerard Bryant while, in a move that would prove typical of the genre, the untried pop star was surrounded by dependable character actors, notably Hilda Fenemore and Charles Lamb as Tommy's parents. Speed was clearly of the essence and, with song-writing partners Lionel Bart and Mike Pratt, Steele pieced together 14 new songs, reputedly in seven days, while scriptwriter Norman Hudis, about to find regular employment with the Carry On films, knocked off the script in ten days. Filming, which began at Beaconsfield Studios in February, was completed in just three weeks – the swift editing and distribution ensuring that, with a total cost of just £15,000, the film made the theatres two weeks ahead of *Rock You Sinners*. Such alacrity was not employed to trump Crombie and Co. but rather to promote Steele's imminent second major British tour: *The Tommy Steele Story* constituted just one element in a successful cross-media marketing campaign that included top ten tie-in single hits with 'Butterfingers' and 'Water Water' and stretched to 'Tommy Steele shoes, shirts, blouses, panties, skirts, ear-rings, bracelets, pullovers and sweaters'.[9] The film was retitled *Rock Around the World* for overseas markets and had its US (Milwaukee) premiere in August.

While it failed to impact on America – no 'primitive' phase British pop film would – elsewhere and especially at home *The Tommy Steele Story* proved itself the 'surefire blockbusting bonanza' the film posters had promised, hitting the year's top ten for UK box-office returns with over £100,000 profit. Critics were united in their praise of Steele's acting ability, the *Sunday Times* reviewer finding him 'a tousled, ebullient teenager whom the screen has not dampened one bit'.[10] Though sparsely reviewed in the national press this clearly was a new cine-cultural phenomenon since the film overcame the 'double whammy' of being British and popular to earn itself a review in *Sight and Sound*, a journal that then eschewed most domestic product for European art-house films. Alongside Steele's 'authentic' and 'charismatic' performance, David Robinson, perhaps eager for the New Wave aesthetic anticipated in the burgeoning Free Cinema movement, found this 'inexpensive and unpretentious film ... notable for brief glimpses of a reality rare in British cinema' and highlighted 'the Steeles' Bermondsey living-room with its cheap ornaments, gaudy crockery and sauce-bottle on the tea-table' as a strategy 'to de-glamorise Steele's private and professional life'.[11] In similar vein, trade advertisements for *The Tommy Steele Story* had lauded 'The <u>True</u> Story of Britain's Most Sensational Entertainer!'

while Sue Harper and Vincent Porter recently further apostrophised the film's accuracy, citing Bryant's later claim that 'all I was doing was making a documentary about a nice working-class lad'.[12] The major problem, however, with such enduring readings is that *The Tommy Steele Story* is 'in reality' almost pure fiction from beginning to end.

The film's plot – polite ingénu comes ashore in London, goes to Soho's 2I's coffee bar, is discovered and becomes an overnight sensation – is just not how it happened. Steele (real name Tommy Hicks) had been a semi-pro for two years, playing London's coffee bars and jazz cellars when on shore leave, and the lengthy battle for his signature – an internecine struggle far more 'authentically' portrayed in *Expresso Bongo* two years later – was eventually won by publicity agent John Kennedy, who features in the film, and his business partner, the successful rag-trader and burgeoning impresario Larry Parnes, who does not. Tommy's management erased his lengthy apprenticeship for fear of harming their new PR creation's carefully forged image as an artless amateur, a fiction further perpetrated by *The Tommy Steele Story*.[13]

Equally questionable is the subsequent *idée fixe* that Steele's movies contribute significantly to the 'castration process' of British rockers. George Melly eloquently mocks a craven complicity:

> Each successive pop music explosion has come roaring out of the clubs in which it was born like an angry young bull. Watching from the other side of the gate, the current establishment has proclaimed it dangerous, subversive, a menace to youth, and demanded something be done about it. Something is. Commercial exploitation advances towards it holding out a bucketful of recording contracts, television appearances and worldwide fame. Then, once the muzzle is safely buried in the golden mash, the cunning butcher nips deftly along the flank and castrates the animal. After this painless operation, the establishment realises it is safe to advance into the field and gingerly pats the now docile creature which can then be safely relied on to grow fatter and stupider until the moment when fashion decides it is ready for the slaughterhouse.[14]

There are myriad examples to demonstrate Melly's theory, but it is debateable when he states that 'Tommy Steele's career illustrates the generalisations I've been trying to formulate with almost text-book clarity.'[15]

Firstly, the case for Thomas Hicks as England's first home-grown rock'n'roller remains non-proven. For instance, his first single release,

'Rock with the Caveman', is a curiously bland effort at 'the devil's music', the word 'rock' being a closer identification than any musical style. Steele's voice was genial before threatening, his stage demeanour more playground skip than bedroom thrust. Colin MacInnes, British pop's first serious commentator, noticed this from the outset, finding with Steele that 'the whole effect, to use a silly word, is so much *nicer* [than Presley] ... in a strange way innocent, even pure'.[16] Tommy Steele, though young and dishevelled, was not an angry young bull: he was little – and white. His early songs, as witnessed in *The Tommy Steele Story*, exemplify quintessentially English variants on rock'n'roll, saxophones blurting in front of a basic rhythm-guitar and piano backing with occasional moderately amplified jazz-style lead guitar, such as on 'Take Me Back Baby' (Figure 2.1). Any sense of Steele as a rocking rebel is rebuffed straight from this opening number. The luxurious Café de Paris location nullifies any notion of revolt against adult mores, while the mise-en-scène securely places Tommy relative to dominant cultural

Figure 2.1   'Take Me Back, Baby': immediate cultural and cinematic containment – *The Tommy Steele Story*

and generational practices. So too do the lyrics: 'I'll be a good boy if only you / Will take me back, baby, / I won't be bad no more.' They constitute an immediate and explicit plea for inclusion and, though ostensibly aimed at a personal and emotional level, the song, especially when performed in such affluent surroundings, carries an equivalent political and ideological charge.

One can also question Melly's depiction of management manipulating a passive, unthinking animal. Steele's direction out of rock'n'roll would prove a typical career trajectory for British stars of the time – as it would for American stars, including Elvis. Much of this can be laid at the door of expediency: nobody could predict how long the teenage fixation on rock'n'roll would endure, and both managers *and* artists were eager to maintain their careers and not become last year's – or last month's – model in an uncertain musical genre. The film is correct in showing how, during November 1956, a proactive Tommy was successfully launched on the sought-for Variety circuit. Steele admired American rock'n'roll, but he liked other forms of music more – in Anglo-Amalgamated's press release he declares himself 'primarily a calypso and ballad singer'[17] – and this Afro-Caribbean influence is foregrounded over the film's opening credits where, in contrast to a confrontational, *Blackboard Jungle*-style introduction, Tommy Eytle's Calypso Band sing how 'This lad from Bermondsey / In show business he made history, / With his heart and soul / He sang his ballads and rock'n'roll.' Ballads first, then rock'n'roll, and all relayed in a calypso rhythm. This opening gambit hardly heralds a rock rebellion.

It is thematically significant that, immediately after its reassuring nightclub opening, the first British pop music film looks to the past and structures all but its final Bermondsey concert through the technique of the flashback. As Maureen Turim has explored, the flashback is a cinematic representation of memory and history that, through its 'naturalising processes', conveys a subjective truth that the spectator cannot question.[18] *The Tommy Steele Story* is not only *about* Tommy Steele but also a story told *by* Tommy Steele, a strategy which authenticates its version of events – suturing the biographical 'fiction' into mediated 'fact'. Susan Hayward notes that the flashback's representation of the past, subjectivised through one person's memories, has clear ideological and indeed nationalistic implications[19] and Turim illustrates how, in times of war or tension, this structural device can lead to patriotic identification.[20] Her example is *Napoléon vu par Abel Gance* (1927) where the flashback, because evaluated through a subjective framing of history, tends to mythologise the 'great man' (sic). It is admittedly a fanciful if not bathetic leap from Napoleon to Tommy Steele, and from Abel Gance to Gerard Bryant, but the difference is one of degree rather than of kind. Robinson, Melly and Andrew Caine have all explained Steele's appeal in terms of charisma,[21] a key concept in Richard Dyer's study on stars and stardom, and one which extends beyond personal qualities to combine aspects of social function and ideology. Dyer highlights how 'charismatic appeal is effective especially when the social order is uncertain, unstable and ambiguous and when the charismatic figure or group offers a value, order or stability to counterpoise this'.[22] Within the narrow socio- and historic-cultural parameters of this study, Steele, at a time of burgeoning generational discord, presents a stabilising agent and signifies as an unmistakable and unifying embodiment of both class worth and filial obedience – 'Grand Entertainment the Whole Family Will Enjoy' the early posters pointedly proclaimed.[23] Equally, at a time of concern at the prospect of an imminent quasi-complete US penetration in both popular music and the music film, Steele is deliberately presented as a man of destiny, a wandering minstrel who helps Britain to find its own contemporary musical style and coherence.

This self-sufficiency is reinforced by the film's total absence of American product. With Britain determinedly patriotic in spite of its international decline – Tommy's 'discovery' coincided with the Suez Crisis in late 1956 – Andrew Caine sketches the optimism represented by teenagers, and how 'youth, through figures such as Steele, could reinvigorate the nation's esteem after the turmoil of the previous two decades'. More pointedly, 'Steele's rise presents a case of youthful Britain fighting back against the upstart Americans, offering resistance to US domination.'[24] If Caine is right, the case is yet again predicated on falsehood. Steele/Hicks' Cunard years included regular visits to the States where in early 1956 he chanced to see Elvis Presley on the Dorsey Brothers' *Stage Show*. A seminal moment in any young rocker's career, the incident, the country and the music are completely avoided in *The Tommy Steele Story*: foregrounded instead are the Caribbean and Calypso. This refusal to become 'Americanised' was a key aspect of incipient English rock'n'roll, a feature again noted by Colin MacInnes, who suggests that UK teenagers transformed it into something of their own, 'in a way that suggests, subtly, that they're almost amused by what has influenced them'.[25]

This sense of humour, of a none-too-serious approach to the new music, is evident in Steele's 'cheeky chappie' verbal and musical performance, but primarily this erasing of American influence equates to a removal of sex. For Harper and Porter this is central to the film's domestic success since it 'neutralises those images of extreme sexual difference which had so alarmed adult viewers of the American rock films'.[26] Steele's lack of provocative movements or signalled sexual interest in his adoring following can again be linked to the structural device of the flashback which reinforces the conviction of Steele's performance, so admired by reviewers. Turim adjudges the flashbacks of male characters more retrospective than introspective: the voice-over represents a subjectivity that controls the past, thus 'exhibiting a self-reliant masculinity'.[27] It is, of course, a clever commercial strategy to present the teen idol as self-reliant, as single (another fiction since Steele was about to become engaged) and it would be often repeated, most notably when the Beatles came to celluloid. This sexual lacuna is also textually evident in audience reception, where there is no sight – and especially no sound – of the mob hysteria recorded in contemporary reviews: Trevor Philpott, anticipating Melly's slaughterhouse imagery, reported that 'When Tommy Steele steps on to a theatre stage, it is like killing-day at some fantastic piggery.'[28] Instead *The Tommy Steele Story* records total silence except for a couple of gentle bursts of laughter during Tommy's comic lyrics.

This (typically English) transformation of sex into comedy links strongly to the film's strategy of dissipating notions of generational conflict. This is not just a case of charming Cockney Tommy loving his mother and obeying his father, though that is important. It is again primarily conveyed through audience responses to his music. When young Tommy, confined to hospital, makes his singing debut at the Christmas concert, all are happy. A young girl in a wheelchair (no holding back on the pathos) is positioned in front of the ward's elected entertainer: an older man is sitting up in bed, swaying to the rhythm as the camera pans across to the proud nurse and approving doctor.

The results of such reassuring, inclusive 'healthy' music would lead directly to the Ruritanian romance of *The Duke Wore Jeans* (Gerald Thomas, 1958) and the fiesta frolics of *Tommy the Toreador* (John Paddy Carstairs, 1959), comedy musicals far removed from the sights and sounds of late 1950s rock'n'roll but vehicles to bring Steele closer to his desired career longevity. Nonetheless, as the first British pop music film, it is instructive to examine the musical numbers in *The Tommy Steele Story*, not just for their narrative and contextual importance, but also to see how – and if – the film experiments to find a fresh grammar of cinematic correlation. To a large extent the grammar is conservative, relying on the established tradition of song performance derived from the classical Hollywood musical. As in the Presley cycle the new sub-genre's musical sequences were mainly based on the lip-synched performance by the solo singer or group which, occasionally combined with minimal on-screen backing sources – for Steele, as for Presley, a guitar – attempted to articulate the illusion of 'real' diegetic performance. Several of the numbers in *The Tommy Steele Story* are straightforward presentations of public performance with the music diegetically realised. Here, again employing the established Hollywood dialectic of inclusion and replacement to create the illusion of attending a live performance, the theatre audience is initially put into the film, the camera centred in the second or third row and creating a spatial continuity that allows the cinema audience first to identify with and then, as the camera twice cuts closer to the stage, to take over from the on-screen audience. A spatial equivalent to the flashback's 'naturalising' processes, the internal audience thus act as 'the celluloid embodiment of the film audience's subjectivity'.[29] It is a generic convention that will be repeated throughout the British pop music film, though it will take *The Young Ones* (1961) to present a more overtly gendered presentation of the internal audience – for the screams finally to be heard.

Elsewhere in *The Tommy Steele Story*, non-theatrical performances provide non-diegetic background music, passably in hospital with 'Butterfingers' and at sea in 'Handful of Songs' where the reflexive lyrics celebrate the power of song, but less satisfactorily in Steele's coffee bar performances where the realistic context is undermined by the unmotivated musical backing. More positively, a third category of pop song performance attempts to play more creatively with the new partner medium of film. The presentation of 'I Like' is a case in point, providing a variant on the Hollywood *bricolage* number where the props at hand are rounded up and danced with, as in the 'Moses Supposes' number from *Singin' in the Rain* (Stanley Donen, 1952). Trying out a second-hand guitar, Tommy spies other instruments in the junk shop. The camera in eye-line matches zooms in on a dusty double bass, cueing a bass solo, then repeats the tactic for drums, piano and saxophone. The dustiness of the instruments shows that they pre-date the rock'n'roll era, and are thus being put to new, revivifying use. This environmental conception of orchestration is also tied in to choreography in 'Cannibal Pot' where Steele's mess-room percussion solo literally enacts Haley's order from 'Shake, Rattle and Roll' to 'Get out in that kitchen and rattle those pots and pans.' (In so doing it ensures a further removal from the sexual euphemisms in Big Joe Turner's original lyrics, cleaned up by Haley.)[30]

There is one number, however, when *The Tommy Steele Story* tackles the issue of correlation in a more complex, ambivalent and purely visual manner. In essence the images accompanying 'Elevator Rock' are a variant on the rise-to-fame montage, seen in numerous Hollywood musicals such as *Lady Be Good* (Norman McLeod, 1941), but whereas the 'classic' montage invariably presents mass distribution as a positive force, Britain's first pop music film is (perhaps) less dogmatic, less certain that (inter)national dissemination outweighs local production. In a scene of skilful compression we witness, not the castration, but the commodification of Tommy Steele. The scene lasts for a total of 52 seconds, and includes 22 edits of increasing brevity, taking us from Tommy's studio recording of 'Elevator Rock' to a succession of 78rpms being pressed, then a shop's shelves full of identical song sheets, each bearing a drawing of Steele plus guitar and the categorisation 'Rock'n'roll Sensation' before, over the closing bars of the song, comes a self-referential *Melody Maker* headline: 'Film Offer to Tommy Steele'. The scene 'economically' conveys the speed of the star-making process, with a conscious scope of editing that demonstrates both graphic relations – the sheet music's proto-Pop-Art anticipating patterns in space – and, more mimetically, rhythmic relations, its patterns in time. As Bordwell and Thompson note, such a systematic and recognisable play of angles and speeds 'impels the viewer's perception to move at an increased pace, and this pace is an essential component in the excitement of the scene'.[31] The celebration of sheer volume, a gaining of pleasure from the glut of product, is probably the ostensible motivation for the film's display of Tommy Steele records and sheet music, but an opposing response, the mechanistic disconnection from emotion concomitant within this process of commodification, cannot be entirely dismissed.[32] These multiple images could even simulate the film itself, slowed down beyond its 'truth at 24 frames per second'. Though it can only be briefly observed on-screen, the overall effect of this express(o) editing is myriad, a modernist moment amidst the stylistic realism that, perversely, evokes the cultural reservations of Richard Hoggart.

The Tommy Steele Story strives to create a distinct indigenous cultural space while, at moments, offering an ambivalent investigation of the new cultural form. No such readings, of course, were critically acceptable at the time. From its first British film sortie, pop music was projected as an aspirational species of variety entertainment. Not only could it not be teenage rebellion: more generally, it could not be politics, it could not be sex, it could scarcely be considered cinema – and it certainly could not be art. Later phases of the British pop music film explored in this study *have* been accepted as explicitly embodying these properties, from the Pop Art stylistics of *A Hard Day's Night* through to the Francis

Bacon-influenced mise-en-scène of *Performance*, a film that, for Colin MacCabe, successfully 'delivered a picture and a soundtrack of that moment' in 1968 when London 'seemed poised between an old and a new world' and fully gathered up the 'aesthetic, political, philosophical and sexual' themes that still dominate our intellectual and emotional lives.[33] This section questions a critical orthodoxy that still largely disregards the pre-Beatles efforts in the British pop music film genre and posits that these 'primitive' films also deliver a picture and a soundtrack of the moment of their making – and as such offer an historical document of the political and – if only through omission – the sexual preoccupations of their time. But they also have, in their own modest (British?) way, aesthetic considerations, a cinematic as well as a commercial philosophy.

The mythology surrounding Steele's discovery at the 2I's, further fuelled by *The Tommy Steele Story*, intensified the coffee bar's attraction for aspiring rock'n'rollers. The film's success ensured that its formula would be swiftly replicated and 19-year-old Steele epigone Terry Williams, renamed Terry Dene (an echo of the rebel James), was signed up by Butcher's Films – a company further down the film food chain than Anglo-Amalgamated – to star in one of their 'occasional first features' – *The Golden Disc*.[34] With a traditionally older, working-class demographic, Butcher's move for Dene reveals an urgent if not desperate need to attract the younger audiences filling cinemas in the late 1950s. However, their preferred 2I's' protégé singularly lacked Steele's determination and charisma. Indeed, Dene's brief career is a perfect exemplar of Melly's paradigm, an insensitively manipulated amateur who could never properly adjust to fame. Dene's off-screen biography – his arrest soon after filming for being drunk and disorderly a sign of incipient mental problems – indicates how precarious pop stardom could/can be, and how film production, even if completed in six months, could fatally delay getting the muzzle into the golden mash. Though his film persona was entirely bland, the press now reviled Dene as a symbol of all that was bad about the new music and its followers and their reaction following the film's Piccadilly premiere on 24 March was predictably negative. Donald Zec in the *Daily Mirror* was typically irate: 'Aren't we getting just a bit too much of this second-rate skiffle-piffle? Teenagers deserve something a little better than the dreary, fumbling picture called *The Golden Disc*.'[35] Dismissed as a pale imitation, a cynical hop onto the coffee bar bandwagon, associated record releases all failed to chart and the film, like its musical lead, quickly disappeared.

The recent resurgent interest in *The Golden Disc* is in part straightforwardly historical: of all the coffee bar films it gives most attention and screen time to the creation, the décor and the social space of a London espresso bar of the period. Though clumsily choreographed, the scene of the transformation of Aunt Julia's Soho café provides the fullest fetishisation of both the gleaming gaggia and frothy coffee. Such clarity is less discernible in analysis focused on issues of genre and gender. For its August US release the film was retitled *The In-Between Age*, the title of a song performed by Sheila Buxton (not Dene, significantly): though referring to misunderstood teenagers it inadvertently signifies as the overriding quality of the film itself which re-presents its ideological compromises at a narrative and musical level.

Narratively, the film is unsure of the extent to which it should showcase its young singing star: scriptwriter Don Nicholl and director Don Sharp understandably transferred the narrative weight from the strangely asexual slant of Dene's demeanour onto Mary Steele (no relation) as singer Joan and her love interest/musical arranger Harry, played by the Canadian Lee Patterson. Patterson's presence indicates a reliance on transatlantic cooperation that is textually replicated: while *The Tommy Steele Story* established a resistant relationship to the United States, *The Golden Disc*'s position can, at best, be categorised as collaborative or 'mutually dependent'. When a hard-dealing British record company nearly ruins the honest amateurs launching Terry, Mr Washington comes to the rescue as a plain-speaking *deus ex* Michigan, offering them the British release of his US roster in return for the American release of their Charm Label. Nina Hibbin's review recognised this homage to the special relationship: 'It's supposed to be a British film, but its message is "Good Old Uncle Sam!"'[36]

Good old Aunt Julia too. For Sue Harper the film 'had a modern veneer … but the gender arrangements were old fashioned':[37] here again the film betrays uncertainty – its 'in-betweenness'. Joan is entrusted with Charm's business arm – but Harry has to forsake his studio work to sort out the mess when she is outmanoeuvred on Dene's contract: she proactively declares her love for Harry – but then seems all too willing to stifle her professional ambitions and revert to the role of (future m)other. Against this, however, Julia is an older self-sufficient woman who at key moments offers both psychological motivation and financial support, notably the initiative and investment for Charm's expansion.

Musically Butcher's – and partner Decca Records – seemed equally unsure and hedged their bets with a score featuring skiffle, rock'n'roll, cool jazz, ballads and even a trumpet solo. But while there are too many musical styles to give the film any sense of direction, cinematically it displays scant variety or experimentation. Dene's songs are all semi-diegetic, with guitar and swaying coffee bar audience, while all guest acts perform their numbers diegetically, mostly in Harry's recording studio. This too annoyed reviewers: 'Why hire a singer like Nancy Whiskey if you're only going to stick her up in front of a camera and mike and photograph her flat?' fumed Frank Jackson.[38] Such plain presentation may reveal more of economic than cultural imperatives, but ultimately the making of Nancy's and others' records *is* the film. *The Golden Disc* functions primarily as a process movie, one that replays the fascination with new technology central to early musicals such as *Show Girl in Hollywood* (Mervyn LeRoy, 1930) which, Jane Feuer notes, 'seems to have been made to sing the praises of sound-on-disc recording rather than the Show Girl herself'.[39] Here one notes a titular shift from artist, 'Tommy Steele', to artefact, the 'Golden Disc'. In its lengthy 'demystification' of the recording industry *The Golden Disc* presents technology as a new form of spectacle, a new show. However, its technological education provides an 'academic' rather than an emotional engagement – scarcely a recipe for box-office success.

The pop music film as parody: *Expresso Bongo* (1959)

If *The Golden Disc* was a limp pastiche of *The Tommy Steele Story*, *Expresso Bongo* was its cruel parody, a swift clobbering of the new teen idol phenomenon. It grew from a satirical short story, based on Steele's 'overnight' rise to stardom, written by East End journalist and playwright Wolf Mankowitz for the *Daily Express*: a pun between the new Italian coffee and the commissioning newspaper helped to cement the common error of pronouncing 'expresso' instead of 'espresso', with its connotations of speed and excitement. Rectifying a major omission from Steele's biopic, Mankowitz's central character, hustling agent Johnny Jackson, was based on Larry Parnes, Steele's Svengali and the man who, Jon Savage contends, 'invented British Pop'.[40] The summer 1958 stage version, starring Paul Scofield as Jackson, James Kenney as his teenage protégé Bongo Herbert and Millicent Martin as Jackson's strip-tease girlfriend Maisie, was an instant critical and commercial hit, reviewers praising its 'adult approach' and 'wit, bite and topicality'.[41] Sensing a popular story in tune with the moment, a film deal was quickly tied up with British Lion Film Corporation, a company recently rebranded as offering 'quality' products such as *I'm All Right Jack* (John Boulting, 1959). As the first coffee bar film from a prestigious studio with a healthy purse, directing duties were entrusted to the experienced Val Guest, today renowned for his sci-fi Quatermass films but then best known for comedy. He had recently written, directed and produced Ted

Heath and His Music in *It's a Wonderful World* (1956), a satirical musical about two struggling songwriters desperate to hit the big time – a theme germane to *Expresso Bongo*. Guest reworked the stage script with Mankowitz, creating new scenes to spoof earnest television documentaries and dropping all bar two stage numbers in favour of new songs composed for the celluloid Steele-like star-to-be.[42] Choreography was entrusted to Sadler's Wells' Kenneth MacMillan (later Sir) while Guest's wife Yolande Donlan landed the lead female role of Dixie Collins, with rising star Sylvia Syms chosen as Maisie. Perhaps most impressively, the lead male role of Johnny Jackson was entrusted to Laurence Harvey, recently catapulted to stardom for playing Joe Lampton in Britain's first New Wave film, *Room at the Top* (Jack Clayton, 1959).

To complement this eminent cast and crew, the producers sought, for the key role of Bongo, an authentic pop star who would attract the teenage audience. Though the work's initial inspiration, Steele was discounted: for Guest 'he didn't have the vulnerability needed for the role of a slightly bewildered teenager rocketed to unexpected stardom'.[43] Instead the director found the desired vitality and 'warmth' when invited to see the 2I's' latest headline act – Cliff Richard. The singer reinforced his appeal by bringing his mother to the contract signing – with life imitating art, Cliff, aged 18, was too young to sign himself.[44] It was also a commercially astute choice, Richard having been voted 'Top New Singer' in the *Melody Maker* pop poll of March 1959.

Shot on location and at Shepperton Studios in September and October, *Expresso Bongo* was granted an A certificate after cuts relating to its strip-club scenes, and premiered at the Carlton Cinema, London, in the presence of Sir Winston Churchill, on 20 November 1959, just 18 months after its West End debut. It went on general release one week later.

By the new year *Expresso Bongo* was 'easily the number one release. Thanks partly to the popularity of Cliff Richard, the teenager's idol, it has taken tremendous money at weekends.'[45] Alongside its commercial success, the film's critical reception was almost entirely valedictory. 'This is, easily, so far, our best musical,' wrote William Whitebait in the *New Statesman*,[46] while Paul Dehn's *News Chronicle* review ran under the heading: 'That Rarity: A British Film-musical America May Well Envy'.[47] Laurence Harvey received blanket praise for his interpretation of Jackson: 'more than believable; he gives an absolute gem of a performance', wrote the *Saturday Review*,[48] while Sylvia Syms was also acclaimed: for David Robinson 'Syms is silly and pathetic and wise – which is as she should be.'[49] With Yolande Donlan shouldering almost all critical reservations – for the *Daily Mail* 'she lacks the emotional depth for the part of the fading star'[50] – the largest ambivalence came with reactions to Cliff Richard's performance. The difficulty of adjudging its 'authenticity' was best exemplified by Isabel Quigly for whom Cliff 'plays his part so straight that there seems no satire about it at all and one is left with the disturbing feeling that here is Cliff Richard in person, as credulous and as nice as Bongo, as simple and as duped. He is either such a clever actor that he actually persuades one he isn't acting or else a boy of such transparent and alarming simplicity that the whole of *Expresso Bongo* has rolled off him like water off a duck's back.'[51] It has proven an enduring response: Ben Thompson, in his mid-1990s appraisal of pop stars on film, admired 'the unnerving blankness' of Cliff's 'noble savage' performance and felt that 'his resolute asexuality in all his dealings with mildly predatory love interest Yolande Donlan is kookier and more disturbing than anything Mick Jagger and Anita Pallenberg can cook up for James Fox in *Performance*'.[52]

Record royalties also rolled in, proving for the first time in a British pop music film the interpenetrative power of cinema and song. Cliff's four film numbers, released as an EP in January 1960, achieved the rarity of eighth position in the singles charts, the more remarkable since one number, 'A Voice in the Wilderness', was simultaneously released as a single and reached number two in the same chart. Within three months the 'Expresso Bongo' EP had sold over 150,000 copies, five times the average EP hit sales. (By the early 1990s global sales finally passed the million mark, thus making it a genuine 'golden disc'.)

Like its tie-in EP *Expresso Bongo* has continued to enjoy popular patronage and a high critical reputation. For Geoff Brown it is 'Britain's most abrasive and entertaining film musical'[53] while Bruce Eder terms it 'the best British rock'n'roll movie of the 50s' and 'probably the best rock'n'roll movie made in England prior to *A Hard Day's Night*'.[54] The rest of this section will work to support these encomia.

The aesthetic superiority of *Expresso Bongo* to its pop film predecessors is evident from the opening establishment shots which, replicating *The Tommy Steele Story* (as had *The Golden Disc*), show night-time scenes of central London. Here, though, their integration with the title credits – the superimposed white lettering of 'Val Guest' and 'Britannia Films' struggling for space and legibility against the neon lighting of 'Coca-Cola' and 'Max Factor'; the camera nudging its way into an amusement arcade on Frith Street, seeking the cardboard cut-out on top of a jukebox then dwelling on the photo and the name inscribed beneath it: 'with Cliff Richard'; a panel of phone-booth adverts for prostitutes hosting, amidst the telephone numbers from Bridgette, Mimi and Carlota, a card

naming the musical composers – constitutes a stunning bravura opening, one minute and 30 seconds of highly skilled mise-en-scène, editing,
dialogue and music that places us centrally in a world burgeoning with
excitement and energy, fads and fancies, and concludes by introducing
us to Johnny Jackson feeding from its scraps. Setting the topography of
the film and yoking together separate lines of narrative into the shape
of our prime protagonist, this exposition both recalls the 'integrated
credit sequences' to *I Know Where I'm Going* (Powell and Pressburger,
1945) and *Hue and Cry* (Charles Crichton, 1947), and will constitute the
inspiration for the opening of Julien Temple's homage to the coffee bar
age, *Absolute Beginners*. Intra-textually though, these credits root the cast
and crew of *Expresso Bongo* within this Soho locale, caustically signalling that they are an integral and, at best, equal component, one more
flickering entertainment advertising/'whoring' its wares and hoping to
deprive the gullible of their hard-earned coin.

Recalling *Expresso Bongo*'s strong theatrical origins, this opening
sequence also negotiates its transformation *into* film, its construction of
a cinematic variant that, as described by Angela Dalle Vacche, 'disassem-
bles language into images and makes language out of images'.[55] Guest
gives both sound and vision a distinct rhythmic flow in many parts of
the film. Aurally, this is evident in Jackson's blustery patter, sometimes
hard to decipher so rapid is the delivery, but whose constant use, whatever problems he encounters, provides as much a 'rhythmic' pulse to
the film as a 'literal' set of meanings. Visually, the cardboard-cut-out
image seen in the opening sequence is later redeployed, though now
enlarged to show the face – and greater financial power – of American
singing star Dixie Collins. This huge advertisement rests throughout
the film in the office of recording manager Meyer (Meier Tzelniker), his
pride and joy of purposeful publicity, her disembodied star-image coming between him and Jackson in the mise-en-scène as later the 'flesh
and blood' woman will separate them in the narrative dimension – until
her own comeuppance.

All is division in the caustic world of *Expresso Bongo*. The gender divide
is reinforced by the music's failure to unite the generations: again exposing the Steele fiction, no effort is made to present older adherents to the
new music's aesthetic. Bongo's parents show no interest in his music:
instead Mrs Rudge remains throughout such a corrosive presence that
Johnny must keep her away from Bongo's breakthrough performance
on the Dixie Collins show where he delivers his carefully rehearsed –
and bogus – lines on being 'a deeply religious boy' in love with his
mother before singing his Oedipal hymn 'The Shrine on the Second

Floor'. In a film where the visual realisation of Bongo's performances are imaginative (and well resourced) but still conventionally diegetic, this sequence stands out, its yoking of such heterogeneous – yet conflating – concepts as religious expression, authentic emotion and a gay-inflected popular culture coming with the screen divided between Cliff, tuxedoed à la Liberace, and tiered choirboys (Figure 2.2). As in the film's credit sequence, though here conducted at a brazenly leisurely pace, we witness the moulding of different and seemingly unconnected systems of communication into new, eccentric yet economically viable configurations. This blending of rock and religion will recur in the genre, most pointedly in *Privilege*. Here the mix is gently debunked, both on-stage with Cliff's carefully choreographed (and critically confounding) performance, and on television with the Reverend Craven, keen to display his trendiness though everything about his appearance – and name – registers otherwise. Generically, the song's cynical exploitation of family values prompts a re-evaluation of *The Tommy Steele Story* and its star's constantly mediated need for parental approval. Biographically, the scene's prescience, given Richard's later finding of God, adds a further, retrospective layer to this textually rich musical number.

The new music's exacerbation of generational conflict is foregrounded at a professional perspective as the older impresarios cynically exploit what they see as an unwholesome here-today-gone-tomorrow trend. It is enunciated when Johnny encourages Bongo prior to his small-screen debut: 'now go out there and kill them. Tonight eight million

Figure 2.2 The new direction: rock and religion – *Expresso Bongo*

telly-hugging idiots are going to fall in love with you – simultaneously.' It is enacted when Meyer registers his contempt for the rock recording in progress by having his secretary put a record of *Aida* on the turntable. Meyer decries a world where he loses his shirt on the opera but makes money from rock tracks: nonetheless, on witnessing Bongo at the Expresso Bar in Soho he straightaway offers Jackson a one-track deal. Just to underline the impersonal nature of the transaction, as Meyer departs a prostitute emerges from the shadows to proposition Johnny.

It is not her first appearance in a film that has commercial sex aplenty. If *The Tommy Steele Story* excised all overt sexual reference and *The Golden Disc* displaced sex onto a chaste romantic subplot, in *Expresso Bongo* sex is central, both to career development and to the music itself – the bang of the bongos that Meyer sees and signs up redolent of *Sapphire* (Basil Dearden, 1959) in its effect on a teenage audience. Sex is present in the opening credits' phone cards and remains as Johnny goes to meet Maisie, performing her historical tableaux *au naturel* where a topless Mary Queen of Scots 'came an awful cropper, / On the headsman's wicked chopper!' Alongside its *double entendres*, the scene renders explicit yet another division, this time in the nation's media since cinema, in the form of *Expresso Bongo* itself, shows – indeed flaunts – this scene (relatively) uncut, but when television celebrity Gilbert Harding (playing himself) visits the club to record for his *Monitor*-like *Cosmorama* the show has to lose much of its fleshy vitality. Quasi-propaganda for cinema as a more 'realist' medium, *Expresso Bongo* glories through contrast in its 'adult' potentialities: the new pervasive medium that Johnny called 'the hot cod's eye which watches every face in Britain' cannot view other parts of the anatomy as more narrowly marketed cinema now can.

This confrontation with television places *Expresso Bongo* firmly in the tradition of the British New Wave films which, as Charles Barr has noted, convey 'a violent animus against television' which they associate with the domestic and the feminine.[56] In *Expresso Bongo* television deprives the male viewer of his visual consummation in the overdressed Soho extracts shown on *Cosmorama*. It also 'feminises' Bongo in the Harley Street psychiatrist's analysis that follows Maisie's dressed-up history lesson, his description of Bongo's 'almost beautiful' face prompting a mock advance from his best mate Beast.

This critique of the rival visual medium is only one of several tropes confirming *Expresso Bongo* as the New Wave pop music film. Its attention to sex and gender is the major link, especially in its narrative and ideological treatment of the older, foreign woman. Dixie's role in *Expresso Bongo*'s unflinching exposé of the world of professional show business is pivotal for, while the film as a whole is concerned with the processes of stardom, it is the American songstress who both articulates the contemporary concerns over pop's longevity and embodies its vagaries. The balance of power shifts firmly towards Bongo's homegrown talents as soon as he appears on Dixie's show, and is finalised when, just after Dixie helps him to sever ties with Jackson, Bongo is contracted to go to the United States *instead of* her. The film thereby concludes (again parodically?) with a clear victory for indigenous pop music over its American rivals, completing a distinct progression in the three 'rags-to-riches' coffee bar films. Where *The Tommy Steele Story* ignored US influence and *The Golden Disc* colluded, at least in economic terms, with the States, *Expresso Bongo* sees America properly shafted: Bongo, not now so innocent, uses on Dixie his personal charm – to borrow a Dene song-title – as a means to professional advancement and ultimate conquest of the US charts.

While Bongo gains his ticket to America, Dixie's fate is comparable to that of the women whose cards were displayed in the opening credits since, at the film's end, she is herself seen as a commodity, desired maybe less for her physical than for the economic advantages she possesses, but just as readily discarded when those advantages disappear. More than this though, the conclusion to *Expresso Bongo* is typically New Wave in its need to labour Dixie's career demise. For all that contemporary critiques perceived a new permissiveness in their depiction of more overt sexual activity, New Wave films' representations of women can now be seen as deeply reactionary.[57] The clearest example of their ideological closure comes in Harvey's earlier *Room at the Top*, where the older, sexually active Alice (Simone Signoret) is killed in a car accident, her 'necessary destiny' for straying from the expected passive gender role. In *Expresso Bongo* the punishment is not so final, the death metaphorical, but it is, if anything, more brutally misogynistic for being openly enacted at a narrative as well as ideological level. Meyer, Bongo's new manager, invites the deposed Jackson to listen in as he rings Dixie to inform her that she too has been usurped, America now interested in Bongo rather than her. We cut to a dropped phone and Dixie's distraught reactions: when Bongo asks who was calling she wryly replies 'An old man with a scythe.' As well as signalling a victory for Britain over the United States, Meyer's message to Dixie, an act of consolatory male bonding, is equally a merciless assertion of the industry's dominant patriarchy.

It is generally acknowledged that British cinema 'changed' noticeably around the turn of the sixties. Arthur Marwick, seeking to 'pin down as precisely as possible the critical point of change' settled on 1959 – the year of *Expresso Bongo*.[58] Marwick detected three renovating tendencies: a perceptive social criticism and satire; an authentic presentation of working-class lifestyles; and genuine innovation both in technique and in breaking away from the purely naturalistic film.[59] John Hill's blessed trinity are sex, class and realism. Adhering to both trilogies of criteria, *Expresso Bongo* merits inclusion as a New Wave venture, stylistically and narratively. Although a music film, every vocal, instrumental and dance number is presented diegetically, reproducing the spectacle of 'genuine' performance and fitting into a realistic framework. Although southern set, the camerawork and mise-en-scène present – until the later digressions with Dixie at the Dorchester – working-class venues for living and leisure, filmed with a distancing aestheticisation equal to that of Richardson, Schlesinger and Reisz.[60] At a narrative level the film's characters are given cogent motivations: even Bongo has a brief biographical hinterland sketched out – an unwanted wartime child, born out of wedlock – that explains if not condones the relative attitudes of a neglectful mother and her resentful son.

It is, though, the candid examination of the world of entertainment and its star products that has garnered *Expresso Bongo* most laurels for realism. The cynical commodification of aggressively ambitious pop performers is the up-front focus of the whole film. Firstly, it shows the expedient view – if not outright contempt – of producers for consumers. Tommy Steele put on a (well-publicised) concert at Bermondsey town hall as a gesture of appreciation to 'the thousands of fans in the thousands of streets' just like his. Bongo, however, is soon enjoying the high life and when Jackson reminds him that 'you're great only so long as the teenage public think you're one of them', Bongo shrugs off the advice: 'What do I care about those grimy yobs!' Bongo is no youthful repository of optimism: instead he forms a bridge to the imminent 'youth-as-trouble' paradigms. Unlike *The Tommy Steele Story*, *Expresso Bongo* also exposes the contempt of producers for other producers, revealing the contract back-stabbings that surround all new potential passports to the gravy train and, as John Mundy points out, highlighting the fiercely hierarchical structure of the British entertainment business.[61] Many of Parnes' acts failed to find lasting success because, for all the arriviste's energy in booking appearances on youth-focused shows such as *Six-Five Special* and setting up provincial Variety tours so dear to Steele (and his mother), Parnes never had access to the top-ranking entertainment circuit owned by Leslie Grade and Bernard Delfont, notably the London Palladium, televised every Sunday night to a national family audience. Johnny Jackson is similarly second division, and Bongo knows enough to realise that he needs a 'better class' of management to become a household star.

With its unyielding exposé of the music industry, *Expresso Bongo* is a coruscating plague-on-both-your-houses satire to match its British Lion stable-mate *I'm All Right Jack*. Its West End pedigree and top-grade casting may have rendered it more acceptable to the elite cultural commentators than other films in the coffee bar collective, but this does not prevent it being the most realistic in its exploitation of rebel rock.

Coffee bar cosh boys

In the late 1950s 'social change was seen as generally beneficial ("you've never had it so good!"), but also as eroding the traditional landmarks and undermining the sacred order and institutions of traditional society'.[62] Youth in particular was seen as the 'underside' of the 'affluent society' with its slavish devotion to consumerism and its absence of rooted, 'traditional' values. This reflected a broader anxiety about the quality of life which was embodied in these new patterns of consumption and the explosion of mass-communications media – television, advertising and pop music. The coffee bar films under consideration here rehearse this dichotomy and can be split into pop musical vehicles and social dramas with added pop numbers, the former investigating the economic and industrial, focusing on the creation of celebrity, while the latter, at the end of the decade, explore/exploit the social and ideological, focusing on the (perceived) practices of criminality. Thus, from the bullish innocence of Tommy Steele, via the charismatic vacuum of Terry Dene, we pass through the ambivalent status of Cliff Richard as Bongo Herbert to the 'jiving, drivelling scum' of *Serious Charge* and *Beat Girl*.

The pop music social-problem film – *Serious Charge* (1959)

Serious Charge again originated on the West End stage, but unlike *Expresso Bongo* it took six years to transfer to the screen. Philip King's play premiered in November 1953 with Nigel Stock in the role of the Reverend Howard Phillips and Alec McCowen playing the juvenile delinquent Larry Thompson who falsely accuses the vicar of making a pass at him. The subsequent drawn-out debates with prospective producers and within the BBFC have been extensively researched by Tony Aldgate, who explains how, even though no 'improper' acts occur, there was no possibility of even a hint of homosexuality in a serious British film at that time.[63] Two important events changed this climate of intolerance – the publication in September 1957 of the Wolfenden Report proposing the decriminalisation of homosexuality and the accession in July 1958 of John Trevelyan to the position of Secretary of the BBFC. With Trevelyan a period of more enlightened liberalism is generally seen to have come to British film censorship: it began with the submission by Mickey Delamar of Alva Films of his script for *Serious Charge*, co-written with Guy Elmes.

Much had changed in British society since 1953, not least the growth of youth culture, and it was for the baldly economic factor of broadening his project's appeal that Delamar added the part of Curley Thompson and commissioned Lionel Bart to write three rock'n'roll numbers. Given the near-certainty of an 'X' certificate, this suggests an uncertain if not confused strategy. Director's duties were entrusted to 43-year-old Terence Young, later to direct early James Bond movies. Young's scouting mission brought Cliff Richard to his attention: 'He seemed terribly self-assured and had a very good stage act. I thought if he could do that, then he could act.'[64] While ostensibly complementary to Cliff, one notes the inauthenticity that Young automatically ascribed to pop music.

A strong – and well-connected – cast was brought together, with Anthony Quayle playing the accused vicar, Andrew Ray the accusing Larry, while the role of Hester Phillips was taken by Sarah Churchill, daughter of Sir Winston. Filming began in December 1958 at the MGM Studios in Borehamwood, with exteriors shot in Stevenage new town. Accompanying the rough cut's submission with claims of serious social intent failed to sway the BBFC's classification: for Trevelyan 'It is pure melodrama and should be treated as such.'[65] The effect of the 'X' certificate on the film's commercial potential was exacerbated when Cliff Richard's stock soared following a celebrated performance of 'Turn Me Loose', complete with menacing leer, on ITV's *Oh Boy!*, transmitted on 30 May. The film opened nationally on the ABC circuit on 29 June 1959, inaccessible to the majority of Cliff's fan base.

Critically *Serious Charge* was damned with faint praise. David Robinson gave a typical assessment: 'It has a passing interest as the first British film to refer directly to the subject of homosexual offences; but the theme is never seriously discussed.'[66] For William Whitebait, echoing Trevelyan, 'the provincial town never comes to life, the Espresso bar is always rocking'n'rolling, and drama develops into melodrama'.[67] The *Sunday Express* found redeeming features in a different focus: '*Serious Charge* is a good British film which tries, a bit shakily, to air the problem of the "juvs" – JDs [juvenile delinquents] – in a growing town who "tool up" regularly with flick-knives and chains.'[68] Dilys Powell, however,

sensed a more exploitative use of the younger generation: 'the translation to the screen is creditable, though I wish the cinema would give
up equating rock'n'roll with juvenile delinquency'.[69] The performances
of the main leads escaped censure but, of the film's 20 extant trade and
national press reviews, only three mentioned Cliff's contribution to the
film. George Sterling homed in on the problematic match of star and
vehicle, noting that 'TV singer Cliff Richard makes his screen debut. His
appearance will please those of his fans old enough to see the film.'[70]

While *Serious Charge* did reasonable box-office business – Josh Billings
categorised it amongst the year's 'Better Than Average Offerings'[71] –
musically the results were far more successful. Underlining the distance
of the film's use of music from its commercial exploitation, however, it
was a re-recorded, slower version of 'Living Doll' that became Cliff's first
number one, selling close to two million copies and redefining him as a
singer. Difficult to sing with a snarl of the lip and pelvic thrust, 'Living
Doll' is Exhibit A to support George Melly's own serious charge that
'Richard is a key figure in relation to the castration of the first British
pop explosion.'[72] Nik Cohn thought so: '"Living Doll" was by far the
most influential single of the whole decade. It was cute and sweet and
bouncy. It was tuneful and ingenuous. It was the British equivalent to
high-school – and it was desperate. In months it took over completely.
No rage, no farce, no ugliness left.'[73] As with Tommy Steele's career
decisions, one has to recognise here that the change of tempo came
from Cliff Richard and the Shadows themselves. This was not industry manipulation, but a performer-led manoeuvre that Cliff himself
acknowledged: 'I parted company with the greasy-haired rock'n'roll
scene and began attracting the mums.'[74] It was a new fan base that
Expresso Bongo would exploit narratively, as well as commercially.

Alongside its 'daring' main plotline, *Serious Charge* has a number of
interesting angles: the urban centrifugal force of new town New-topia
with society mutating into something far too large for parish cohesion
and patriarchal control; the 'nature versus nurture' axis in its debate on
criminality; the melodramatic speed of narrative development, character reaction and 'dynamic use of spatial and musical categories'.[75] The
employment of the Cliff Richard character – here sporting a damning
JD leather jacket and jet-black Elvis-style duck's arse quiff – and his
rock-inflected musical numbers undoubtedly provide an additional and
potent ideological charge. This was largely ignored in initial censorship
and critical responses but constitutes the focus of this analysis. It is
best explored, following Trevelyan and Whitebait, through the signifying mechanisms of melodrama, a genre which, Susan Hayward notes,

centres on the victim, staging 'persecuted innocence and the drive to identify the good and the evil'.[76] The victim in *Serious Charge* is ostensibly the wrongly accused vicar, Howard Phillips, a 'man of God' trying to comprehend teenage motivations. But the film houses other victims too. Hester Peters holds a high position in the pecking order, rejected in her love for Howard. In male-focused melodramas, however, the central strain is 'the protagonist's unwillingness or inability to fulfil the Oedipal trajectory'.[77] The failure to fulfil this trajectory – put bluntly, to struggle but finally find a girl and settle down – is evidenced in the characters played by James Dean:[78] in *Serious Charge* Curley is a similar victim, unable to meet society's expectations of male adulthood.

Nor does he fit smoothly into generic models. Curley's presence was ostensibly a pretext for including some audience-generating rock'n'roll: the corollary of Delamar's (frustrated) ploy was the need to integrate pop music numbers into a predominantly non-musical product. Here there were no opportunities for coffee bar auditions, stage performances or recording studios. As such its grammar of cinematic correlation is revealing, though like much else in *Serious Charge* the most effective epithet is 'contradictory'. For both 'No Turning Back' and 'Living Doll' Cliff sings along to his own records which are played on the radio and jukebox respectively. This is a tried and trusted strategy to contain the pop-song performances within a semi-credible diegetic scenario. But later brief snippets of 'Mad About You' and 'Living Doll' come direct from the machinery, leading in a literal interpretation to the conclusion that Curley has become a successful singing artist with an alacrity beyond even a Tommy Steele. It is an ambivalent articulation of the songs, revealing a deep uncertainty in integrating pop songs and dramatic performance.

Even within this division, different fates befall the musical performances. The first, 'No Turning Back', is undoubtedly the most successful, an exciting montage of music and movement that, as in *Sapphire*, scares the representative of moral decency out of understanding. The gang's arrival at the church hall and Curley's singing engenders a more energetic dancing style between the table-tennis tables, notably from Michelle, the vicar's French maid. After close-ups of her face revealing the sensual pleasure she is experiencing, an eye-line match from Howard shows Michelle, shot from the chest down, twirling so that her skirt rises up to her waist – a framing close to pornographic in its reduction of the woman to waist and thighs. At which point all stops as Howard (literally) pulls the plug. Within less than two minutes the filming of the dance contains 24 edits of jiving feet, girls jumping into boys' arms, plus three reaction shots of the hot-under-the-collar cleric. The rhythm of the montage and the close-ups of Michelle convey the dual message of rock'n'roll and sexual promiscuity. It is an explosion of pent-up passion in a parsimonious setting – delirious or dangerous depending on your age and inclination, but undeniably constructed with considerable skill.

'Living Doll', *Serious Charge*'s most celebrated number, is, by contrast, a cut-up, constricted affair. Though Cliff here has the screen and the girls to himself, the camera merely shows its specially imported star sitting in a chair, his leg swinging casually over the lap of one of the three girls who are all performing a hand-jive. Even in the film's more up-tempo version, there is no inherent rage or ugliness. But context is all: after just a few bars of Cliff's performance, the camera leaves him and the music decreases in volume so that we view and hear the dia- logue between two other 'juves'. Performance is sacrificed to the semiot- ics of the social-problem film as the music is employed as a sign, here unequivocally overlaying the discourses of rock'n'roll with juvenile delinquency – all in the charged coffee bar setting.

After this, it is as though the film loses nerve, or interest in Cliff as pop performer. Instead his narrative function grows, illustrating Geoffrey Nowell-Smith's observation that melodrama is 'fundamentally concerned with the child's problems of growing into a sexual identity within the family, under the aegis of a symbolic law which the father incarnates'.[79] In *Serious Charge* the tyranny of the patriarchal leather belt is reserved for the unrepentant elder sibling Larry. Instead Howard stays in town to stand surety for Curley. Does this make him a new custodial father figure for the reformed rocker? Or are there other motivations?

The notion of homosexuality lowers over the second half of *Serious Charge*. The eponymous accusation brought by Larry is, we know, not true, but why are Hester and the town so quick to believe it? Stephen Bourne has suggested that Howard 'is probably unconsciously gay' and offers supportive evidence ranging from his love of shopping to 'a rather matey relationship with the lesbian probation officer' and how 'the knowing, teasing presence of his mother would seem to suggest that he has not had girlfriends in the past, nor had she encouraged any'. Bourne concludes that 'Perhaps the film might have been more honest if Cliff had played the vicar's would-be nemesis, as the young pop singer does occasionally smoulder with loose-limbed, pouting eroticism.'[80] It is an astute analysis of the film, but Bourne's closing conjecture could be pursued to include Curley in a gay reading of *Serious Charge*. In a film eager to exhibit teenage coupling, Curley is distinct in never being

Figure 2.3   He's got the look: Cliff and the film's final, serious charge – *Serious Charge*

paired off with a girlfriend – he sings alone at the church hall and during the erotically uncharged 'Living Doll' his 'roving eye' pointedly never fixes on the girls around him. Thompson senior will only support his elder son in court and is indignant when informed of Larry's accusation: 'you mean we've got *one of them* down at the vicarage?' The camera cuts from the father, not to his interlocutor Larry but to Curley who opens the door and makes to enter the room: he is dismissed with equal intolerance. Above all, there is the decisive concluding look from the back seat of the probation officer's car up to the reverend (Figure 2.3). Is it shyly respectful, or coyly sexual? As in *Expresso Bongo*, is it clever acting or transparent simplicity? Whatever the motivation, its effect is searing, allowing a final recognition of the reverend's personal torment.

As in the social-problem melodramas *Sapphire* and *Victim* (Basil Dearden, 1961) that bracketed its release, the issue of 'passing' can finally be identified as central to the meaning of *Serious Charge*. Marcia Landy points out how *Victim* 'plays with the game of identification. Not only does the film postpone recognition of the character's gayness, but it denies the audience access to information.'[81] *Serious Charge* has a different overt agenda to *Victim* and is less explicit in its treatment of the accusations made against the lead male. But the comparison can be pushed. Andy Medhurst praises the strength of delivery by Dirk Bogarde in *Victim*'s 'confession' scene where he tells his wife that 'I stopped seeing him because I wanted him!', calling it 'the moment when irresistible sexual desire finds, literally, its voice'.[82] Anthony Quayle remains silent and does not stop seeing him: he offers a more restrained, understated – 'typically' British – acting style, but here too 'the containment of desire breaks down'[83] and rips through the ostensible social message of the film. The charge we leave the cinema remembering is that generated by the exchange of looks between the reverend Howard Phillips and pop singing Curley Thompson.

The pop music exploitation film – *Beat Girl* (1960)

Amidst its censorship travails, Cliff Richard's first film venture employed rock'n'roll as a culturally acceptable metaphor for 'youth-as-trouble'. This uncertain template was repeated with the late addition to a further self-professed social-problem film of another 'pretty boy' 2I's' graduate – the adenoidal Adam Faith.[84] The renamed Terry Nelhams was noticed on Jack Good's *Six-Five Special* by prospective film producer George Willoughby (or rather his daughter)[85] while planning a cheap exploitation film centred on the Soho coffee bars and its 'beatnik' culture. Faith had a distinctly minor role, but between casting and production his singing career blossomed and his part was rewritten to capitalise on his involvement: 'Adam Faith Gets With It!' the posters would (eventually) proclaim. Willoughby was persuaded that, for the musical numbers, it would make sense to employ the man who had arranged all of Faith's records thus far and so, significantly for film (music) history, John Barry was commissioned to write his first film score.

Beat Girl is a prime example of the pop music vehicle giving a chance to emergent – and émigré – talent. Alongside British stalwarts David Farrar and Christopher Lee, the eponymous Beat Girl Jennifer marked a debut performance by French-educated Bardot lookalike Gillian Hills. Behind the camera, Berlin-born New Wave cinematographer Walter Lassally worked with the Anglo-French Edmond T. Gréville, whose previous directing included the stylish thriller *Noose* (1948), another film with a female lead and a Soho nightclub owner. Alongside its continental cast and crew, *Beat Girl*'s financial provenance also promised transgression. Its credit sequence opens with 'George Minter Presents': executive producer Minter's Renown Pictures Corporation had debuted with the notorious *No Orchids for Miss Blandish* (St. John Legh Clowes,

1948), 'greeted' by the *Monthly Film Bulletin* as 'the most sickening exhibition of brutality, perversion, sex and sadism ever to be shown on a cinema screen'.[86] Perhaps Minter was looking to create a similar potent mix when story and screenplay duties for *Beat Girl* were entrusted to Dail Ambler, a glamorous blonde aka prolific pulp-fiction crime writer Danny Spade.[87] *Beat Girl* was her first film script – and it met with severe resistance.

When Ambler's initial treatment, entitled 'Striptease Girl', was submitted to the BBFC in March 1959, the first reader followed his précis thus: 'The summary gives little idea of the degradation of this story: the author may pose as a realist or a reformer but this seems to me to be machine-made dirt – the worst script I have read for some years.'[88] Unsurprisingly, the project entered a lengthy process of 'consultation': even after a rewrite that toned down the nudity John Trevelyan demanded further changes, insistent that 'the youngsters seem to us to be too "beat", too irredeemably nasty'.[89]

As with *Serious Charge*, the bulk of filming took place at the MGM Studio at Borehamwood, Hertfordshire, while exteriors were shot at the Chislehurst Caves, Kent, and in Soho. Whether in deference to the censors' more muted protests to the 'beat generation', or else foregrounding the lately added pop music score, the film was submitted to the BBFC on 30 November under a new title – *Beat Girl*. The change in nomenclature did not placate the censors who insisted on several cuts: on viewing a dare-scene redolent of *Rebel Without a Cause*, they demanded Renown 'delete all shots of boys or girls on railway line and all references in dialogue to "chicken"'.[90] Exhibition difficulties now emerged, probably because of a log-jam on the ABC circuit – Rank would not show X-rated films at the time. Thus, rather than *Beat Girl* serving as a symbiotic vehicle with record promotions, the tie-in single and album came and went unaided. Meanwhile Faith became a major pop star, matching Cliff Richard hit for hit throughout 1960: he even had a later film released, a straight acting role in *Never Let Go* (John Guillermin, 1960) – and *Beat Girl* stayed on the shelves. It finally made the cinema circuits in late October 1960, except in Warwickshire, where the local authority banned it as, more famously, they did *Saturday Night and Sunday Morning*.[91] The film was released in the United States in October 1961, retitled *Wild for Kicks*.

When belatedly exhibited *Beat Girl* was reviled in the national press. Alongside Margaret Hinxman's diatribe cited in the introduction, the *Daily Express* confidently concluded that it was a film which 'no one could like'.[92] Only the trade press lauded the 'Jean-age melodrama', concluding that 'No mistake, *Beat Girl* will "send 'em" to the box-office.'[93] Faith's own retrospective judgement combined both camps: '*Beat Girl* was no film epic. But it has been coining money since its release. The reason is, I suppose, that its rather lurid story appeals to teenagers' tastes.'[94] Its musical content also contributed to the coining: Faith's 'Made You', largely because coupled with the newly released *Never Let Go*'s credit accompaniment 'When Johnny Comes Marching Home', reached number three in the singles chart before the BBC banned it when appraised of the more demotic meaning of having 'made' somebody. More lastingly, *Beat Girl* was also the first film in Britain to have its soundtrack released on LP: bearing a production still on its cover, it peaked at number 11 during a three-week stay in the album charts, but has retained a 'slow burn' income due to Barry's later career.

Similarly, in the wake of the Sex Pistols and the Mod revival, the eighties saw a new interest in Gréville's film. For Ehrenstein and Reed, writing in 1982, *Beat Girl* is 'a definite must for scholars of teen attitude and rock-to-punk evolution'.[95] In academic exegesis, however, the frames of reference for *Beat Girl* have remained relatively unchanged from its initial censorship and media reception: it continues to be viewed as part of a cycle of exploitation attractive for its sordid sensationalism. Lez Cooke, for instance, reiterates a divide present in John Hill's pioneering *Sex, Class and Realism* of 1983 by contrasting late 1950s–early 1960s 'serious' social-problem films with fare such as *Beat Girl* that 'exploit the issue for public consumption' and 'where sensationalism rather than seriousness seems the objective'.[96] However, Peter Hutchings has critiqued the way Hill omitted or marginalised more blatant generic offerings such as *Beat Girl* in favour of films like *Sapphire* because of 'an undefined "seriousness" on the part of the filmmakers involved in the latter'.[97] The following analysis will attempt to show firstly that *Beat Girl* is equally as 'worthy' and contains as much 'seriousness' as films more resistant to a blatantly commercial imperative; and secondly that the musical component, still critically untreated, is, though crudely integrated, central to imparting the film's *complex* – and censored – ideology. To do this, it is germane, as with *Serious Charge*, to read *Beat Girl* as a 'jean-age' (musical) melodrama.[98]

Susan Hayward has indicated how melodrama, exposing the decentred subject caused by alienation under capitalism, 'attempts to make sense of modernism, and of the family'.[99] Issues pertaining to modernism, especially the anxieties produced by urban change, are explicitly addressed in *Beat Girl* through the character and career of Jennifer's father, Paul Lindon, an obsessive, 'sociological' architect whose living room is dominated by a model of his projected City 2000, an abstract architectural pattern with a regular, indeed obsessive repetition of rectangular units in its grid of skyscrapers. As Paul intones to his new French wife Nicole over what Jennifer calls the family 'coffin' how his design will reduce human contact and hence social ills, image undermines his peroration. On the right, looking down on his creation, is the wealthy technocrat. To the left is his new family – wife eager to share and daughter in distant indifference. Behind them, centre-screen, lies the open door into the more sharply illuminated dining room where the old maid is clearing away after the meal. As Paul talks of a new society envisioned on social equality, we witness how his present time and space are predicated upon capital and labour. The mise-en-scène 'centres' the decentred subject of the hired servant.

Thus, through narrative and mise-en-scène, concerns over social spaces – and the socialisation of spaces – are enacted with and through a family context. But also, and more explicitly, these concerns are conducted outside the home, in settings and set-pieces unacceptable to the BBFC but (retrospectively) enriching to the characterisation and meaning of the film. Following *Expresso Bongo* – a record sleeve for the original West End production decorates the coffee bar wall – *Beat Girl* deploys a Soho location to run together the teen world of coffee bars with the illegitimate sexuality of the strip club. The Off-Beat café is different, though, in being represented as largely a *feminised* space. Here the gang do not tolerate alcohol or violence and give free rein to their emotions: one beat, Tom, whose mother died in the war, can here escape his father's implacable gender codes: 'Don't cry for your mother, boy, it's not manly.' As her male friends openly reminisce on their wartime misfortunes – these are all children of the bomb, hence their atomic nihilism – Jennifer asserts that this environment, with all the people, noise and energy that her father's City 2000 would suppress, is where she belongs: this is her life.

It remains a distinctly privileged life. *Beat Girl*, for all its stylisation and excess, provides the fullest cinematic treatment of the 'beatnik' scene in the Soho/Chelsea district in the late 1950s–early 1960s[100] and, by focusing on teenagers from upper-middle-class backgrounds, it reveals the ubiquitous nature of youth problems. Though part of this affluent existentialist enclave, Jennifer strives to assert her individuality, to be a self-sufficient woman who, again in a trope familiar to melodrama, refuses to conform to a submissive gender role. This can (now) be seen when the gang play 'chicken' on the railway line and Jennifer keeps her head on the track the longest. She wins.

The scene, though, was cut from the film initially released. The musical numbers remained, and evidence a further development in the grammar of cinematic correlation as strong emotion is displaced via music. If *The Tommy Steele Story* was noticeable for the removal of sex, the songs sung by Adam Faith in *Beat Girl* could claim – especially post-censorship – to be the central repository for the film's X-rated sexual atmosphere. Faith's first number, 'I Did What You Told Me', is innocent and unadventurous, sung upstairs in the coffee bar after Jennifer has put a record on the jukebox, ostensibly to provide a diegetic backing track. 'Come on, Dave,' she exhorts him: 'Make the banshee, I'm music minded.' As Dave (Adam Faith), sitting at the table, sings, Jennifer is transfixed, eyes shut, luxuriating in a song that, pertinently, tells of male obedience. For Faith's second number, however, the setting and sentiment are different. In the candle-lit cellar-bar, as the John Barry Seven play the title music, a young couple stop dancing and walk off to an isolated alcove. The camera follows but any voyeuristic pleasure is removed when the girl blows out the candle and the screen descends into total darkness. Jennifer again dictates terms, telling Dave to 'sing that number and make it cool'. Dave again obeys, beginning with a crude cut across the John Barry Seven's own performance, evidence of the social-problem film's continued uncertainty with musical integration. The song 'Made You' can be interpreted as referring both to the relationship between Dave and Jennifer and to the content 'within' the black screen that preceded the singing. Characteristic of the melodrama is how the undischarged emotion which cannot be accommodated within the action is traditionally expressed in the music and in elements of the mise-en-scène.[101] The chorus of Dave's song, the significance of which eluded both BBC and BBFC authorities, declaims 'I never can relax until I've made you' – an instance of the 'beat' teenage argot employed to circumvent adult constraints, and an example of the (male) sexual frustrations that need to be 'siphoned off'. Whilst the guitar solo generates the expected cut to the cellar-bar dancers, elsewhere the camera remains fairly tight on Faith and cuts to reaction shots of Jennifer, again swaying enraptured to the music. The song is applauded by most of the dance floor, while Tony is effusive in his praise: 'Great, dad, great! Straight from the fridge!'[102] For the viewer, though, following on from the blackout on the young couple, the music here has not heightened the sexual possibilities of the setting: it has substituted for them.

That the Beat Girl *belongs* to no-one is enacted in the film's choreographed sections: where all others pair up, Jennifer finds fulfilment in dancing alone. In the opening scene, a young Oliver Reed can only dance behind rather than with her, apeing her movements but excluded from her self-enclosed pleasure. When he later invites her downstairs – 'Say, baby, you feeling terpsichorean?' – the film's opening is reprised, though now with more rapid editing as increasing close-ups of Jennifer are intercut with shots of the music's source, the drums, bass and saxophone, then the tapping foot of a musician – exhibiting the height of 'beat cool' in his Jesus sandals. Finally a full close-up, the screen filled with Jennifer's eyes, precedes her move onto the floor to dance – alone. This concentration on her eyes highlights that all is being viewed from the female perspective: the male performers are 'dismembered' and objectified, their hands – and feet – there solely to serve *her* pleasure.

This 'pop pornography', the reduction of people to objects of untouchable pleasure, leads Jennifer inevitably to 'Les Girls' strip club opposite the coffee bar. The reinstated version of this scene allows us now to see the enriching ambivalence with which it was composed – editing and mise-en-scène echoing earlier scenes and revealing differing approaches to exploitation. The appeal of the striptease for Jennifer is conveyed as empowerment as she witnesses the performance of Pascaline on-stage, wrapping a sheet into a phallic form, stroking and kissing it, then throwing it away dismissively. The composition of the scene, with its frequent cut-backs to Jennifer, establishes a formal parallel with the musicians in the cellar-bar. The curt discarding of the wrapped-up sheet suggests a use of men for pleasure, all conducted on the woman's terms, and it is this sense of 'control' which Kenny, the club's owner, employs to sell the idea of stripping to Jennifer. The mise-en-scène, however, again undercuts his words. As Kenny tells Jennifer of the job's allure, they stand either side of his two-way mirror which allows a view of the acts on-stage and their audience. In the centre, visually privileged as in Paul's modernist home, is the distant image of the working woman, again dressed as a maid, though this time it is not the tableware that she is removing. Without the singular female perspective, on display is an economy of masculine desire operating on and through the aestheticised and commodified bodies of women. In his negotiations Trevelyan had expressed his preference for a film *about* rather than *of* exploitation, and the mise-en-scène here fulfils this role, again focusing attention on the decentred subject – the woman forced to sell her labour for the benefit of affluent men.

When Paul returns home late and witnesses how Jennifer, stripping in response to her friends' taunts, has imported this perceived potentiality into the domestic setting, he carries out the standard, symbolic act of generational conflict by smashing the young gang's record – and declaims Andy Medhurst's favourite, 'treasurable line' from the film: 'Get out of it, you jiving, drivelling scum!'[103] He then slaps Jennifer on the face. Music and dance prompt Paul's first act of uncontrolled emotion in the film, his first genuine contact with his daughter. It signifies, though, as a clear condemnation of the deficiencies of established patriarchal modes of discipline – and censorship.

Their results are shown to be counterproductive, precipitating Jennifer's flight into the eager arms of Kenny and the exploitation film's manipulated, 'transparent' conclusion – a jealous lover stabbing Kenny to death and Jennifer's safe return home – that continues to exercise critical responses. Laura Mulvey has distinguished between the James Dean-style 'masculine melodrama' with its relative resolution and the 'female melodrama' with its function of excess and unresolved contradictions – it is 'as though the fact of having a female point of view dominating the narrative produces an excess that precludes satisfaction'.[104] The unresolved conclusion to *Beat Girl* continues to confuse. John Hill writes that once the police arrive, Jennifer's only escape route is to cry for 'Daddy', thus fusing state and paternal authority.[105] It is an interpretation repeated by John Mundy who sees Jennifer 'rescued by patriarchy and the reassertion of the family unit'.[106] This is a questionable reading: as Jennifer fights her way to the front door of the strip club she calls out: 'Daddy! Nicole! Come back! Help me!' It is a cry to *parental* rather than patriarchal control. As the family disappears into the London night, the father centred, his arms around Nicole and Jennifer, the image can equally be read as the man being supported by the stronger women on either side of him, the soft street lighting suggesting a softening in family relations. It is again a familiar trope of female melodrama: 'For family life to survive, a compromise has to be reached, sexual difference softened, and the male brought to see the value of domestic life.'[107] More than anyone, it is Paul who has learned his lesson. Whereas at the start of the film he looked down God-like on the maquette of his social creation, now the high camera looks down on him, a lost creature in an alien landscape, being led by Nicole and Jennifer to a life of more 'organised disorder'. The right angles will have to go.

The events surrounding Jennifer's friends again support this softened, more 'feminine' interpretation of the ending. Nowell-Smith explores the 'syphoning off' of unrepresentable material via Freud's concept of conversion hysteria – the return of the repressed – and notes that, while the repressed for the woman may be female desire, for the male it is the fear of castration. Acceptance of that fear or possibility is repressed at the level of the story but again reappears through mise-en-scène and/or

Figure 2.4   From breakneck racer to broken-necked guitar – *Beat Girl*

music.[108] The former is found with the wifeless Paul where, to put it bluntly, the building of skyscrapers compensates for an inactive phallus. Its musical manifestation is centred on Adam Faith's Dave, who has most forcefully (over-)expressed his masculinity through singing with his guitar and bravado drag-racing with his friend's car. In the closing reel, subcultural – and class – divisions appear as a group of Teds smash the car and, when confronted by Dave, take his guitar and break that too. Dave refuses to retaliate: 'Fighting's for squares!' Preceding the shot of the reunited family, we see Dave throwing his broken guitar into a bin (Figure 2.4). George Melly's accusations of the castration process of British rockers perhaps find a symbolic home here – but not in a way to be condemned.

To label this as emasculation seems too harsh for, as Pam Cook notes, melodrama's sexual softening provides 'a merging of masculinity and femininity'.[109] It is there in the independent, defiant Jennifer. It is there in the film's conclusion, with a chastened Paul. Above all, it is there in the musician Dave who, like Jennifer, has the courage not to live up to gender and generational expectations. For Andrew Caine 'the movie's cocktail of sex, deviance and crime arguably has more similarities with *Performance* than with *Expresso Bongo*, despite the latter's strip-club scenes'[110] and Dave's final stance indeed pre-echoes James Fox's gender-softening and final merging with Mick Jagger a decade later. In *Beat Girl* Faith gives an attractive, positive performance as a young man not afraid, in modern parlance, to reveal his 'feminine' side. From all the coffee bar films this pop star performance earns the greatest respect.

That such a recuperative conclusion to the 'coffee bar quintet', with its belated use of pop music as a metonym for 'youth-as-trouble', could still elicit intransigent opposition from the censors and vituperative criticism from the national press indicates the extent of the *dialogue de sourds*. The pop music melodramas *Serious Charge* and *Beat Girl* were more complex, probing and ambivalent in their depictions of the young and their music than the censors or the critics first allowed. But one of their pop idol actors would heal the socio-industrial divisions.

Cliff Richard

As cinema changed in the late 1950s so did music, though in an opposite direction. Alongside the ostensibly radical style and content of New Wave cinema came a transmutation of rock'n'roll into more traditional musical forms. Critics again debate the precise year of this change. Charlie Gillett sees rock'n'roll as having 'petered out' around 1958, absorbed by the music industry,[111] while for Nik Cohn 1960 was the *annus horribilis*: with Chuck Berry in jail, Elvis a post-army balladeer and Little Richard with religion, 'It was a wholesale plague, a wipe-out.'[112] Cliff Richard was a prime mover in Britain's musical recuperation with 1959's 'Living Doll' the perfect illustration of a slower 'rock-pop' hybrid which, as Cliff well knew, 'appealed to parents who had money'.[113] For the likes of George Melly this was a showbiz sell-out; for others, though, Cliff was the Saviour of British Youth, with the blending (gelding?) of rock'n'roll into more expansive musical discourses duplicated in a social rapprochement of the generations. Cliff's three pop musicals of the early 1960s are a key component in this 'merger' of rock'n'roll with established modes of entertainment, both in sound, with the styles of music deployed, and in vision, with the reassuring images presented of the young, not now JDs but 'just good kids'. Employing structures far more unflinchingly formulaic than their 'exploitative' coffee bar predecessors, out went Brando, Dean and Presley; in came Rooney, Garland and Astaire.

This musical and moral makeover, with money at the root, inevitably also employs the ideological underpinnings of the Hollywood musical. The musical is not just a film 'type'; it brings with it spectator expectations, structures, codes and conventions which combine to indicate its ideological function as, in Dyer's phrase, a 'gospel of happiness'. Within this gospel, the cultural practice of the Hollywood musical is, as Susan Hayward summarises, 'selling marriage, gender fixity, communal stability and the merits of capitalism'.[114] Initially it may strike that these strategies fit ill with the perceived newness of pop music, the radical, iconoclastic nature of its performers and young audiences. But the 'selling' that Hayward categorises would prove all too easy for Cliff and his various leading ladies to perform.

Especially in its British context, the musical's 'gospel of happiness' establishes a contrast between the new and old decades. Vigour, joyfulness, expansiveness, fun and games are all re-presented/reflected in the look and plotlines of the early 1960s Cliff Richard trilogy. The 1950s had been a decade of post-war negativity, a time of grumbling, bitterness and pessimism: a black-and-white decade. The new decade was going to be different – and in colour. Generically, however, Cliff's mainstream musicals hark back to the 1940s, even the 1930s. In *The American Film Musical*, Rick Altman defines three sub-genres, each concretising a particular form of make-believe: *fairy tale*: to be in another place (whence the travelogue semantics); *show*: to be in another body (whence the emphasis on stage illusion); and *folk*: to be in another time (whence the focus on America of yesteryear).[115] Cliff Richard's 1960s pop music films do not stray into the 'folk' category since the producers sought a topical narrative drive, be it property development, the expanding tourist industry or the film industry itself. But *The Young Ones* can be categorised as a straightforward show musical, *Summer Holiday* a fairy-tale musical, while *Wonderful Life* employs a generic synthesis, conjoining elements of both fairy-tale and show genres. This section will apply the seminal critical works of Altman, Richard Dyer and Jane Feuer, all largely predicated on the classic period of the American musical, to demonstrate just how completely the Cliff trilogy enacts a capitulation to the syntax of its 'parental' generic form.

The pop music film as utopia – *The Young Ones* (1961)

A reported £10,000 pay-out released Cliff Richard from his three-film contract with Mickey Delamar and Alva Films, and cleared the way for his first starring role in a big-budget film musical. This was masterminded by independent film producer Kenneth Harper who secured an initial six-figure budget from the major studio ABPC (Associated British Picture Corporation) and gathered together a strong creative team. For the screenplay and production numbers he hired West End revue regulars Peter Myers and Ron Cass, with Sid Tepper and Roy Bennett commissioned to write three teenage-attracting pop numbers. As director, Harper chose Sidney J. Furie, a 28-year-old Canadian with a growing reputation, and paired him with the experienced director of photography Douglas Slocombe. Even more prestigious in this generic context, Herbert Ross, resident choreographer with the American Ballet Theatre, was brought across the Atlantic to sort out the dance numbers.

None of the team were interested in a rock'n'roll film but all shared an affection for MGM musicals and attention soon focused on *Babes in Arms* (Busby Berkeley, 1939). This Rodgers and Hart musical, starring Mickey Rooney and Judy Garland, told the tale of youngsters putting on a show to raise money: for Cliff it was updated into a group of teenagers putting on a show to save their youth club from being torn down by a property developer. Plot secured, the next step was casting, important since Cliff himself felt unsure of a move to centre-screen.[116] To surround this core fragility, the services were secured of Robert Morley to play property developer Hamilton Black, while Richard O'Sullivan, Teddy Green and Melvyn Hayes became key members of the youth-club gang. Selecting a female lead proved more problematical, with the part finally going to Rhodesian dancer Carole Gray: it was felt that, while pretty, she was not an unduly threatening presence to Cliff's female following and, while talented, she would not upstage the star. Cliff's permanent backing group the Shadows, deprived of strong acting roles, contributed two instrumentals to the soundtrack, supported Cliff on several numbers and wrote the climactic 'We Say Yeah'.[117]

Pace the satirical *Expresso Bongo*, *The Young Ones* was the first British pop music film not conceived as an exploitation 'quickie'. Filming at Elstree Studios lasted from late May to mid-August, its vaudeville finale shot at the Finsbury Park Empire. A mark of ambition if not accounting, the final budget was £230,000, more than double Harper's original estimate. The gala premiere of *The Young Ones* took place at London's Warner Theatre in Leicester Square on 13 December 1961, and opened nationally in January 1962. Across the Atlantic, the film, retitled *It's Wonderful to be Young*, premiered on 13 March but only found exhibition in October 1962. A concerted campaign was mounted to break into the lucrative American market, with Cliff and the Shadows giving hour-long live shows after selected film showings. Sadly, the plan proved a total failure – touring in the middle of the Cuban Missile Crisis may not have helped – with theatres normally holding over two thousand less than half full. Cliff and the Shadows would never tour the States again.

At home, though, *The Young Ones* was hugely successful, commercially and critically. The trade press reported the film 'fairly packing them in' straight from its release[118] and it was ranked second in 1962's top grossing films, only behind *The Guns of Navarone* (J. Lee Thompson, 1961) which had cost £2 million to make. On the strength of this one film, Cliff Richard was seen as the UK's top box-office draw, beating Elvis' three 1962 releases in *Motion Picture Herald*'s annual survey.

Critical response was, for the most part, ecstatic. Paul Dehn's review began: 'I pick my words as cautiously as I burn my boats: this is the best screen-musical ever to have been made in England.'[119] For Nina Hibbin also it was 'easily the best British musical I've seen'.[120] Even the august *Monthly Film Bulletin* called it 'a rare and robust shot at a British musical'.[121] While much of the credit for this success was given to director Sidney Furie, not all agreed: for David Robinson 'derivative choreography' and 'timid shooting' meant that 'the film ends up looking like a Hollywood film of the 'forties (though that in itself is not bad)'.[122] Though his singing escaped censure, there were also differing opinions as to the strength of Cliff's performance. For Dehn it was significant that 'he can now lock horns with Mr Morley and emerge uncrumpled' though Patrick Gibbs felt that Cliff's 'talent hardly enables him to carry a film on his own shoulders'.[123] Hibbin approved of the film's message, a demonstration that 'today's people are a bit of all right' while Gibbs again dissented, pining for the exploitative: 'Artistically I would have preferred them to find the cash with the help of a cosh, flick knife or bicycle chain, for what has started so well ends up ignominiously as yet another back-stage musical.'

The soundtrack album matched the film's commercial success. It topped the UK charts for six weeks in early 1962, selling an unparalleled 110,000 copies in that period, and spent ten months in the top ten. The title track, released in January with 'We Say Yeah', entered the singles charts straight at number one – then a rare achievement – with a record advance order of 524,000 copies, and by March sales passed the million mark. Abroad 'The Young Ones' rang up 2.5 million sales, Cliff's biggest international hit until the late 1970s.

An analysis of the exposition to *The Young Ones* reveals its different scope and ambition from its pop music predecessors. A slow panoramic view of the London cityscape pulls in to reveal its vantage point as the top floor of a skyscraper, still under construction but already dwarfing the historical buildings around it: an embryonic Manhattan-on-the-Thames. A hooter sounds, labour cedes to leisure and Britain's first colour pop music film flaunts its breakthrough feature in the opening credits, all conveyed to a full orchestral score that mirrors architecture by importing a brash American musical influence. Unlike *Expresso Bongo*'s semiotic integration of titles and setting, here the building site with its straight lines of black scaffolding and dull grey concrete is all but obliterated as major players, such as Richard, Ross, Harper and Furie, are named in wavy multicoloured capitals: it is spelled out straightaway that, with high production values, colour (displayed in CinemaScope) will count.

The same colours come into – and out to – play as the opening number is sung against green shopfronts, yellow doorways, red phone boxes and obligatory double-decker buses. The film is at pains to show that hard-working youth, from waitresses to legal assistants, has earned its right to dance on 'Friday Night' while the presentation of their preparations forms its boldest cinematic moment, the screen gradually splitting into eight oblong panels with slabs of colour replaced by the leading players getting themselves ready. Each addition is matched to the rhythm of the music, providing a visual octave, a metonymic keyboard. Sound and vision synergise, demonstrating how music plus colour equals entertainment. The distance from the New Wave realism of a work such as *Expresso Bongo* is confirmed in the first duet, where Cliff's Nicky both advocates and illustrates the 'classic' musical's utopian power. 'Nothing is impossible as long as you believe,' he tells Toni, illustrating the conquest of Everest by jumping to the top of a phone box and Gagarin's conquest of space by swinging vertically around a Belisha beacon. Disappearing into the night sky without even attempting a goodnight kiss, Nicky is respectful to the point of chasteness, a leading man reminiscent of Gene Kelly in what Rick Altman terms his 'eternal youth' and 'adolescent energy' with 'childlike qualities'.[124] Here is a utopia free of Newtonian principles *and* of teenage promiscuity.

For Richard Dyer this utopian sensibility consists of five main categories: community, transparency, abundance, energy and intensity.[125] Dyer has shown how songs from musicals such as *Gold Diggers of 1933* (Mervyn LeRoy, 1933), *On the Town* (Stanley Donen, 1949) and *Funny Face* (Stanley Donen, 1957) fit into each of these categories: by making a similar application to *The Young Ones* this section will demonstrate how wholly the Cliff musical imports the codes and conventions of its Hollywood template.

Dyer defines community as 'all together in one place, communal interests, collective activity', while its main showbiz form constitutes the singalong chorus numbers.[126] This is most clearly demonstrated in *The Young Ones*' first chorus number which follows on Cliff's call that

they hire the theatre for one night and 'show Mr Black that he's dealing with every young kid in town'. Jane Feuer notes of Hollywood that
'over and over again in these backstage films we see the "kids" triumph-
ing over greed, egotism and all those puritanical forces which would,
in the name of the community, conspire against entertainment'.[127]
Employing Dyer's terminology, this triumph is the utopian solution to
fragmentation – '(job mobility, rehousing and development, high-rise
flats, legislation against collective action)'.[128] In a precise match, this
fragmentation is the social tension which provides the narrative motor
for *The Young Ones*. Whilst a dominant, divisive subplot in *Beat Girl*, *The
Young Ones* is instead cut from the same cloth as the Rooney–Garland
vehicles since, in mounting the show that will save their youth club, the
theatrical community inevitably conquers – and unifies – all.

Dyer admits that the weakness of his analysis is the omission of class,
race or patriarchy.[129] To these 'give-away absences' *The Young Ones* adds
age since, as part of its entertainment utopia, the film seeks to dissipate
any notion of generational conflict – even Hamilton Black views the
economic clash with his son Nicky primarily as a training exercise for
the heir apparent: Sue Harper terms it 'oedipal by-play between Cliff
and his father'.[130] Narratively, this unity is foregrounded in the reaction
to the broadcasts of the mystery singer's ballad number 'When the Girl
in Your Arms'. Functioning like Tommy Steele's hospital-ward audience, a fan base stretching from boarding-school girls to bridge-playing
pensioners, and even (stretching credulity) a smoky cellar-bar cabal of
beatniks, listens attentively to the radio. This device of synchronised
simultaneous radio listening is a commonplace of later musicals: Rick
Altman compares its use in *American Hot Wax* (Floyd Mutrux, 1978), creating a 'constellated community' of otherwise heterogeneous people, to
earlier musicals' most characteristic throwback device, the passed-along
song, where 'all succeed in making music together because of their
commonality'.[131] *The Young Ones* employs both devices. The film begins
with a passed-along song: in a strategy similar to the start of *Porgy and
Bess* (Otto Preminger, 1959), 'Friday Night' establishes both the gang's
post-work aspirations and the film's long-standing generic conventions,
the orchestrated city symphony moving us from one contented citizen
to another, common interest synchronising their every sound and
movement. Thus *The Young Ones'* vision of societal coherence incorpo-
rates both new and established methods of musical sharing. Young and
old sing in the same key, tune in to the same waveband.

More intimate numbers illustrate Dyer's second category, transparency. For the performance of 'Lessons in Love' Nicky sings to Toni

and they dance close but chastely together. This replicates the familiar musical trope of rehearsal numbers becoming courtship rituals rather than performances for an audience. When ousted by the buxom star Dorinda Morrell, Toni tearfully flees the club though, true to Hollywood conventions, the leading lady gets her solo number, with 'No One for Me but Nicky' enacting Toni's determination to fight Dorinda for her young man's affection. Wandering up and down the street, she is filmed through a misty halo, a Doris Day effect that adds an American aura to the home-town girl. It also, paradoxically, illustrates Dyer's sense of 'Transparency – (open, spontaneous, honest communications and relationships)' with its 'links to sincerity' and its showbiz forms in 'sincere' stars, love and romance. For Dyer this forms the utopian solution to 'Manipulation (advertising, bourgeois democracy, sex roles)'.[132] The consciously performed sexuality of Dorinda, part of a cynical media stunt to 'exploit' the group's plight, provides the manipulation against the 'honest' performance of Nicky to Toni, the dedicatee of his composition and the only partner with whom he can 'sincerely' perform the song. Sue Harper notes that the film's 'gender arrangements are symmetrical. Good girl Toni has managed hair and a flat chest. Bad girl Dorinda has ebullient hair and breasts. Poor Cliff has no choice at all.'[133] True, but not as Harper implies: it has to be Toni with her tomboy name, her wholesome demeanour and dressed as a city gent in the finale's tap-dance number. Not for the first time in a British pop music film, sex doesn't come into the picture – not yet.

Dyer defines Abundance as 'the elimination of poverty for self and others; equal distribution of wealth' and well-being with its showbiz forms residing in spectacle, décor and costume.[134] *The Young Ones* displays a confident British variant as abundance is flaunted on-(wide)screen throughout the film. Its benefits are most openly evidenced in the title song, filmed at the Reigate lido: there, as Nicky sings to Toni, we see around them the affluent young at play, sunbathing and water-skiing. There is no need, or desire, to vandalise the lido, as perpetrated by the gang in *Serious Charge*: instead teenagers legitimately enjoy the benefits of capitalism and sensuous material reality. The song goes further, though, working musically and lyrically to provide again an equal distribution of generational values. Its instrumentation derives from rock'n'roll while foregrounding Norrie Paramor's string arrangement that (harmoniously) answers each sung line of the verse. Its lyrics advocate both *carpe diem* – 'why wait until tomorrow?' – and adult care – 'then we'll teach the young ones of our own'. These twin tenets are visually reinforced as hedonistic teenagers cede to Cliff picking up a young child and adopting the pose of pseudo-dad. His depiction has softened considerably from the flick-knives and coshes of which Hamilton (exaggeratedly) speaks earlier in the film.

Dyer's fourth category, energy, is defined as 'work and play synonymous' and sources its showbiz forms in tap and American Ballet Theatre.[135] Backstage musicals have always quoted liberally from theatrical sources: *Cover Girl* (Charles Vidor, 1944) flashes back to vaudeville, while the 'Born in a Trunk' sequence from *A Star is Born* (George Cukor, 1954) offers a virtual history of musical theatre. In similar fashion, *The Young Ones* maximises choreographer Herbert Ross' expertise by foregrounding its own 'Ballet Theatre' antecedents, notably in the extended music-hall sequence of 'What Do You Know We've Got a Show'. This is crucial to *The Young Ones* establishing its credentials and conventions, advocating continuity between the music in the film – and thus the film itself – and traditional, adult forms of musical entertainment, British and American, which the visual media – including this film – are in the process of superseding. In a lengthy number eclectically sourcing and acknowledging vaudeville, melodrama, the country house mystery and Astaire and Rogers, the music and choreography conclude with Nicky, to accompanying female screams, high-kicking his way centre-stage and singing the chorus of 'Living Doll'. The set-piece thus climaxes with self-quotation, Cliff placing himself seamlessly into its long multimedia genealogy. This process of quotation also plays on the audience's feelings for the performers of yesteryear, creating a sense of continuity and instilling a communal bond. As Feuer notes, 'The earlier form is recycled into the contemporary form, in the process cancelling through quotation any discontinuities between the audience and the entertainment industry.'[136]

Dyer sees his final category, 'Intensity – (excitement, drama, affectivity of living)', as closely linked to ideas of 'authenticity' and coming from the intimacy the spectator takes pleasure in while watching the body perform.[137] In *The Young Ones* this is most noticeable in the climactic show's brief shining affirmation of rock'n'roll independence. 'We Say Yeah' is arguably the most raunchy, transgressive song treatment in a British pop music film thus far. Especially given its surrounding discourse, it is strong stuff, providing an affective cinematic correlation with rhythm and lyrics. Establishing shots of Cliff with the Shadows, and then the audience, precede a medium shot of Cliff singing of teenage rebellion: 'Momma says no, daddy says no, / they all gotta go, coz we say yeah,' a musical reaffirmation of Tommy Steele's initial 'Rebel Rock'. The camera cuts first to ecstatic female fans screaming back 'yeah', a reminder that passionate, quasi-sexual adulation preceded the arrival of the Beatles, then back to the object of their ardour, its new low-level footlights position providing what Rick Altman terms a 'crotch shot' (Figure 2.5).[138] During the second verse and chorus, a view from behind Cliff focuses on his legs as he dances, then provides a further close-up of the pop idol and a further reaction shot of his fans screaming back their affirmation before Cliff retreats towards the Shadows, the curtain is drawn and the audience applaud rapturously. It is, compared to what has come before, an audacious sequence: the fast pace of editing and juxtaposition of images accentuate the sexuality of the performance, the 'danger' of the rock performer, far different to the chastened Tommy Steele. It achieves this by allowing what Feuer calls a 'doubled identification' as 'We feel a sense of participation in the creation of entertainment (from sharing the perspective of the performers) and, at the same time, we feel part of the live audience in the theatre.' Feuer reiterates Dyer's terminology: 'Only a reflexive form such as the musical can lend so much *intensity* to our experience of a simple song and dance.'[139] In this generic context, the level of 'intensity' conveyed by the performance both on-stage and from the director's chair constitutes by far the most achieved expression yet of celluloid rock and is a harbinger of Richard Lester's more celebrated concert climax to *A Hard Day's Night*.

The structure of the climactic show is significant, however, subsuming Cliff and the Shadows into consensus as it moves straight into the choreographed stage version of 'What Do You Know We've Got a Show', replete with music-hall tempi and temporal nostalgia. With Hamilton

Figure 2.5 One brief shining moment: Cliff as cock rock – *The Young Ones*

Black invited on for a further 'take-over bid' and then shuffling centre-stage between Nicky and Toni, the number's simple choreography demonstrates that the errant son will settle down with his father's loving – and economic – blessing. Altman sees the Hollywood musical as an 'ode to marriage' and the marrying of riches (as exemplified by the male) to beauty (in the form of the female).[140] *The Young Ones* fits exactly within this paradigm, Nicky having the rich father, Toni the sensible good looks. The family and the firm are reconciled, the Oedipal trajectory has been completed, and the genre can realise its ideological strategies, selling marriage, gender fixity, communal stability and, not least, the merits of capitalism. It comes, though, at the cost of instant musical castration, a trend that continues with Cliff's next film, *Summer Holiday*.

The pop music film as fairy tale – *Summer Holiday* (1963)

The success of *The Young Ones* led the financial backers to prepare an immediate repeat. Producer Kenneth Harper kept the same creative team from *The Young Ones* though Sidney Furie was committed to working on *The Boys* (1962), a social melodrama featuring a Shadows score. In his place Harper appointed 33-year-old debutant Peter Yates, fresh from the Royal Court – and later to find international success directing Steve McQueen in *Bullitt* (1968). A fuller budget, over half a million pounds, was secured, and the team set to work, hopeful that, in Cliff's own words, their 'successful formula could be squeezed a little harder'.[141]

Harper sought a film voyage to Greece to reflect the increased interest among young British people in travelling abroad for their holidays. Writer Ron Cass' inspiration to employ a London RT double-decker bus can be traced back to British Transport Films' 1955 *From Shepherd's Bush to Zurich*, a record of two such buses touring around Europe.[142] The rest of the script fell quickly into place, Cliff leading a group of London Transport mechanics who convert a bus into a mobile home and drive it across Europe to Greece. Cliff's gang were also retained, though Richard O'Sullivan was unavailable and Una Stubbs proved a notable, lasting addition – her working partnership with Cliff would extend to his 1970s television shows. After rejecting choreographer Herbert Ross' first Broadway recommendation, Barbra Streisand, the producers awarded the part of the female lead to 19-year-old Lauri Peters, a classically trained dancer who had played James Stewart's daughter in *Mr Hobbs Takes a Vacation* (Henry Koster, 1962). Again recommended by Ross as a passport to potential American distributors, Peters was, as with Carole Gray in *The Young Ones*, not the anticipated glamorous lead.

For Tony Meehan this was an entrée for Cliff's fan base: 'The notion was to pick girls who were quite plain and who wouldn't threaten the fans. I think the girls liked leading ladies who they could identify with.'[143] Interiors were shot at Elstree Studios but almost all exteriors, supposedly crossing Europe, were filmed on location in and around Athens, testimony to the resourcefulness of art director Syd Case. Filming began in Greece in late May 1962, though the 'Bachelor Boy' scene was later added at an Elstree mock set-up when it was discovered that the final edit was three minutes too short.

There was no shortage in marketing, however: *Kinematograph Weekly* noted how 'one of the most ambitious and far-reaching exploitation campaigns ever planned for a British film is now under way to launch the film'. Alongside extensive media coverage and pre-release screenings in 70 UK venues, this included a 'Summer Holiday' range of summer fashions, and well-publicised 'special appearances' by the converted double-decker bus.[144] The film was given a gala premiere at the Warner Theatre in Leicester Square on 10 January 1963, with Cliff driving the bus up to the theatre entrance. The film opened nationally two weeks later, and throughout Europe in March. Its low-key US release, through AIP, did not come until October.

Arguably the single best marketing ploy had been brokered by Kenneth Harper who deliberately scheduled a winter release in the hope of increasing the film's escapist appeal. The weather duly obliged and *Summer Holiday* proceeded to break all box-office records for a British film and for the year 1963 was only out-grossed by another sequel, *From Russia with Love*, directed by *Serious Charge*'s Terence Young.

Cliff considered *Summer Holiday* the peak of his film career,[145] and most critics agreed. Margaret Hinxman, full of praise for his previous year's 'breakthrough in British musicals', wrote that 'miraculously this follow-up film is even better',[146] while Penelope Gilliatt stated that *Summer Holiday* 'must be the most cheerful and skilful British musical of our generation'.[147] While the *Daily Mail* was typical in acknowledging that 'the film owes much to the professional punch and pace of Peter Yates's direction and Herbert Ross's choreography',[148] the slimmer Cliff – a passing 'chubby' comment on *Coronation Street* occasioned a sustained work-out – was roundly praised. Felix Barker was not alone in emphasising the star's cross-generational appeal, finding that 'every mother would be proud to have him for a son, every daughter as a boy-friend'.[149] Penelope Gilliatt hypothesised that the 'rock-bottom reason' for *Summer Holiday*'s box-office appeal would not be Cliff Richard or the love story but the fact that Myers and Cass 'have embedded in it the

great characteristic that is overlooked by everyone who abuses teenagers: their solidarity and tolerance towards each other and their belief
in a casually communistic way of life'.

Maybe: *Summer Holiday* certainly reiterated a capitalist solidarity
between the film's commercial success and affiliated record sales. The
soundtrack album beat *The Young Ones* album to one million sales, both
its 14 weeks at number one and 36-week chart run the longest of Cliff's
career. The album spawned three number one singles, again unequalled
at the time, each selling over a million copies. In every popular and
commercial aspect this was the apogee of the British pop music film
thus far.

Summer Holiday immediately plays with the expectations set up by
The Young Ones. Where Cliff's previous film highlighted its Technicolor
status, the new offering teases the audience by beginning in black and
white. In an opening redolent of New Wave style and content (and
Harper's exhibition strategy), we are presented with shots of a pier and
windswept beach, where a brass band is playing 'Summer Holiday' to
a handful of spectators before rain and storms send all running for
cover. Here is no idealised nostalgia for working-class leisure; not here
the warmth or communality of the trips to Blackpool in *A Taste of
Honey* (Tony Richardson, 1961) or Southport in *A Kind of Loving* (John
Schlesinger, 1962). *Summer Holiday* attempts instead a social topicality
by presenting these British seaside resorts as a colourless world, far short
of the utopian foreign holiday destinations sought by the young ones
of the sun-seeking sixties.[150] The film relocates to a London Transport
garage yard and, as a bulky shape slowly materialises through the rain,
the image subtly changes to colour. It is a swift transition with a lengthy
genealogy. Jane Feuer shows how the Hollywood musical 'progressively
added colour to provide more entertainment, that is, to increase the
voluptuousness of those parts of a film which were supposed to represent fantasy'.[151] Most famously, it is there in the contrast between the
dream of Oz and the reality of Kansas. In Britain's latest musical that
'glorious' colour first materialises not with a yellow brick road but with
the totemic patriotic bright red bodywork of the London Transport
double-decker bus WLB 991.

There are two issues to emphasise here. This transition encodes
Summer Holiday as Cliff's 'fairy-tale musical' *and* emphasises the film's
bolder espousal of British values. Whilst *The Tommy Steele Story*, the
only previous pop film to visit foreign shores, eliminated all reference to the United States, *Summer Holiday* reveals a renewed sixties
confidence in British identity by setting up an early contrast between

British and American values, emotionally and musically. To investigate this interaction with American socio-cinematic models, it is beneficial to view *Summer Holiday* through the paradigm structures set down by Rick Altman in *The American Film Musical*. Altman again defines the Hollywood musical corpus through five main syntactical categories: Narrative Strategy; Narrative/Number; Couple/Plot; Image/Sound; and Music/Plot. Each can be applied to Cliff's song-and-dance road movie, the contrast between transatlantic values setting up the first category.

Summer Holiday, in apeing the Hollywood musical, borrows its narrative strategy from what Altman terms dual-focus structures, largely conducted between the male and female leads, each identified with specific cultural values: 'only by reading these films from the point of view of courtship and male/female parallelism can we discover their operation as musicals'.[152] For Altman these characters generate a chain of oppositions – sexual, background, national origin and temperament – which must be resolved for marriage to occur.[153] Applying this to *Summer Holiday* we see Cliff's Don, happy to be single, contrasting with Barbara, looking for love and commitment and, though national differences are not unduly problematic, a chasm exists in social status: motor mechanic versus successful star. *Summer Holiday*, however, *reverses* the set of societal oppositions that Altman sees as typical of a Hollywood musical such as *Top Hat* (Mark Sandrich, 1935) where the British are categorised as: aristocrat, closed society, silence, formality, repression, business, legality; whilst the American is termed as: commoner, open society, noise, informality, freedom, pleasure, love.[154] Here, set in 'neutral' continental Europe, it is the Americans who are, if not aristocratic, possessed of wealthy pretensions, who restrict the pleasure and the freedom of their young and look for money from a marriage: it is Don, his factory-working colleagues and the three British girls on their way to Athens who sing, have the freedom to travel, dress informally, and fall in love without parental – or societal – obstruction.

Barbara's final declaration that, irrespective of their respective social status, she would love to marry Don links with Altman's second element of musical syntax. For narrative/number 'the musical does not just combine realism and rhythmic movement, dialogue and diegetic movement', but also 'creates continuity between these radically different areas'. For Altman this continuity is founded on the bonds of marriage: 'In societies heavily dependent on mythical thinking, marriage is openly conceived as a mystical phenomenon, a magic moment permitting the union of the two into one. Even in the more practical traditions of western capitalism, however, the basic arrangement remains the same.'[155] Both the mythical and capitalist approaches to marriage are presented in *Summer Holiday*, through the Yugoslav wedding dance and the final press-witnessed engagement. The film plays on both societal views of marriage and, whilst the depiction of the Yugoslav peasant ceremony met with contemporary criticism for its 'casual racism',[156] the Western capitalist view, solely valued by Barbara's mother as regulating the transfer of capital, does not necessarily profit from the comparison.

However motivated, the young couple's concluding kiss sanctions the third of Altman's syntactic quintet, the couple/plot. 'The formation of the couple is linked either causally or through parallelism to success in the ventures which constitute the plot.'[157] With Stella Winters' final acceptance of Don as son-in-law, the trip is successfully completed, the marriage and the transport contracts earned. In keeping with Hollywood practice, the relationship between male and female lead is not a mere adjunct to the musical's overall plot. 'Time and again, to solve the couple's problems becomes synonymous with, and thus a figure for, a solution for the plot's other enterprises.'[158] Most of these revolve around boy–girl relationships, and *Summer Holiday* presents a challenging, if uncertain, demonstration of gender roles.

Firstly, whatever her failings as a mother, Stella is a forceful figure of power and persuasion: there is no Mr Winters and seemingly no need for one. The three girls driving over to Athens also convey a sense of independence and empowerment: the dance routine to the song 'Let Us Take You for a Ride', in the style of French director Jacques Demy, stresses that any agreement to travel with the boys will be on the girls' terms. This initially places the sexes in conflict, a plot strategy that Altman defines as 'sex-as-battle'.[159] However, it does not last beyond this first Ross rumpus: once on the bus, the girls assume traditional roles by preparing the food and sewing buttons, suggesting that their mobile living quarters have become a feminised space in a less than liberating manner. Overall, though, the film can be seen as more positively gendered, fitting closest to Altman's category of 'sex as adventure' which he sees as 'aimed primarily at a female audience'.[160] Like the first great fairy-tale musical *The Desert Song* (Roy Del Ruth, 1929), 'the film fashions out of the clichés of exoticism a coherent thematics, a syntactic bond between the spectator's overt fascination with unknown lands and that same spectator's unavowed but intense interest in the uncharted seas of sexuality'.[161] It is the same for Barbara Winters, the female audience's unthreatening screen representative, who meets a man possessing the novelty and excitement that she craves. She is frustrated by the nature of her reality; he seems identified with the exoticism and danger of the very land around him.

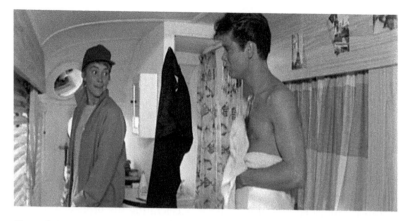

Figure 2.6   Beefcake on the bus: Cliff inviting the fe/male gaze – *Summer Holiday*

Barbara's refusal to return home, declaring that, 'Mother, I'm having more fun than I've ever had!,' is generalised by the girls' dismissal of the boys' Athens apologies: 'We wouldn't have missed it for the world!' It is in this presentation of excitement for the female characters – and female audience – that *Summer Holiday* most closely replays the template established, not by Rooney and Garland, but by Nelson Eddy and Jeanette MacDonald, especially in a film such as *Naughty Marietta* (W.S. Van Dyke, 1935) which, for Altman, 'seems to possess every element requisite for a sex-as-adventure success'.[162] There are numerous plot comparisons, but *Summer Holiday* can offer (briefly) a more open view of sex, with the newly lean Cliff happy to be seen topless emerging from a shower on the bus (Figure 2.6). Barbara, disguised as a boy, is given a close, privileged view of the torso, like the (predominantly female) audience she represents. The scene sets up complex sexual and gender ambivalences. Responding to Laura Mulvey's influential work on the male gaze,[163] Mary Ann Doane sees the female spectator as masochistic or transvestite,[164] a position equally applicable to Barbara. *Summer Holiday* takes many of the tropes of the musical comedy, using disguise and mistaken identity/ transvestism, not just to further the plot and provoke laughter, but also as 'a psychological crutch, an invitation to "dress up" mentally, to try on other, normally forbidden roles'.[165] In *Naughty Marietta*, disguised as her own maid, a young lady may speak more frankly than normal and express a hidden but desirable side of her personality. Disguised as a boy, Barbara uses the mime sequence to intimate her true gender. This foregrounds the implicit connection between make-believe and theatrical or filmic illusion, explicitly identifying the viewing pleasures of the audience with the desires of the film's characters. The travelling mime artists are the more openly artistic equivalent of Cliff and his bus crew and they help to complete what Altman calls 'the fairy tale musical's triangle of desire', namely, the exotic – travel; the forbidden – (sexual) adventure; and artistic illusion – the right to sing.

Altman notes that 'the traditional classical narrative hierarchy of image over sound is reversed at the climactic moments of the musical'.[166] This fourth element of syntax, where language is lifted to a more expressive realm, is evident when Don enters the press conference and, abandoning speech for song, finally declares his love in 'Big News'. More globally, *Summer Holiday*'s 'melding' of its visually and narratively encoded oppositions is replicated at a musical level, accelerating the process begun in *The Young Ones* and moving Cliff Richard into more traditional popular music modes. Again the film functions as a musical compromise, though with the balance swinging (in both senses of the word) more towards traditional, ballad, and revival jazz rhythms. *Summer Holiday* is by far the most musically 'rich' of the pop films investigated in this study, containing a total of 18 musical sections. With 11 song-and-dance sequences, three Shadows instrumentals, credit accompaniments, and musical numbers linked to a Yugoslavian wedding and courtroom mime, by the standards of any musical the film reveals a complex sonorous texture. The duet 'A Swinging Affair' is here pivotal in providing a stylistic linkage between the Myers–Cass show songs and the Shadows' compositions that reinforces narrative developments: as Don realises his desire to be with Barbara, so his smooth low-key pop voice joins with Lauri Peters' more brassy, theatre-style vibrato.[167]

Indeed, 'A Swinging Affair' constitutes the full fulcrum of *Summer Holiday*. It occurs halfway through the film, with the bus and its crew at the top of the Alps: after this, it is, literally and musically, downhill all the way. In particular the waltz sees a capitulation to traditional orchestral discourse. At least the film feels constrained to provide a lyrical apology for this 'emasculation' of the English Elvis as the four young couples rise and take to the dance floor, almost involuntarily: 'As the music flows through me / I belong to the song with the one-two-three beat,' Cliff intones. With a change of time signature we move from rock'n'roll to Johann Strauss. For aficionados of the recent rock tradition, this must have signalled the point of no return, the *pointe assassine* from which there could be no forgiveness. Diegetically, though, the musical style and lyrical reluctance are all part of a greater good: as in *Top Hat*'s 'Isn't it a Lovely Day to be Caught in the Rain', it is not so much words or song: 'the magic of dance has brought their love along as no dialogue ever could'.[168] It is a magic directed towards dominant systems of social – and generic – ideology.

The whole sequence illustrates the fifth and final of Altman's syntactic elements of the musical, namely music/plot. This is not just music's primacy over plot at emotional junctures, but 'music's tendency to enter into structured relationships'.[169] In the American genre competing musical styles fight it out: for example, all-black musicals from *Hallelujah* (King Vidor, 1929) through to *Cabin in the Sky* (Vincente Minnelli, 1943) commonly set up an opposition between church music and jazz. *Summer Holiday* half-heartedly lines up rock against orchestral jazz rhythms, though after brief moments from the Shadows in a Parisian cellar-bar the contest is all but conceded, the camera leaving them to focus on the film's main protagonists dancing amongst the audience. The group's marginalisation – their own musical castration – is complete with Bachelor Boy's late addition to the film: while Cliff sings presciently of his planned celibacy, the guitar-rocking boys lose their instruments altogether and uncomfortably perform what Bruce Welch would look back on as 'a real wally dance'.[170]

Cliff has remained a bachelor boy, which leads to a further contextual factor where cinema can deliver a picture and a soundtrack of a moment. This relates to the star's 'extra-filmic' dimension, the material connected to a performer's life and reputation outside the film itself. Recent sing-a-long DVD releases suggest an added cult audience for Cliff's colour films, rather than the 'mainstream' audiences of the early 1960s. Cult audiences for musicals are difficult to define but one can be readily located in the gay male urban subculture. A major problem with Altman's generic theory, based on ideas of normative heterosexual coupling, is that it does not address how 'resisting readers' can transform a musical: his 'mass audience' reading strategies involve an acceptance of what by the early 1960s were already debatable gender-based conventions of partnering. Though this is the one film of the trilogy that does not have the squabbling camp 'couple' formed by Melvyn Hayes and Richard O'Sullivan, *Summer Holiday* continues a thread of 'coded' gay iconography running from a look at the end of *Serious Charge* and through a stage outfit at the centre of *Expresso Bongo*: indeed it constitutes the Cliff film most conducive to a gay reading. One must omit here the question of gay personnel or authorship, an orientation lengthily denied by Cliff himself. 'Queer' readings of musicals shift the emphasis from narrative resolution as heterosexual coupling – the comic plot – onto readings based on non-narrative, performative and spectacular elements – the numbers. Thus, the Greek 'look' as a well-toned Cliff sings 'The Next Time' on the hills outside Athens matters over and above the narrative codes. This is the one film where we see Cliff topless – and as he emerges from the shower a 'young boy' passes him his towel. All of which returns us to Judy Garland, though minus Mickey Rooney and far from Kansas. Referencing instead Vincente Minnelli's European-set *The Pirate* (1948), one could suggest that *Summer Holiday* similarly embodies a 'queer' sensibility in its movement away from a constrictive heterosexuality and towards a liberating androgyny. Thus, while conforming to an ideology that ostensibly sells marriage and the merits of capitalism, its vision of utopia is a perfect world of freedom *from* the constraints of gender. For Richard Dyer, 'only *The Pirate* seems to use Garland's campness in a sustained fashion in its play with sex roles and spectacular illusion, two of the standard pleasures musicals offer'.[171] The mime scene with Orlando's players, Cliff's enjoyment of the company of other men while singing his creed of Bachelordom and Lauri Peters' cross-dressing are all-important here. Heterosexuality and femininity as masquerade are perennially important themes and they find an intriguing articulation in that liminal space of personal liberation and exploration, the *Summer Holiday*.

The pop music film as conservative reflexivity – *Wonderful Life* (1964)

In December 1963 Cliff Richard left for the Canary Islands to complete the third of his films for Harper, Cass and Myers. Intended as the crowning achievement of a trilogy that had taken the box office by storm and the critical press by surprise, problems were apparent from the outset. Cast and crew were initially secure: though Herbert Ross had returned to the United States, choreography was entrusted to the up-and-coming Gillian Lynne, and Sidney Furie was free to resume directing duties. Cliff had Melvyn Hayes, Richard O'Sullivan and Una Stubbs around him, while a more charismatic and conventionally beautiful leading lady was employed, Susan Hampshire progressing from her brief deb appearance in *Expresso Bongo*. Timing, though, was a severe problem. To maintain momentum, it was known that filming should have taken place the previous summer, with a release date early in 1964, but Cliff had been signed to a summer season in Blackpool and the cinematic impetus was lost. So too, given the seismic events on Merseyside, was the audience's musical tolerance. The script then failed to cohere. The original plot, centred on Mexican banditry, had to be abandoned due to the cost of filming in central America. A relocation to the Canary

Islands led to a total rewrite – and a loss of orientation. Suddenly working against the clock, Cass and Myers' resultant scenario had little thematic unity, with scenes changing almost daily to accommodate prevailing on-set weather conditions and other contingencies, such as a sudden chance to film on the docked Queen Mary liner. Then an unreliable Dennis Price had to be replaced by former Rank front man Derek Bond, while Una Stubbs and Melvyn Hayes both had lengthy absences due to illness and injury. At least for the cast in situ their 15-minute 'The History of the Movies' sequence – described on call-sheets as 'the bad-weather standby' – had greater attention, and success. Interior scenes were filmed back at Elstree Studios in February and March, and *Wonderful Life* was premiered at the Empire Theatre in Leicester Square, London on 2 July 1964 in the presence of HRH Princess Alexandra. The film opened nationally on 7 September. It was retitled *Swingers' Paradise* for its inevitably low-key American release.

Wonderful Life was to prove the least rewarding of the colour trilogy, coming in at a relatively disappointing number five in the list of top-grossing films for the year 1964. Cliff admitted that 'it wasn't the best end to a trilogy of British musicals!'[172] and critical opinion broadly concurred. *Films and Filming* stated that '*Wonderful Life* is a sad little picture' and highlighted the production problems of an 'improvised' film musical: 'A live musical can be tightened up as it is run-in on a provincial tour; but not a film, it has to be with-it from the opening shot to the last.'[173] In the national press Leonard Mosley, so fulsome in his praise of *Summer Holiday*, headed this review: 'Even Cliff Can't Sing His Way Out of This!' before trashing 'this bloodsome bore of a film' in which 'they've sabotaged the boy. Torpedoed him. Drowned him in drivel.'[174] John Coleman noted a tiredness in the formula, a slipping from the *Zeitgeist*: 'what looked pleasing domestic mateyness and frolics in *The Young Ones* now comes over as desperation'.[175] Cliff passed through it all, his reputation if anything enhanced. Dilys Powell found him 'brasher, snappier in action, but still the boy Galahad',[176] while Michael Thornton's assessment revealed enduring hierarchies of taste: 'Now, for the first time, he shows the ability to outlive his original pop-idol status and endure as a serious artist.'[177]

Musically the soundtrack album was again the trilogy's least successful, reaching 'only' number two behind the debut, eponymous album of *The Rolling Stones* and staying in the charts for just 23 weeks. 'On the Beach', the sole single release, reached a relatively disappointing number seven in Britain, though worldwide it brought in close to one million sales. Like the film, however, it lacked the longevity of its two predecessors.

The opening to *Wonderful Life* immediately enacts the capitulation of rock'n'roll to traditional musical styles, as Cliff and the Shadows, happy enough as a jobbing string quartet, lose their jobs when their electric guitars blow the ship's generator. Cliff's previous title songs had some pretension to a pop-rock format, but 'Wonderful Life', with strings and chorus foregrounded, establishes the film's musical discourse as mainstream, unelectric. While the narrative combines show and fairy-tale musical structures, elsewhere *Wonderful Life* is notably non-dialogic as interplay between emergent and established musical discourses cedes to a repertoire of devices taken wholesale from Hollywood, with large-scale dance numbers such as 'In a Matter of Moments' and sexually based duets such as 'All Kinds of People' reaching saturation point.

'On the Beach' alone possesses anything remotely resembling a rock-style 'intensity', allowing Cliff to erode the film's boy-meets-girl tentativeness as he pulls Jenny out to dance. We move from the pleasure of watching their easy, assertive poses to the Shadows and Hank Marvin who, the centre of musical attention for the one time in the film, proceeds to quote the chords of the middle-eight from The Beatles' version of 'Twist and Shout'. It is a significant shift from *The Young Ones'* confident self-quotation of 'Living Doll': the moment of admission that both Cliff and the Shadows' time has gone, that the baton of popular music – and music film – has passed to Liverpool. Even in the textual confines of *Wonderful Life*, the song's much needed vitality is immediately contained, ending with a graphic cut from Cliff to Douglas (Bond), the older generation with which Cliff will work so comfortably as an on-screen 'brother' at the film's finale as they perform 'Youth and Experience' to their film premiere's audience. As if to literalise this equivalence of values, one-half of this audience is shown to consist of the older generation, including Chelsea pensioners, singing that 'We don't understand the young' or 'the hair styles they like'. Instead of a row of quiffed cosh boys or even mop-topped Merseybeats, the film audience's other half, that unknowable Youth, is revealed as a group of smartly dressed boy scouts and girl guides, grandchildren to be proud of as they sway in quasi-military unison. Never did the final credit 'The End' seem so appropriate.

The most fully realised spectacle in *Wonderful Life* is considered to be its lengthy 'We Love a Movie' montage. In truth, there are many aspects of this section that one could criticise: the infantilism, the anti-intellectualism, the US-centrism, the repetition of procedures seen both in previous Cliff films and even in this film's earlier 'With a Little Imagination' sequence. Let two examples suffice. The Shadows start and close the sequence dressed as the Keystone Cops: pop stars, elsewhere portrayed in British pop music films as juvenile delinquents, are now slapstick upholders of law and order. Lauri Peters' transvestism in *Summer Holiday* occasioned mild examinations of gender fixity: here great film beauties turn out to be the Shadows in drag, the pretext for a cheap gag. Overall it seems that *Wonderful Life*, rather than catching the excitement and renewed *danger* of contemporary British popular music, has a pedagogic agenda: educating the young in its (imported) cinematic heritage.

This could be considered an easy target to denigrate, with more ostentatious results obtainable by placing the sequence in a more radical perspective. To that end, Jane Feuer's *The Hollywood Musical* will be central to the rest of this investigation. For instance, *Wonderful Life*, just like *An American in Paris* (Vincente Minnelli, 1951), acknowledges an element of fantasy within the musical's structure. To reapply Feuer's observation on Gene Kelly's work in general: 'each film places a secondary, more stylized fictional world into a primary, less stylized fiction'.[178] This structure in *Wonderful Life* could be investigated, not as an impoverished apeing of classical Hollywood, but rather as a 'modernist' distancing device. Film theorist Peter Wollen has employed the term 'multiple diegesis', signifying multiple narrative worlds, to refer to the heterogeneous narrative levels in the late sixties films of Jean-Luc Godard.[179] Applying this radical framework to Cliff's film, one could set up a series of hypotheses. Is the 'We Love a Movie' montage deconstructive? Does it separate elements, lifting spectators out of their transparent identification with the story and enforcing a Brechtian concentration on the film's overall artifice?

Alas, it is not possible to establish *Wonderful Life* as Sidney Furie's version of *Weekend* (1967): they are diametrically opposed – 'worlds apart' – in their ambitions. In a Godard film, multiple diegesis calls attention to the gap between fiction and reality or history, as seen in his later British pop music film with the Rolling Stones. Within the Hollywood musical, however, and English epigones such as the Cliff Richard trilogy, heterogeneous levels are created only to be finally homogenised through the union of the romantic couple. This holds true with a degree of aesthetic satisfaction for the first two Cliff musicals: the great disappointment of *Wonderful Life* is that it can only claim this unification at a clumping structural level. The soundtrack lacks a correlative contrast in discourse, while a contrary viewing of the film allows scant 'intellectual' distantiation. This is not to decry Furie: it is the same with all Hollywood musicals, especially the backstage or behind-the-camera variant which, as

Feuer reveals, is congenitally reflexive. Instead of any modernist motivation, *Wonderful Life*'s mish-mash of sub-generic elements represents a form of random quotation and pastiche that strives to make the film pleasurable in all the ways that Brecht would have censured. It possesses what Feuer calls a *conservative* reflexivity.

Self-reflexivity as a critical category is largely associated with aesthetically or politically radical films that call attention to the codes constituting their own signifying practices. The classic Hollywood musical, however, employed reflexivity to 'conserve' rather than deconstruct the genre's codes: Feuer suggests it sought to 'keep pace with a fickle mass audience by including within itself different generations or species of entertainment'.[180] This remystification in a sentimental vein has, Feuer notes, a common name, 'nostalgia', 'frequently used in reference to musical comedy'.[181] Numerous Hollywood musicals try to evoke nostalgia for a bygone entertainment era, while asserting that entertainment itself is eternal: above all other strategies, it is in this play with nostalgia that *Wonderful Life* and, though more dynamically, *The Young Ones* and *Summer Holiday* are very much in the Hollywood tradition. They display how the musical is a continuing cycle of conservation within innovation or, as Feuer states, 'of innovation *as* conservation'.[182]

This conservative reflexivity, an uncritical borrowing from existing sources in an attempt to reaffirm continuity, marks a key difference between *Wonderful Life* and the next phase of pop music films that sought to invert or negate previous generic hierarchies or values. 'Conservative' or 'constructive' quotation implies the cancellation of the march of time and in this lies the real failure of *Wonderful Life* since it cannot hide the fact that time had caught up with Cliff. 'On the Beach' stands out like a voice in the wilderness, but there is nothing in *Wonderful Life* to match the vigour of 'We Say Yeah', let alone original late fifties rockers such as 'Move It'. It constitutes a bathetic and definitive conclusion of the first, 'primitive' phase of the British pop music film. It was time for others to take up the mantle of positive rebellion, to move things on, to sing not just 'Yeah' but 'Yeah, Yeah, Yeah'.

3
The Mature Pop Music Film: Bombs, Beatlemania and Boorman

Introduction: rockets and rehearsals

The primitive British pop music film was conditioned under a Conservative government. The Labour Party, out of power since 1951 and long divided over nationalisation and the H-Bomb, found new hope with the election of a new leader in 1963. Harold Wilson knew how to drag the party away from its internecine quarrels and simultaneously rid it of its old-fashioned cloth-cap image. In his first speech as leader to the party conference he spoke passionately of his belief in a New Britain forged in 'the white heat of a technological revolution' and hitched his scientific promise to the country's extant youthful energy and swagger, claiming that 'we want the youth of Britain to storm the new frontiers of knowledge, to bring back to Britain that surging adventurous self-confidence and sturdy self-respect'.[1] While governments changed, the British pop music film continued to 're-present' the preoccupations of the society it sought to entertain. From Gene Vincent's hankering after a 'Spaceship to Mars' in *It's Trad, Dad!* and past NASA naming such a vessel after Herman's Hermits in *Hold On!* (Arthur Lubin, 1965) – without stopping at the sci-fi/pop film hybrid *Gonks Go Beat* (Robert Hartford-Davis, 1965), skilfully 'cult' marketed on its 2007 DVD release as 'the *Plan 9 From Outer Space* of film musicals' – the pop films of the period tapped into the new energetic and scientific *Zeitgeist*. Divisions remained, though, and concerns over a nuclear (non-)future increasingly 'contaminated' any proffered 'gospel of happiness'.

The foregrounding of the technological base to popular culture also helped the genre to attain a *creative* self-reflexivity in its mature age: set largely in front of the television camera, these films repeatedly exhibit the filming of popular music. Earlier pop music films had largely eschewed the process of mediation – Terry Dene's rise towards *The Golden Disc* is indicated by a brief appearance on an unnamed television show hosted by David Jacobs – but the mature pop music film more openly acknowledges its interdependence on the small screen. *It's Trad, Dad!* begins in the obligatory coffee bar, but its teenage clientele now follow music on television, not a jukebox, and the film ends with them hosting a self-organised and professionally televised concert. The Beatles' later landmark television appearances accelerate this shift in emphasis towards the visual aspects of popular music. At the same time, an awareness of and uneasiness with this presentational format is newly highlighted: *A Hard Day's Night* concerns the Fab Four's fan-filled journey south to a televised Variety concert while *Catch Us If You Can* provides a journey south-west to escape the ubiquitous presence of and presentation through the television cameras.

At all levels popular culture discovered itself inexorably linked with and exploited by media, commercial and marketing enterprises. Philip Norman notes that 'newly Socialist Britain in 1965 is remembered, not for "white heat" or "driving dynamism" but for short-sighted euphoria and feather-headed extravagance ... the hallucination of "Swinging London"'.[2] With the country now edging closer to economic ruin, this opiated hallucination was again media driven, the new colour supplements publishing regular features on the bright young things of fashion, taste and style. With a doubleness that will come to define this middle phase, the media-inflected practices of Pop Art are explicitly employed by the budding auteur directors: narratively, however, *A Hard Day's Night* punctures this parasitic relationship, while annoyance at the manipulation of youth – simultaneously held as 'fun' and 'trouble' depending on generational outlook – provides the plot motor for *Catch Us If You Can.* The one pop film to replicate the look of Swinging London, Grenadier Guards and all, will begin with a heartfelt call for more meaningful personal relationships, John Lennon's B-minor plea for *Help!*

Generic development is not temporally secure, however. Cut-price 'primitive' efforts continued into the Wilson era, as with Tommy Steele's *It's All Happening* (Don Sharp, 1963). The extent to which Steele had already distanced himself from rock'n'roll is underlined by Robert Murphy, who summarises 'Tommy in a Max Bygraves-like role as an ex-Barnados Home boy putting on a show with Russ Conway, the George Mitchell Minstrels and long forgotten balladeers Johnnie de Little and Dick Kallman to raise money for similarly deprived children'.[3] Other releases, though, while presenting 'residual' form and casting, can be seen to offer 'emergent' ideologies, more in tune with the imminent 'mature' phase of the pop music film genre.

Play It Cool (Michael Winner, 1962) was the first film vehicle for Robert Wycherley, a Liverpool rock'n'roller signed up to Larry Parnes' management stable and renamed Billy Fury. Fury plays singer Billy Universe who, with the Satellites, help heiress-on-the-run Ann Bryant (Anna Palk) to find her banned fiancé – and their hero – rock star Larry Grainger (Maurice Kaufmann). Their search is largely an excuse to visit Soho's nightclubs and feature the moment's pop acts – and the latest dance craze, the Twist – but the narrative concludes with the discovery that their idol Larry is a grubby womaniser, chasing Ann only for her money. Cue a *Beat Girl*-style cry for 'Daddy!' and a touching family reconciliation.

Play It Cool was critically slated – or ignored.[4] Andrew Caine, who has discussed why such low-budget revue-format fare was treated with particular disdain by the press and its 'elite commentators', nonetheless has to agree that Winner's film shows 'little idea about how mise-en-scène can enhance the overall theme and mood of a film'.[5] For all its emphasis on 'cool' London, the film also retains a 'safe' mix of musical styles, exploiting current chart hits and dance trends, but still placing them in the commercial cadre of Variety-style performance. Thus the guitar and sax sounds of Shane Fenton's twist number 'Like Magic' are juxtaposed with American crooner Bobby Vee and Lionel Blair's cabaret floor show. Even Fury is contained within a fictional group of children and gauche adolescents. *Play It Cool* does, though, have strengths in its understated outlook on personal and professional relationships: Bruce Eder later commended the picture's 'pleasing earthiness and knowing cynicism about the music business'.[6] This is more in line with *Expresso Bongo* than Cliff's early sixties fare but it also looks *forward* to the more complex cultural investigations of the mid-decade. *Play It Cool* originated from the same studio and producer – Anglo-Amalgamated and David Deutsch – that would next make *Catch Us If You Can*, and it contains several thematic similarities – or rehearsals – for its more applauded successor. Both films star a pop group helping a woman on the run from a domineering patriarch; both feature 'picaresque peregrinations'[7] and confront a group of beatniks; both conclude on a note of disillusion, with neither quest ending in success. Atypical above all for the genre thus far, in neither film is the girl 'given' to the hero at the end: here, as Ann returns to her father and the airport, Billy skips off down the runway with the band, reprising the title song. *Play It Cool* has its artistic faults, but its singular denouement distances the film from the chaste communion of the Cliff Richard musicals and prepares the way for more complicated interpersonal relationships in later phases of the pop music film.

John Mundy interprets *Play It Cool* as a forerunner of the Swinging London films which offer 'unprecedented narrative emphasis on female pleasure and sexual identity'.[8] The following year another pop film would again rehearse this genre/gender development. Hammer executive and occasional director Michael Carreras released *What a Crazy World* – from his own Capricorn Production company through Associated British – in December 1963. Based on Alan Klein's stage musical which was developed through Joan Littlewood's Theatre Workshop, the film relates the 'rags-to-riches' story of Alf Hitchins, a young idler who lives with his parents in an East End tenement block and divides his time between the local gang and his on-off girlfriend Marilyn, who hates his friends and wants Alf to settle down. One day Alf puts all his frustrations into a song, 'What a Crazy World': when released, the number immediately becomes a hit, to the delight of all – except his family who remain distinctly unimpressed.

Alf was played by Joe Brown, a singer and distinguished guitarist whose easy-going stage manner and cheerful Cockney image led to a career that 'ran parallel to, though less successfully than, Tommy Steele's'.[9] Gang leader Herbie was played by Reginald Smith, repackaged by Parnes as Marty Wilde, and a stalwart of early British rock'n'roll. Cast as Brown's girlfriend was singer Susan Maughan, while there was also a guest slot for comedy beat group Freddie and the Dreamers, later to star as a boy-scout troop in the perversely primitive *Cuckoo Patrol* (Duncan Wood, 1965). For Andrew Caine the casting of Parnes' (near *passé*) protégés gives *What a Crazy World* a 'residual' feel:[10] contemporary reviewers also saw few 'emergent' aspects in the work. 'The British New Wave rides again', bemoaned the *Monthly Film Bulletin* of 'this would-be "musical with a difference", which turns out to be merely an amalgam of pop music, Cockney *sparrer* and teenage clichés'.[11] Alexander Walker was more assertive, though, declaring it 'the best native musical since I saw *The Young Ones*', largely because of the way the film 'doesn't let the neighbourhood try to ape Broadway'.[12]

Alongside its formal duality – social realism yoked to musical theatre – *What a Crazy World* may also have divided critical opinion by employing a split narrative/ideological presentation of opposed teenage motivations: the dual focus on Alf and Larry offers a synthesis of the tropes of 'youth-as-fun', embodied in the 'overnight success' of the lovable Brown, and 'youth-as-trouble', evident in the threatening delinquency of the aptly named Wilde who is not even *working* class, but lumpen, parasitic. This dual focus anticipates later phases' exploration of these twin tropes. The film also anticipates 'mature' treatments in its dual attitude towards generational difference: here there is no reconciliation finale, as the communal closure is undermined by constant arguments between brothers and sisters, husbands and wives, and especially teenagers and parents, all underscored by the mockery of authority figures.

Where *What a Crazy World* stands alone, though, is in its treatment of gender. Simon Frith and Angela McRobbie suggest that 'male domination of the music industry leads to exclusive representations of masculinity in contemporary pop music'.[13] Thus the masculine is represented as the norm, the feminine as its binary opposite, the 'other'. This approach is considered equally pertinent to the film industry and would therefore apply in double measure to the pop music film: Susan Hayward emphasises how cinema's essentialist approach to these binary oppositions, with the female more emotional, economically inferior and more associated with the domestic and reproductive spheres, 'fixes gender and leads to a naturalising of gender differences'.[14] *What a Crazy World*, however, openly interrogates these fixed divisions. Already not all had it so good as Harold Macmillan had promised and the male characters are, with the exception of Alf's father (Harry H. Corbett), unemployed. Though the lack of work is seen as an individual before a social problem – with jobs still available the unemployed man is considered a 'layabout' – the film is reminiscent of *The Full Monty* (Peter Cattaneo, 1997) both for premise and placement, with every character performing a song set in the Unemployment Exchange being male. Even Alf's song-writing is *re*productive in that it recreates his daily experiences, and is composed at home, typically the female sphere of influence. By contrast, Marilyn and Alf's sister Doris are both in work, with Marilyn quickly promoted to a managerial position. Again echoing Cattaneo's post-industrial film, the women are here the possessors of authority, responsibility and financial power.[15]

What a Crazy World equally problematises a male-dominant ideology in the sexual domain. The male teenagers ostensibly embody an adventurous self-confidence in their relationships with women but, with the exception of Alf, fail to initiate a relationship – here again it is Doris and Marilyn who are successful. Doris is clearly sexually active: Alf, writing about what he knows best, pens 'Sister, sister, every feller down the street has kissed her. / She's a goer.' Such revelations may include 'poetic' licence, but Doris confirms her sex life when, after preparing a meal for her boyfriend, she lies back on the couch and tells him that

'I kept it hot for you, Fred.' Annoyed when Alf fails to call her, Marilyn goes out instead with another man, asserting to Alf her right to see whoever she wants: their relationship is conducted entirely on her terms. It is *female* sexuality which is successful in the film and the women who exhibit confident gender dominance.

Susan Hayward writes that 'until the 1960s and 1970s the musical did not question itself – it indulged in narcissistic auto-satisfaction. Arguably, the rock musical of the 1960s started the questioning of the codes and conventions of the genre.'[16] *A Hard Day's Night* is the key film in this generic interrogation, but while formally and ideologically innovative, its attitudes to gender are conservative, even retrenched, upholding a viewpoint that is consistently male, white and heterosexual. Both *Play It Cool* and *What a Crazy World* postulate an alternative potential, though, like most of the latter's males, they did not 'bring home the bacon'. Cue instead the lucrative 'Lesteroid'.

The pop music film as political allegory: *It's Trad, Dad!* (1962)

'It's a passing phase. I give it five years.' The sentiments of the probation officer in *Serious Charge* towards rock'n'roll were shared by record industry executives. Although rock'n'roll achieved international penetration in the latter half of the fifties, the music moguls were already looking around for the new style which, they thought, would inevitably replace this bright but briefly profitable blue-jeaned fad. When interest did dip as the decade closed, the record industry invested in a whole new series of musical novelties, hoping to be the first to find the latest golden goose. Two of the most successful turned out to be, as Cliff Richard sang, Youth and Experience, early teenage singers and traditional jazz. There was also a series of new dance crazes, the Creep, the Cha-Cha and the Locomotion choreographing a pathway for the Twist, which sold millions of records worldwide and spawned its own 'exploitation quickie', Sam Katzman's *Twist Around the Clock* (Oscar Rudolph, 1961). These novelties converged in a film that presented the calling card of the British pop music film's most inventive director: *It's Trad, Dad!* by Richard – then Dick – Lester.

An intellectual and musical prodigy, Lester was an undergraduate at 15 and at 23 oversaw production duties for Associated Rediffusion's pioneer jazz programme, *Downbeat*, followed by *The Dick Lester Show*, a first attempt to recreate for television the ad-libbed humour typical of the Goons. While the latter led to a series of comedy shows with

Peter Sellers, Spike Milligan and Co. and an Oscar nomination for the 11-minute Goons home-movie *The Running, Jumping and Standing Still Film* (1959), the former brought him to the attention of film producer Milton Subotsky. Known for giving young (and cheap) talent its chance, Subotsky thought that Lester, having shown confidence and innovation in filming musicians, would be a good choice to direct his latest project. The 20 pages that Subotsky mailed through were not, as Lester thought, a plot summary but the complete shooting script, the skeletal storyline a pretext to fit in 20-plus musical numbers in the allotted time. Lester agreed to the assignment, and set to work for the British arm of Columbia Pictures on his first major feature.

It's Trad, Dad! presents an unconsciously valedictory snapshot of the state of British popular music in that doldrums period between the original 1950s rock and the arrival of the Beatles. Starring 'school-girl singing sensation' Helen Shapiro and 'boy next door' Craig Douglas, the film's roll-call, more uncertain even than *The Golden Disc*, stretches from the 'twister' Chubby Checker to the Edwardian pastiche of the Temperance Seven, evidencing the total lack of musical direction that came to define the 1961–62 period. As such the film does *not* primarily showcase trad jazz but reveals a 'buckshot' technique of booking, aiming at a vast range of targets in the hope that something worthwhile would eventually be (a) hit.

To gain sufficient footage with almost no plot and a three-week shooting schedule allowing little time for retakes, Lester drew on his television experiences, shooting each number three times with three cameras, on an adaptable honey-combed set. This procedure allowed for speed and security, a 'live' feel to the musical numbers, and facilitated Lester's preferred staccato rhythm of editing. Completed to schedule the film was released in the UK on 28 March 1962. For the US market, less in thrall to trad jazz, it was retitled *Ring-A-Ding Rhythm*.

It's Trad, Dad! impressed the critics with its energy and visual flair. Accorded 20 words by Dilys Powell, her summary highlighted 'jazz for the tweenagers, deafening, orgiastic and dashingly shot'.[17] This was indicative of the general trend: the music's decibel-enhanced drive being varyingly patronised or pilloried, but the filmmaker's 'tricks' receiving plaudits. Felix Barker, for instance, noted how 'first-rate cutting, clever photography, and an unusual interpolation of stills almost made me forgive the unholy Juke Box volume of notes'.[18] The film was also, in its own terms, a clear commercial success. Made for £50,000, the film took £300,000 in Britain alone. Alone: its returns abroad proved slight, especially in the United States.

The revue format had been a staple of low-budget musicals since the 1930s – see Will Hay's *Radio Parade of 1935* (Arthur B. Woods, 1934) – and pop had continued the largely unimaginative trend with a theatrical spin-off of the television show *Six-Five Special* (Alfred Shaughnessy, 1958), notable for allowing skiffle pioneer Lonnie Donegan his only solo film appearance, *Sweet Beat* (Ronnie Albert, 1959), notable for promoting Al Burdett's Stork Club, the venue where Terence Fisher first sighted Tommy Steele, and a further outdated E.J. Fancey offering, *Climb Up the Wall* (Michael Winner, 1960), not notable at all and erroneously considered by *Kinematograph Weekly* 'just the thing for the Espresso coffee bar trade'.[19] *It's Trad, Dad!* marks a sharp advance both for style and content on its 'primitive' peers, and remains far ahead of Douglas Hickox's two 1963 compendium pieces which, frankly, do not even *try* to create a framing narrative: *It's All Over Town* has Lance Percival and Willie Rushton merely dream that they see Frankie Vaughan, the Hollies and the Springfields, while *Just for You* has Sam Costa sitting in bed, awake at least, calling up at the push of a button the Applejacks, Freddie and the Dreamers and the Merseybeats. *It's Trad, Dad!* is superior also to its own 'follow-up', *Just for Fun* (Gordon Flemyng, 1963) – where the youngsters set up a Teenage (political) Party and cram 21 different artists and 27 songs into 84 minutes – as it is to the narrative-free clip compilation *Pop Gear* (Frederic Goode, 1965) and the alien investigations of *Gonks Go Beat* and *Popdown* (Fred Marshall, 1968). Perhaps its closest (retrospective) rival can be found in *Live It Up* (Lance Comfort, 1963), more accurately lauded by the trade press as a 'Pop-music parade tagged onto a local-boy-makes-good story' that 'should send the kids home twanging'[20] and intermittently preparatory for the genre's 'mature' phase with Mary Quant's 'swinging' costume designs and the distinctive production numbers of Joe Meek (later 'awarded' biopic status in the faintly pantomimic *Telstar* (Nick Moran, 2008)). Above all, these variously narrativised revues, however, Lester's style particularly shines through since, as Alexander Walker observed, '*It's Trad, Dad!* was the first feature film that successfully made the presentation techniques of television commercials and the pop shows on the small screen designed for the teenage and sub-teenage audiences into an integral part of its jokey structure.'[21] Where Shaughnessy's more considered production values had abandoned the editorial spontaneity of Jack Good's original, *It's Trad, Dad!* is the first British pop music film to utilise the 'Good grammar' of television's techniques and its audience's expectations. Others would replicate a conservative tv-style presentation; none would match Lester's 'mature' mediation.

With a sensibility well attuned to musical presentation, Lester could 'instinctively' match if not enhance the performer's skills with a correlating artistry in direction, photography and editing. In the opening number where Terry Lightfoot and his New Orleans Jazzmen perform 'Tavern in the Town', the screen is sectionalised, drawing the audience's attention as each new patch of image appears. Instead of focusing only on the leader Lightfoot, this 'virtuoso' technique introduces all members of the band. Music is a communal activity and the 'democratic' sectional editing honours that interdependence. Lester is equally adept at presenting pop performers. For Gene Vincent, abandoning his black leathers and hard rock sound on 'Spaceship to Mars', the scene begins with a close-up of the neck of a guitar screen left, the neck of a saxophone screen right, while between them, out of focus, is the white shape of Vincent, almost indistinguishable against the white background. The song that follows sees a constant interplay of form and focus between the singer and the stylistic polarities of rock guitar and jazz saxophone, with Vincent mostly small and distant, an uncertain player in a tentative song of jazz-rock fusion. By contrast, the next number, 'Double Trouble', fills the set with photos of the Brook Brothers who repeatedly preen at their photographic image or even sing to it. Neil Sinyard notes how 'It is a nifty elaboration of the self-adoration lurking in both song and delivery, the style providing an appropriate support for a performance that oozes glutinous narcissism.'[22]

Elsewhere, while Lester repeatedly focuses in close-up detail on numbers that showcase instrumental virtuosity and the professional's pleasure at music making, the film also displays a secure knowledge of the imperfect processes of musical performance. Where *The Golden Disc*'s structural repetition inadvertently conveyed the boredom inherent in the recording business, *It's Trad, Dad!* supplies detailed and deliberate instances of both routine and risk. In John Leyton's 'Lonely City', the romantic lyric is undercut by Leyton's casual flipping over the music and taking a few quick drags on a cigarette between verses, while during Acker Bilk's rehearsal session, we see the trumpet player make a wry grimace after fluffing a high note.

Alongside inside knowledge of the music industry, Lester layers on eye-catching effects taken from contemporary art practices. For instance, Bilk's 'Frankie and Johnny' is filmed with a wire mesh placed in front of the camera: this gives the impression, as Philip French noted at the time, 'either of news photos or Lichtenstein prints'.[23] Like Lester's cinematic style, Roy Lichtenstein's style of painting was largely based on commercial techniques and subject matter. Employing the quotidian, discredited images from advertising or adult-oriented romance and war comics, his work invested these simple, repetitive narrative signs with an aesthetic detail normally reserved for museum-housed 'high art' while simultaneously contrasting their overwrought emotional scenes with his reduced, industrial 'cool' style. Such Pop Art strategies did not meet with general approval, the critic Max Kozloff adjudging these 'New Vulgarians' as the inventors of 'the pin-headed and contemptible style of gum-chewers, bobby-soxers and, worse, delinquents'.[24] An apt style, it would seem, for the visualisation of pop music. Here Lester similarly treated a subject matter with a repetitive regularity of image, quiffed hair and pointed shoes, goatee beards and Edwardian dress, his nuanced mise-en-scène establishing variety within the repetition of musical styles and allowing a focus on each performer's distinctive import. Does this presentation expose Acker Bilk as another 'new vulgarian'? Philip French's observation is acute in pointing up the doubleness that functions throughout Lester's films and the mature phase of the pop music genre, as here the image simultaneously suggests that Bilk's work possesses more lasting qualities, proves itself art amidst the commerce; and/or that he too is part of the ephemeral cast list, soon to be consigned to the press archives as musical taste moves on.

The film itself is aware that it is dealing with transient phenomena, and emphasises the point at both structural and visual levels. The sheer number of performers, each gaining a maximum of a couple of minutes, some having their performances overlaid with plot dialogue, gives a sense of the here-today-gone-tomorrow nature of the musicians and their wares. The film's closing titles are presented in the form of grainy newspaper photographs, again an ambiguous summation: the performers are frozen in perpetuity but are also soon to be yesterday's news (as a number of these artists already were). This latter reading is reinforced when, during the final number, the camera highlights a dancing girl trampling all over a newspaper on the floor – a visual comment on the insubstantial nature of pop fame. That this dance is to a saxophone solo of a distinctly modern jazz idiom, courtesy of Sounds Incorporated, only adds to the idea that the film is aware that it is already a historical document.

Alongside the innovative mise-en-scène, a key ingredient of *Its Trad, Dad!* is its humour. With so many musical numbers to cram in, the film has little time to exploit comedy of situation or of character: its negligible, but consciously clichéd plot concerns the efforts of Helen Shapiro and friends to organise a music concert to save their coffee bar from mayoral bureaucracy. Instead it is packed with visual gags, many of them straight from the Goon school, with speeded-up film – the parents at a buffet; stills – Acker Bilk and band dashing for a cup of tea; and captions – arrows pointing out 'Boy', 'Girl' and 'Mayor' from a crowd scene. This demonstrates Lester's respect for the visual inventiveness of silent cinema, coupled with a disregard for linear narrative. This constant in Lester's work has, as with Lichtenstein, brooked dissent. For Roy Armes 'façade is a key word in any summing up of Lester's achievement: the bright glossy surface, the quirky visual gimmicks ... an act of conscious manipulation by a man used to the need to pep up the surface of his work to make it more immediately enjoyable'.[25] This critique is misleading, though, as there is usually a point to the wisecracks. Lester stands at an oblique angle to the fledgling pop music film genre, setting up a knowingly playful discussion with his material and audience. For example, while looking to enlist a disc jockey at the BBC, Helen and Craig enter the music department, only to find musicians stacked on shelves, waiting for their call. This can work solely as a device for Lester's reduction to absurdity of the film's diegetic world – Lindsay Anderson would repeat the effect when the headmaster pulls a chaplain out of his study locker in *If....* (1968). But metaphorical interpretations are also evident: the utilitarian manner in which the corporation hires and fires musicians; a reiteration of the boredom and hanging around consistent with the profession.

Of thematic interest for this genre study – and Lester's later films – is the enduring axis of generational conflict. Robert Murphy notes how *It's Trad, Dad!* takes 'a more radical stance on the clash between the generations than the Cliff Richard musicals' with the adults remaining throughout 'grumbling killjoys',[26] while Alexander Walker sees in the film's title 'the flip, mocking emphasis of a generation growing more aggressively conscious almost daily of their own identity and creating heroes who were certainly not those of their fathers'.[27] However, an inclusive ambiguity is equally present: the titular rhyme can also suggest a generational compatibility, both the appropriation of the music from a previous decade as one's own *and* the recuperation of that new trend by the older generation. The concluding concert is, short-term, a victory for the young, but the mayor's hypocritical acquiescence suggests how easily new cultures can be appropriated by the dominant ideology. As such the film's ending can be more cynically read as indicating the way politicians were coming to realise the merits of media presentation: it is certainly an astute anticipation of Harold Wilson sharing 'purple heart' jokes with the Beatles two years later.

This ending also highlights a new aspect that *It's Trad, Dad!* brings to the British pop music film – the political dimension. Lester's film feeds off its socio-political context, then predominantly known as 'the atomic age'. Britain's successful H-bomb testing in April 1957 and its subsequent strategy of nuclear retaliation provoked from a concerned public the formation, in January 1958, of the Campaign for Nuclear Disarmament (CND). The movement thrived and its series of marches from Trafalgar Square to the atomic research establishment at Aldermaston was, for participant Jeff Nuttall, notable for its teenage majority and how 'trad jazz floated out over the sodden Berkshire fields'.[28] An awareness of this political appropriation of trad jazz conjures up new notions of teenage rebellion. With a recognised channel for protest, CND was far removed from duck's arse quiffs, smashed windows and coshes. Instead it represented 'a new synthesis ... an imminent counter-culture that merged personal expressiveness with political activism'.[29] Nigel Young's summation could read as the 'essential' message of Lester's first pop music film.

In 1962 the political connotations of *It's Trad, Dad!*'s eponymous music would have resonated strongly. When the mayor's roadblock is breached, the appearance of the jazz band's arrival at the coffee bar is heralded by an uplifting rendering of 'Keep the Red Flag Flying'. The film's finale has Northern Ireland's Ottilie Patterson singing 'Ain't gonna study war no more' no less than nine times as she accompanies Chris Barber in 'Down by the Riverside'; it is topped with the Aldermaston regular 'When the Saints Go Marching In'. Sinyard comments that the film ends 'with editing and music marching often to the same rhythm':[30] it is, in memory at least, a recreation of the march to Aldermaston's 'carnival of optimism',[31] a redolent evocation of anti-bomb protests.

Central to this evocation is the figure of Acker Bilk, a middle-aged clarinettist who, for George Melly, 'may have represented some kind of chauvinistic revolt against American domination; that the mixture of Edwardian working-class dandy and rural bucolic came to stand for a pre-atomic innocence when we were on top'. More pertinently, while Bilk was carefully presented as apolitical, 'it was his bowler which the less thoughtful and more emotional fringe of the CND movement adopted as their symbol'.[32] Bilk's performances in *It's Trad, Dad!*, alongside their Pop Art filtering, are illustrated with variously angled close-ups, fetishising the objects that construct the Bilk persona – the cigarette, cider bottle and, especially, that politically charged bowler. Visual interest is enhanced through negative shots of his hands working at the clarinet, a 'trick' reserved for Bilk alone (Figure 3.1). Is he the reverse of the seemingly innocent, apolitical musician, embodying instead our biggest musical rebel to date? In the film's narrative, Bilk is

Figure 3.1   Acker Bilk and the apocalypse – *It's Trad, Dad!*

the catalyst for the youngsters' successful thwarting of authority, their meeting with the disc jockeys and final persuading of the mayor to rescind his anti-jazz policy. Less obviously germane to a popular music compendium, the switch to negative is also the 'traditional' cinematic grammar for nuclear holocaust, as in the apocalyptic ending to Robert Aldrich's nuclear noir *Kiss Me Deadly* (1955). David Robinson's thought-ful review of Lester's debut movie began by noting that 'in his television days, it sometimes seemed as if Lester was not quite in key with his stars' H-Bomb age surrealism. Clearly though, something of it rubbed off on him.'[33] The influence had sunk deep as evidenced by *It's Trad, Dad!*

One could even argue that Lester has made from the film's fractured narrative an allegory of nuclear disarmament. The disenchanted, voice-less young rally behind the sounds of trad jazz to engage in active protest against the establishment: they break through police barri-cades; they finally break down the boundaries of age and class as the gruff working-class police sergeant (Arthur Mullard) spontaneously joins the dance while the mayor (another Aldrichian 'Nameless One') more calculatedly pulls the sting of their protest by accepting – and no doubt then amending – their proposals, leaving the young activists happy (if again purposeless), as the final credits roll. In particular, one could highlight the scene where the artists' van approaches the police blockade, conveyed through a parodically tense countdown from ten to one: though openly ironic, the scene uses the cinematic grammar of imminent explosion. That catastrophe is averted is due entirely to the skill and determination of the protestors. Stylistically and narratively, *It's Trad, Dad!* marks the moment when the pop music film, like the teenagers on the march to Aldermaston, attained – through peaceful rebelliousness – a respectable maturity.

The canonical pop music film: *A Hard Day's Night* (1964)

With only John Leyton enjoying sustained future success, *It's Trad, Dad!* illustrated how quickly musical trends could slip from popularity: *A Hard Day's Night* demonstrates the opposite direction, capturing a national phenomenon on the verge of global penetration – a feat which the film would help to realise.

Six months after Lester's debut feature, the Beatles released their first single in Britain. 'Love Me Do', though only a modest success, presaged a seismic shift in a domestic industry previously dominated by balladeers and London-based groups. By the close of 1963 they were enjoying unprecedented popular success: the 'youth quake' that had struck America in 1956 with Elvis Presley and rock'n'roll now hit Western Europe with the Beatles and the 'Merseybeat'. These shock waves initially failed to trouble the United States, largely because EMI's American label, Capitol Records, had farmed out the latest UK wannabes to small and ineffectual independent labels. However, Noel Rodgers, the British representative for United Artists Records, had seen Beatlemania for himself and knew that American success was inevitable: on discovering that EMI had failed to cover film soundtracks in their contract with the group, Rodgers approached George 'Bud' Ornstein, production head of United Artists' European film division, with the proposal that they quickly offer the Beatles a three-picture deal in order to obtain three – lucrative – soundtrack albums. Thus, in its conception, the apogee of the British pop music film was akin to almost all its generic predecessors: a low-budget exploitation movie to milk the latest brief musical craze for all it was worth.

With a cheap and cheerful product in mind, Ornstein approached Walter Shenson, an independent American producer who had shown with his first UK features – the Peter Sellers' vehicle *The Mouse that Roared* (1959) and its (now Richard) Lester directed sequel *The Mouse on the Moon* (1963) – the knack of making British product accessible to the US market. He was therefore a logical figure for Ornstein to approach with, as Shenson later revealed, no brief other than to make a film 'with enough new songs by the Beatles for a new album'.[34] Brian Epstein was very much in favour of the new venture, but the Fab Four would prove harder to convince. As John Lennon recalled: 'We'd made it clear to Brian that we weren't interested in being stuck in one of those typical nobody-understands-our-music plots where the local dignitaries are trying to ban something as terrible as the Saturday Night Hop.'[35] Given that this put-down seems an almost perfect plot summary of *It's Trad, Dad*, it might seem perverse that that very film's director would be approached. However, Lester won the group's approval, not for his previous pop music film, but because of his Goons' credentials: the Beatles loved *The Running, Jumping and Standing Still Film*. With all parties happy, a standard low-budget ceiling of £200,000 was agreed – with the Beatles on 25 per cent of the net profits.

Lester brought with him cameraman Gilbert Taylor whilst the Beatles provided the film's musical director, George Martin. Screenwriting duties were entrusted to Welsh-born but Liverpool-reared Alun Owen. Best known for North-set television dramas such as *No Trams to Lime Street* (1959), Owen spent several days with the group to get a sense of their rapport and routine. It had been decided from the off that the film would constitute an exaggerated 'day in the life', a fictionalised documentary of the Beatles' real-life relationship to fame. This called for black-and-white photography to replicate the footage now flooding the media, a format that Owen also felt best suited the quartet's personalities: 'They are immediate people and I knew from that that it couldn't be a colour film. The boys are essentially black-and-white people.'[36] Owen paid two further visits to the group on tour before handing in a widely approved first draft in late January 1964.

By February 1964, though, a day in the life of the Beatles had changed – dramatically. It forms potentially the greatest pop story ever told. With Capitol finally giving a full release to 'I Wanna Hold Your Hand', the Beatles had wowed the press the moment they touched down at New York airport, had been seen on the *Ed Sullivan Show* – by the highest viewing figures ever for a television broadcast – and, in the space of just two weeks, had conquered the hearts and pockets of America. The richest nation had been shaken out of its post-Kennedy mourning; the home of rock'n'roll had finally succumbed to 'the British invasion'. With their faces known from coast to coast and their full back-catalogue about to occupy every spot in the Billboard top five the Beatles had suddenly become the most bankable pop stars on the planet. And they were due to start working with Richard Lester on a rock-bottom-financed exploitation quickie in ten days' time.

With a new product to handle, all parties were of a mind not to alter existing arrangements. Alongside an extremely tight shooting schedule there was a limit to what a fuller budget could add to the desired 'faux-documentary' filming style besides generating more footage that would take longer to edit. They were adamant that they did not want to change the film to colour. There was one agreed addition, though: following the enormous success of the Beatles' airport-lounge press conference in February 1964, Owen added a press buffet in a theatre lounge, a scene to allow the boys to shine in similar fashion. With speed of the essence, Shenson eschewed big-name stars – and drawn-out contract negotiations – and awarded the largest non-Beatle role to character actor Wilfrid Brambell. As ever, an experienced team was assembled, including Norman Rossington, John Junkin, Anna Quayle and Victor Spinetti, who could be relied upon to deliver the 'tight' script whilst most attention went into directing the pop star debutants. The Beatles also 'prepped' quickly: in the week prior to filming they worked up the tapes of nine songs from which Lester would choose six to film.

On Monday morning, 2 March, a train left Paddington Station, with John, Paul, George and Ringo plus the film crew all on board. From the outset they were besieged by hoards of hysterical fans: this rather interfered with production schedules, but provided suitable raw material for the expedient Lester. In one scene, for instance, he turned the cameras on a bunch of screaming girls who had surrounded the Beatles' limo after a long day's shooting. This footage was then knitted into the film, explaining a continuity error where the boys wear different clothes on and off the train. Thus, at times, the fictional documentary became factual – or vice versa. For the closing concert sequences, shot at London's Scala Playhouse, Lester now had the confidence – and finance – to employ six cameras shooting simultaneously as the Beatles performed. The subsequent editing of John Jympson would provide a visual energy equivalent to the music being played.

The Beatles' success in Britain had been swift but successive: in America it was instant and total, as evidenced by the response to the film and its motivational music. United Artists had initially programmed 500,000 pressings of the soundtrack album but the momentum created by radio previews culminated in advance orders of over two million, making *A Hard Day's Night* potentially America's largest selling album to date. Before the laboratory release of the film's final print, the tie-in soundtrack album, itself still at the presses, had not only guaranteed itself number one position in the charts, but had ensured the film's £200,000 budget had already been doubled in profits. This

LP hysteria fed back into film demand, with America alone demanding 700 prints, Britain 110, while worldwide an unprecedented order of over 1500 prints was made. With only three and a half weeks left after shooting to complete the editing and get the prints made, United Artists announced confidently that *A Hard Day's Night* would be shown on a saturation basis in every available market around the world, with 'more prints in circulation than for any other pic in history'.[37]

In Britain, the film was given a royal world premiere at the London Pavilion on Monday, 6 July 1964. On 2 August the film went on general release in Britain and the rest of Europe. In America, it was officially premiered at the Beacon Theatre in New York on 12 August and opened in 500 cinemas throughout the country the next day. However, special previews at over one hundred cities had already brought in over half a million dollars. Such had been the demand for product associated with the Beatles that *A Hard Day's Night* had become the first film in the history of the motion picture industry to ensure a profit while filming was still in progress.

The critics were equally captivated. Michael Thornton enthused that 'Walter Shenson's 85-minute production is not, I am relieved to say, the usual kind of British pop musical in which a series of hit songs are linked loosely by an incredible plot and unspeakable dialogue.' Instead he judged it as possessing 'all the ingredients of good cinema – wonderful photography, imaginative direction, and excellent character performances'. Thornton was not alone in praising the writing: 'in a diamond-bright script full of laconic, incisive wit, Alun Owen captures, better than anyone else to date, the strange, elusive idiom of the Merseybeat'.[38] Dick Richards was one of many largely to credit Richard Lester: 'He has directed with vital speed and inventiveness and has splendidly brought in the atmosphere of mass juvenile hysteria without overdoing it.'[39] Not least in the list of those receiving encomia were the Beatles themselves who drew lofty comparisons with past comic quartets, Cecil Wilson asserting that 'the Marx Brothers exploded back on the screen last night'.[40] Especially for older critics the film succeeded in characterising its individual members: Isabel Quigly noted that initially 'I seemed to be gazing at indistinguishable quadrupeds' before asserting that 'after half an hour the confusion was over for ever'.[41]

This 'tabloid' movie earned itself a maturely reflected review in the UK's doggedly intellectual *Sight and Sound*. If one excepts *Expresso Bongo* with its respectable literary antecedents and established cast-list, *A Hard Day's Night* was the first low-rent British pop music film to be reviewed by the heavyweight journal since *The Tommy Steele Story* seven years earlier. The critical establishment was coming to realise that the Beatles' enormous success required that their film debut should be taken as a significant and prominent artefact of popular culture. Geoffrey Nowell-Smith's review noted that, whatever one's reservations, '*eppur si muove*: And yet it works'. Indeed, for Nowell-Smith it works 'on a level at which most British films, particularly the bigger and more pretentious, don't manage to get going at all'.[42] As to its place in the pop music genre, sister publication *Monthly Film Bulletin* found *A Hard Day's Night* 'streets ahead in imagination compared to other films about pop songs and singers'[43] while, in the ultimate – and enduring – critical soundbite, Andrew Sarris of the American magazine *Village Voice* described the film as 'the *Citizen Kane* of jukebox musicals'.[44] The analogy to an American masterpiece is doubly apposite since it not only suggests a qualitative evaluation but also *A Hard Day's Night* constituted the first ever British pop music film to conquer the American market. Prior to their February tour of the States, the Beatles had been worried about their chances: Hunter Davies noted that 'George said he'd seen Cliff's film *Summer Holiday* reduced to the second feature in a drive-in in St. Louis.'[45] By the time the film was completed, though, they knew that such fears were groundless.

Box-office profits were phenomenal. The film brought in $5,800,000 in US rentals in six weeks, and around $14 million world gross. As well as the album and single tie-ins, the film was shrewdly released just prior to the Beatles' second US tour in August. It was the second most profitable film of 1964 in Britain, just behind Guy Hamilton's *Goldfinger*. However, while *A Hard Day's Night* is a British film by dint of employing a British cast and crew, its financing came from and therefore its profits went to United Artists, an American company. In this, it set the trend for the rest of the sixties: as with the James Bond films, *Alfie* (Lewis Gilbert, 1966), *Georgy Girl* (Silvio Narizzano, 1966) and others, *A Hard Day's Night* may have been quintessentially British in ideology, but its economics were entirely American. As were its ultimate critical accolades: uniquely for a British pop music film, two British contributors received Academy Award nominations, Alun Owen for original script and George Martin for soundtrack.

There was a similar, symbiotic domination of the music charts. The singles 'Can't Buy Me Love' and 'A Hard Day's Night' topped both UK and US charts, while the soundtrack album, the film's initial *raison d'être*, achieved unparalleled success. In Britain, *A Hard Day's Night* remained at number one in the album charts for 21 weeks (to be replaced by *Beatles for Sale*), selling 700,000 copies in its first year of release, with

European sales well over one million. In America an advance order of one million was quickly doubled in sales as it topped the album chart for 14 weeks. Global sales of the soundtrack to *A Hard Day's Night* can be totalled at around four million. None of the Beatles' compositions were nominated for Academy Awards, however: in 1964 that honour went to 'Chim-Chim-Cheree' from Robert Stevenson's *Mary Poppins*.

In addition to its financial success, *A Hard Day's Night*'s cultural capital has grown to the extent that, in 1999, it was voted 88th in the BFI Top 100 British films, flanked by Ken Russell's *Women in Love* (1969) and Humphrey Jennings' *Fires were Started* (1943). Lester's take on the ardent female desire kindled by the Beatles has latterly attracted detailed, if largely synchronic, academic treatment.[46] The following textual analysis adapts my own monograph on the film, adding a fuller diachronic reading of its relationship to previous pop product.

The opening chord of 'A Hard Day's Night' – a G7 with added ninth and suspended fourth – has, for Ian MacDonald, 'a significance in Beatles lore matched only by the concluding E major of "A Day In The Life", the two opening and closing the group's middle period of peak creativity'.[47] It also heralds the true opening of a middle phase in the British pop music film, a phase that will problematise the status of pop fame and the media images that promote it. As part of that media these films know that they contribute to the mythologising of its stars but simultaneously subject that process to a distanced, critical analysis. It is a doubleness, a resistance to closure, that permeates every aspect of *A Hard Day's Night*, even its paradoxical title, and that prompts an active and collaborative engagement with a teasing, ironic complicity. Lyrically, songs such as 'Can't Buy Me Love' deal with highly duplicitous forms of exchange, echoing those between stars, spectator and film while visually Lester's knowing use of quotation and connotation, of clichés in verbal and photographic form, further contributes to an ironic questioning of any literal understanding of realism. From the outset the cinema-verité style is thrown into doubt, with a duality inherent in the filming of the public space: are the Beatles filming or really fleeing their ubiquitous aficionados, or does such a division become meaningless in the context of their effect on young extras?

This is a key aspect of the film's ambivalence: the boys are shown to have the whole world at their feet yet cannot walk the streets in safety. The opening shots of *A Hard Day's Night* illustrate that the film will explore the phenomenon then sweeping the media: Beatlemania. Armed with privileged behind-the-scenes access, it investigates the response to this unprecedented cultural happening by the caught-unawares media machine and records the nature of the fan base feeding into this mass hysteria. Above all, though, this 'process' movie allows us to see how Beatlemania affects the boys themselves – and for the most part it is not seen as a pleasurable existence. Those opening frames mark a clear distinction from a rags-to-riches biopic like *The Tommy Steele Story*: here running straight towards us are recognisable celebrities, enduring the trappings of stardom; here are Lester's 'revolutionaries in a goldfish bowl'.[48]

An auteurist reading of Lester's work would highlight the recurrent thematic investigation of the idolised hero. Flashman in *Royal Flash* (1975), Robin Hood in *Robin and Marian* (1976), Superman in *Superman 2* (1981) are all subjected to a degree of fan worship that precludes the ability to live a normal life. Stylistically, Lester's cinematic treatment of the Beatles advances his signature experimental camerawork and consciously artistic appropriations. Again this is no mere 'pepping up' but rather a probing beyond surfaces. For instance, freeze-frame photography is used to capture the image of the moment: a repetition of photographs is seen during the group's press conference – and on the film's publicity poster. It is a device that elicits comparisons with the work of Andy Warhol as each image is mechanically stacked to mirror the industrial process that first brought the group to public attention. Each shot, while underlining the similarity in the group's dress and hairstyle, is subtly different, working to individualise the quartet. With the appearance across and down the screen of the posing George Harrison we see both a Warholian celebration of the visual rhythm of contemporary 'packaging' – the boys are as manufactured as a tin of soup – and, simultaneously, a celebration of variation within standardisation. More specifically, this patterning also signifies in parallel to a Warhol painting like *Jackie* (1964), his repeated portrait of the widowed Jackie Kennedy. Eric Shanes notes that Warhol's reproductions of Jackie showed his objection to the way television and other media were programming everybody to feel sad.[49] In *A Hard Day's Night*, itself part of America's collective expiation, everybody is being 'programmed' to accept the Beatles' youthful enjoyment and irreverence. These equivalent 'processes' of programming are suggested by the use of a repetitiousness that is metonymic of how the mass-communications industry disseminates pained or joyous images through a multitude of printed and electronic media to the world.

Beyond this, however, these images, through their visual rhythm, approach the condition of abstraction. Emotion is disseminated but ultimately dissipated since, as Klaus Honnef comments on Warhol, 'continual reiteration undermines the exceptional nature of the original subject matter. Its uniqueness is dissolved.'[50] The image is consumed, but the 'real' person escapes. Such is also the case in *A Hard Day's Night*, which highlights the medium's inability to 'capture' the four young individuals behind the fashionable façade. This again illustrates the film's core duality: Lester's appropriation of Pop Art, photography and even cinema-verité serves only to demonstrate that, for all its privileged access, the Beatles remain beyond our grasp, ultimately unknowable.

A 'Pop Art' treatment of the Beatles is germane to the plot of *A Hard Day's Night* which investigates how a commercially oriented 'artistic' generation – the middle-class media professional – tries to exploit and tame this latest craze. Press conferences framed *The Tommy Steele Story* and undercut Dixie Collins in *Expresso Bongo*: here the sequence represents a generational confrontation between the values of the 1950s and the 1960s. Where Tommy Steele would reply politely to the condescending questions of Fleet Street's finest, the Beatles answer back irreverently. In *A Hard Day's Night* the press (two women in flowery hats seem straight from Tommy Steele's Café de Paris interview and many were real journalists roped in for the sequence) now constitute an age, class and mind frame that suddenly seem to be way off the pace.

Though itself a commodification of the Beatles, *A Hard Day's Night* is not afraid to attack that cynically programmed process. In a scene that astutely critiques the merchandising of youth, Kenneth Haigh appears as professional style-guru Simon, looking to identify and exploit the teenage market. His discussion with George, mistaken for their latest male model, reveals a patronising parasitism; his bewilderment at Harrison's rejection of their new shirt range does not prevent his noting George's descriptor 'grotty' as a new term of 'pimply hyperbole'. In a satire of the perceived transience of new fashions, Simon consults the calendar, is reassured that trends won't change for another three weeks and so George and his 'utterly valueless opinions' are sent packing. 'The new thing,' he retorts, 'is to care passionately and to be right wing.' Harold Wilson's triumphant entry proves the style-guru's error of judgement in the political sphere; George's casual exit ('I don't care!') shows him wrong on the current personal stance. More than this, though, the whole scene serves to show that George, like the other Beatles, is 'real', 'a natural', and not just a marketed product. Which is, of course, both true and not true.

The dualities of the film text are most evident in its generic characteristics, both documentary realism and musical comedy. Each 'discrete' genre reveals *A Hard Day's Night* as borrowing from and building on existent pop music film strategies. The film's claims to present a 'realistic' insight to life on the road for the Beatles are at best *partially* supported by a comparison with the concurrent television documentary shot by Albert and David Maysles. *Yeah! Yeah! Yeah! New York Meets the Beatles*, broadcast February 1964 in Britain and November in America, records the Kennedy Airport press conference, the hotel and car sieges, even a train journey and escape to a nightclub, plus of course inter- spersed footage of performances to a chorus of hysterical fans. There are, though, major differences: the documentary shows a fuller social realism by providing evidence of the 'real' public and private side to life on tour, notably the relentless and ruthless hawking of wares to radio stations and the girls being smuggled into the group's rooms late at night. By contrast, Lester's version can appear more as a cleaned-up 'Capitalist Realist' tract, propaganda for the latest pop stars of pop not that dissimilar to *The Tommy Steele Story*.

For Bob Neaverson the narrative construction and pacing of *A Hard Day's Night* are 'in effect (if not intention), closer to that of the French "new wave" than to any previous British or American pop musical'.[51] Technical parallels are evident in the use of hand-held cameras, freeze-frames and jump cuts, but, as contemporary critics noted, several of these mostly comic effects connote the silent-movie practice of Chaplin and Keaton as much as if not more than the *Cahiers du Cinéma* cohort. For all this comedic innovation and quotation, however, the Beatles' first movie must also be read as a traditional musical comedy imbued with Hollywood conventions. Just like Cliff's earlier *The Young Ones* and his concurrent *Wonderful Life*, *A Hard Day's Night* functions primarily as a backstage musical and through its formulae we access both the public and the private lives of the stars. In essence, the film *is* about putting on a show since, in a move that would have delighted Tommy Steele and his mother, the Beatles headline a Variety show with a bill including Lionel Blair and his dancers, operetta singers, even Derek Nimmo and his performing doves. (Realism: as Michael Braun reports on their tour of France: 'Shortly after midnight the Beatles were introduced, but then a juggling act came on stage.'[52])

For all this residual 'baggage', however, there are two ways whereby *A Hard Day's Night* demonstrates its advance on primitive pop music films and registers its inherent modernity. The first is by removing this backstage show from a theatrical, or even cinematic, context. As in *It's Trad, Dad!* we are here thrust into the electronic – and then innovative, unknown – processes of live television transmission. It is a further dual-ity: a traditional backstage musical set in the white heat of technology.

Figure 3.2 Mediation and generic maturity – *A Hard Day's Night*

As when rehearsing 'And I Love Her' the Beatles are constantly mediated through a camera viewfinder or control-room monitors: the new medium of television is everywhere foregrounded and fetishised (Figure 3.2). It is an apposite presentation: from televised Variety shows such as *Sunday Night at the London Palladium* and the *Ed Sullivan Show*, the Beatles were the first group to be fully marketed through television: *A Hard Day's Night* knows not to upset that successful strategy.

The second 'modernist' strategy employed is in taking a critical stance towards its textual material. Cliff Richard's *Wonderful Life* is also predicated on the filming of musical numbers yet, as seen, its random quotations and pastiche of the past Hollywood tradition demonstrate an inherently 'conservative reflexivity'. By contrast, the Beatles' film calls attention to the codes that constitute its own signifying practice. When John Lennon cries out 'Hey kids, I've got a great idea! Why don't we do the show right here?' he is deliberately distancing *A Hard Day's Night* from the Rooney–Garland-inspired product of Cliff and the Shadows. John is exposing the structure itself at the expense of a transparent transfer of the ritual value contained within the genre: as such the film adopts what Jane Feuer terms a 'critical reflexivity'.[53] Lennon, duplicitous as ever, is having his generic cake and eating it. The film declares its ironic distance from the plot structures of the backstage musical, but still entertains a broad family audience by utilising those very structures.

Although for the most part conventionally motivated, *A Hard Day's Night*'s cinematic correlation again does much to advance the pop genre to new levels of sophistication. The opening title track instantly signposts that the film will repeatedly employ musical numbers without tying them to musical performance. A break with the conventions of musical presentation is again noticeable during the first number in the train carriage, 'I Should Have Known Better'. As the boys' playing cards suddenly – surreally – transform into musical instruments, the presentation of the song both is and is not diegetic, rupturing any reading of the film as generically coherent and inducting us into an overall viewing strategy. Coupled with the earlier high-jinks where the group suddenly taunt the commuter from outside the train, the cinematic correlation advocates a move towards alterity, generic hybridity, a constitutive duplicity.

The film concludes in conventional fashion with the group in concert. The climax repeats the format of *The Tommy Steele Story*, *The Young Ones* and *It's Trad, Dad!* but here the forum has altered considerably. Francis Wheen notes how 'the Beatles resembled Tommy Steele both in the speed of their success – from obscurity to royal Variety performance in one year – and in their ability to appeal equally to mums and teenagers'.[54] Steele, though, was mostly filmed singing to the older generation: the teenage hysteria expunged from his stage performance is now predominant in the Beatles' televised show. Here, not uniquely nor immediately undercut as with Cliff's 'We Say Yeah', we sustainedly see and hear Trevor Philpott's 'killing-day at some fantastic piggery'. During the second verse of 'Tell Me Why' a slow tracking shot behind Ringo's drums presents for the first time both the group in performance and their teenage female fans. It is the crowning moment in *A Hard Day's Night*. Lacking the traditional romantic subplot, the final 'boy–girl' union is revealed to be that between exultant fans and excited players: within the agreed parameters of the stage and auditorium, the concert provides a clear exposition of the musical's generic and ideological function as we finally attain the utopian 'gospel of happiness'.

Above all else, though, the filming to accompany 'Can't Buy Me Love' constitutes the single moment of breakthrough for the pop music film – its mid-phase 'paradigm shift'. Just as the Beatles escape their incarceration, so is the musical number freed from its generic restrictions, and subsequent films are legitimised to employ the pop song as 'traditional' instrumental music had always worked, as an enhancement to the mood of a scene. Here also is the most complete example of Lester's empathy with the music: his creation of a visual correlative to the emotion contained in McCartney's composition. Occurring after half-an-hour of increasing claustrophobia, the song structurally represents a massive release of pent-up energies: as Ringo notices a door marked 'Fire Escape', the second word acts like a signal, and the group dash down the metal staircase and onto the field below. As they cavort in Goon-like release from the rigours of convention, Lester uses varied angles and speeds to convey the quartet's energy. When they jump over discarded props, the film momentarily speeds up to help them run and stumble their way into the open air. An aerial shot down onto the square concrete heli-pad follows one of the boys down a long path and back again: the run leads to no special sight gag – it is the sense of achieved release that matters. When the filming gets down amidst the group dancing together, Paul runs up and into the camera, smirking out at us as he breaks the ultimate taboo. Not all is ad-libbed anarchy, however: a slow-motion shot of John, Paul and George jumping from a height references the Beatles' existing photographic iconography, notably Dezo Hoffmann's Sefton Park shot of the group leaping in the air. Following another arching dash, we cut to a final shot from the air as the foursome run and leapfrog. Their fun is abruptly ended, however, as a large middle-aged man appears, dressed in raincoat and wellingtons. The groundsman's role here is identical to that of the policeman at the end of Gene Kelly's 'Singin' in the Rain' routine – and Howard's at the church hall in *Serious Charge*: he is the representative of elderly authority that will not accept such Dionysian exhibitions of self-abandon. His reprimand – 'I suppose you know this is private property' – resonates since it is the treatment of the Beatles as *public* property that has prompted their flight. The tension between public figures and private spaces here motivates the Beatles' own Running, Jumping and Standing Still Film – and helps to cement their economic pulling power.

The phenomenon known as 'Beatlemania' was a commercial enterprise whose boundaries transcended the cinematic into the worlds of music, fashion, even language and a life-enhancing credo. These examples of a 'totalising' culture may have struck the knowing George as 'grotty', but style-guru Simon was right that everyone would want to buy in. And this constitutes the final, overarching, duality of *A Hard Day's Night*'s harmony of opposites. As the socio-economic context demonstrates, the film, despite its widely publicised stylistic innovations and thematic insurrections, can but serve to reinforce the dominant capitalist ideology. A swift sequel was inevitable.

The colonial pop music film: *Help!* (1965)

When their first film deal had been contracted, the Beatles were a local success: now they were an international phenomenon. Consequently, the budget for their follow-up film was doubled to £400,000, and the shooting schedule raised from eight to 11 weeks. United Artists were now more 'hands on' in their investment, wary lest a radical concept alienate their adoring public: see The Monkees' later *Head* (Bob Rafelson, 1968). All were happy for Walter Shenson to continue as producer and Richard Lester as director, though elsewhere there were three changes of note from the first venture. Cameraman Gilbert Taylor, unimpressed with the hysteria on set, withdrew and was replaced by David Watkin, lighting cameraman on Lester's previous movie, *The Knack* (1965). George Martin again produced all the film's musical tracks but, seemingly due to personal differences with Lester, lost out on instrumental scoring duties to Ken Thorne. An Oscar nomination clearly signalled the kiss of death as, largely because of the Beatles' growing antipathy, Alun Owen was not rehired.

An early corporate decision meant abandoning the cod-realism of *A Hard Day's Night* for a more mainstream fully fictional product, but one where the Beatles could still largely play themselves with any proper 'acting' reserved for the more willing Ringo. An important factor here was to keep a lead on other British pop groups that had slavishly copied the Beatles' blueprint. Jeremy Summers, for example, regularly visited the set of *A Hard Day's Night* before directing Gerry and the Pacemakers in *Ferry 'Cross the Mersey* (1964), an identikit pastiche where the group's loss of their instruments rather than their drummer jeopardises their appearance at the grand (Cavern Club) finale. Contextually, Beatles fans now knew too much to accept a retread of their debut feature's faux-innocence: John Lennon admitted that any fresh insight into their lives would have meant a version of *Fellini Satyricon*.[55] The basic storyline, of an Eastern cult chasing Ringo for his sacred ring, was worked up first by the American Marc Behm, then amended and 'anglicised' by Charles Wood, the adaptor of Ann Jellicoe's stage play for *The Knack*.

Here, though, is the first evidence of a distancing of the Beatles from their second film. Unlike Owen, who had been invited in to observe the boys on tour, Wood conducted his research entirely from repeated viewings of *A Hard Day's Night*. Thus, a caricature was drawn from an original caricature – John as sardonic, Paul as sexy/cocky, George as mean and Ringo ever-amiable – with 'safe' set-piece witticisms imposed on the group rather than working up examples of their own irreverent humour.

Secondly, with a significant budget now at stake, the Beatles were no longer allowed to 'make or break' the film on their own. Instead a team of experienced comic actors were contracted, not this time for cameo parts but as integral motors for the plot. As well as inviting back Victor Spinetti, in came Leo McKern as cult leader Clang, plus John Bluthal, Patrick Cargill and television satirists Eleanor Bron and Roy Kinnear. The effect of this 'heavyweight' casting was that, whereas *A Hard Day's Night* had been a film 'about' the Beatles, their second project was, to quote their second album title, a comic extravaganza 'with the Beatles'. John Lennon's summary appeared accurate: 'I'm an extra in my own film.'[56]

Cast and crew flew out to Nassau on New Providence Island on 22 February 1965, then mid-March decamped to the Austrian ski resort of Obertauern. One week later all returned to Twickenham Studios, in and around which the rest of the film was shot, plus three days on Salisbury Plain. Though affording the group some requested sun and snow, the third problem with the Beatles was their own distance from a film shoot that was no longer a novelty and a storyline that failed to capture their imagination. Constantly high on their new discovery, pot, the group would often corpse during takes, pushing Lester to distraction and Ornstein close to abandoning the shoot, but the commercial momentum was too great and so the project continued. The Beatles' second royal premiere took place at the London Pavilion on 29 July, with a crowd of 10,000 people blocking Piccadilly. The film opened at 250 leading cinemas throughout the United States on 11 August.

That unstoppable commercial momentum was confirmed by *Help!*'s box-office returns, close to $6 million in the United States and $14 million worldwide. In the UK the film was the second highest money-maker of 1965, bettered only by *Mary Poppins*. Its performance was on a par with *A Hard Day's Night*, though one might have expected better with a now global phenomenon to market. Musical returns were equally profitable, though not now solely for the United Artists: EMI renegotiated its contract and, uniquely in North America, the full soundtrack album was released on its own label, Capitol. With advance orders of well over one million dollars, it entered the Billboard charts at number one and stayed there for nine weeks. In total, it spent 44 weeks in the charts, won a gold disc and topped two million sales in the USA and Canada. A different *Help!* album, released in the UK on 6 August, had a record advance order of over 250,000 copies. This was not strictly the soundtrack album, for the instrumental numbers were excluded in favour of supplementary Beatles tracks, including 'Yesterday'. Though seen as one of the Beatles' weaker albums, it too entered the LP charts at number one and stayed there for nine weeks. This diluted *Help!* sold over one million copies worldwide, again just about equal with the album of *A Hard Day's Night*.

Contemporary critical reception picked up on the overall sense of anti-climax. Michael Thornton's *Sunday Express* piece was typical: 'this isn't a nose-diving flop, that's for sure. But there is nowhere in evidence the special exciting quality of *A Hard Day's Night*'.[57] This time the pacing was considered just too frantic, Penelope Houston complaining that 'around half-time, ridiculous as it seems, you really could do with a pause'.[58] Patrick Gibbs attributed Lester's 'frenetic style' to a lack of confidence in Behm and Wood's script, 'a preposterous piece into which, it seems to me, any old pop group might have been dropped, so little is made of the Beatles' individual qualities'.[59] Nor did the plusher production values help to convey the boys' character: Alexander Walker thought that 'colour cushions their impact, gives their anarchy a kind of cotton-wool softness'.[60]

The biggest critical regret concerned the loss of comedy. Rather than Merseyside Marxes, Hollis Alpert damned with the faintest of praise: 'the humor reminded me much more of the old Abbott and Costello movies'.[61] Nonetheless, there are several successful comic moments in *Help!* An early scene follows the Beatles up their separate paths to their separate houses on an unassuming working-class street characteristic of monochrome New Wave cinema, then cuts inside where the four houses have been transformed into one huge palatial corridor with innumerable gadgets, an inside lawn and even a sunken bed. With its early play on appearance versus reality, the scene establishes the film's elegiac epistemological core. For all its surface difference, *Help!* furthers a key trope of *A Hard Day's Night*: while earlier British pop music films presented young men on the make – either as stars or as juvenile delinquents – here they have made it, and again at times seem unsure if it has been worth the effort. It is an ambivalence at the heart (and home) of the film.

Where it *is* still worth the effort – and where most current encomia concentrate – is evident in the musical numbers, even if, à la *Twelfth Night*, they convey much of the comedy's melancholy. One of many lyrically sad, if musically upbeat numbers, 'Ticket to Ride', is rightly considered the most inventively filmed sequence in *Help!* – the visual partner to 'Can't Buy Me Love'. Here Lester again uses the Beatles' music as a non-diegetic accompaniment to action sequences, but now adds a ground-breaking rhythmic montage: entirely fashioned post-production, its splicing together for pace and rhythm uniquely replaces any prearranged choreography. Pauline Kael was of the opinion that *Help!* is Lester's 'best edited, though not necessarily best film'[62] and this editing is best seen in the inventive cinematic correlation for Lennon's first heavy-metal track, the synaesthetic exposition of the white heat of technology. When the camera zooms in on four black specks moving up the snowy mountainside then cuts, first to the four Beatles hurtling down the slope on ski-bikes, then falling back into the snow, it is apparent that the images are being edited to fit the lyrical movement of the song. During the second chorus each Beatle places a ski pole up against the camera, screen left, a simple effect that foregrounds the cinematic process itself. On the repeat of the first verse, a long shot accompanies the skiers with an animation of the song's notes along the overhead telegraph wires: the Beatles literally presented through cartoon strokes. The next verse puts the Beatles on a train, not entrapped as in their first film, but in control, Paul driving, George stoking, John a toreador swinging a cape before it. A sense of light-headed liberty is conveyed, the contrast with previous 'on the road' footage reminding us that this is pure fantasy. As the final kicker fades, the quartet again descend the slope on their snow bikes, moving now away from the camera, leaving behind a scene of improvised, unskilled fun – though one carefully and skilfully edited – and riding back into the constraints of narrative.

They also ride forward into music film history: a precursor for much pop visual product that followed, the sequence fits seamlessly into the non-stop, fast-edited pop videos of, if not MTV, then VH1 (Figure 3.3). Yet 'Ticket to Ride' employs a tableau of black on white: elsewhere the film foregrounds its new medium of colour. This is narratively signalled from the outset when, after the film's exotic, unexpected opening in the Eastern temple of the Goddess Kaili, the Beatles begin the title song with a return to the black-and-white stylisation of *A Hard Day's Night*. Just as we debate how these contrasting discourses will be unified, Ringo is hit in the eye by a coloured dart but does not react. A cut-back reveals a screen within a screen, the musical footage being attacked by the outraged swami Clang in his sacrificial chamber. As further darts hit their target, the opening credits spring into colourful existence, distracting attention from the Beatles and their monochrome grammatical correlation. Generically, the scene functions as a 'conservative' reprise of Cliff's first colour credits in *The Young Ones*, informing us that the spectacular 'fantastical' Eastern plot of ritual sacrifice will supersede the 'reality' of the Beatles' life. It also makes clear that plot (sadly) will win out over

Figure 3.3   Alpine anarchy: an early airing for the pop video – *Help!*

performance. There will be fewer diegetic numbers than in *A Hard Day's Night*, none in a concert setting, and none devoid of plot interference. The pattern of the opening track will be constantly repeated: indeed, the plot of *Help!* constitutes a reiterated attempt to stop the Beatles performing. Even heavily armed performances on Salisbury Plain of 'I Need You' and 'The Night Before' are halted by underground explosions and a farcical pitched battle. As Neil Sinyard comments, 'the authentic voice of the Beatles is finding it difficult to make itself heard – which is the point'.[63]

Nonetheless, the musical numbers shine, with colour, critically panned as an obstacle to character and narrative clarity, here offering clear benefits. The second song sequence, 'You're Gonna Lose that Girl', is the genre's first colour recreation of a studio recording. After establishing that the recording process replicates the spatial arrangements of the group's live performances, George and Paul sharing one mike with John alone at another, a series of colour filters create a quasi-abstract choreography, first blurring George and Paul in blue, balancing John screen right with a left-side slab of pink, staying with pink for close-ups of George and Paul before ending on John where a shaft of pink shines through the blue until the light whites him out. It constitutes the film's first play of editing to rhythm, and a singular visual patterning for the mise-en-scène: Steven Soderbergh boldly pronounced the sequence as 'the birth of modern colour photography'.[64]

This pioneering use of colour, be it through filters or geographical setting – 'Another Girl' is filmed naturalistically in warm shades of yellow, blue and pink – accentuates the film's rich visual composition. At the time, Lester summarised *Help!* as 'Wilkie Collins' *The Moonstone* as drawn by Jasper Johns.'[65] The comparison to Collins' 1868 novel, centred on the retrieval of a precious stone originally stolen from an Indian shrine, is straightforward. Foregoing Victorian realism, *Help!* presents a variant on Collins' plot portrayed in the style of a pop collage, with heterogeneous fashions and colours yoked to captions, animation and fast cross-cutting. Why, though, Jasper Johns? Robert Hughes admits that the artist's game of conceits *could* be seen as 'art complacently regarding its own cleverness, in an emotional void'[66] – an accusation frequently levelled at Lester himself. However Hughes sides with Johns for shaking art out of its Abstract Expressionist lethargy 'by forcing his viewers to think about representation and the paradoxes it entails, instead of merely producing evidence of turmoil'.[67] Though he has later distanced himself from Johns' explicit influence,[68] Lester's comparison is useful since Johns' main tropes for an exploration of the hermeticism of signs are also investigated in *Help!*, the first Pop music film with a capital P.

The clearest example of Johns' Pop Art influence on Lester's pop music film comes with the titles that enumerate the five attempts to steal Ringo's ring. For Johns the stencilled numbers in a work such as *0 through 9* (1961) revealed an interest in the shapes' abstract quality. Employing a set of signs that are given, common and impersonal, the succession of numbers in *Help!* provides a steady and predictable container for the chaotic action that is initiated inside them, a collaged play with graphic data where Jean-Luc Godard meets the Goons. Johns created a series of studies of targets, most famously *Target with Plaster Casts* (1955), a canvas like an archery target. In the Salisbury Plain sequence a shot from inside a tank shows a similar target – trained menacingly on the Beatles. Above the target in Johns' composition is a wooden construction with four boxes each containing a plaster cast of part of a human face, truncated across the bridge of the nose and across the chin. The filming of 'You're Gonna Lose that Girl', cutting between extreme close-ups of John Lennon's chin and forehead, provides a commensurate fragmentation of the human face, the deconstruction of the public persona. Seeking to explore the song's lyrical message, the varied repeated close-ups signify as a vain attempt to get beyond the image to the human, epistemological core.

Johns' most memorable images were arguably his flags, reduced through paint to abstract signs in 'the ideal space of art'. Hughes points out that in a work such as *White Flag* (1955), one of Johns' many versions of the Stars and Stripes, 'we see the painting first, that pale, perfect skin; but the flag beneath it, the sign, has lost its power to command'.[69] In particular one could cite its power to command to kill, to register and reinforce the new Imperialism. Flags feature constantly – and impotently in *Help!* The Union Jack is worn by Mal Evans' lost swimmer trying to get home (just as Britain post-Suez is seeking a new direction?) and hangs limply at Wembley Stadium (pre-1966 of course) as the packed terraces sing the 'Ode to Joy' from Beethoven's Ninth (an indictment of Britain winning a war but losing the peace?). Similarly, Clang ensures his flag is flying proudly on his army jeep only for the vehicle to lurch off in the wrong direction, a symbol of pride and achievement that is literally misdirected.

Alongside its subtly subversive Pop Art influences, *Help!* is feverishly responsive to contemporary cinematic practice. Paul's play with baseball glove and ball while sequestered in Buckingham Palace references Steve McQueen's solitary confinement in *The Great Escape* (John Sturges, 1963), while Alexander Walker saw the same sequence's endless rubber tubing as 'a nodding tribute to a similar Jacques Tati gag in *Mon Oncle*' (1958).[70] More prevalent within the film's examination of epistemology is a play with the codes and conventions of espionage, and the clearest influence on the second Beatles' film is its United Artists sibling, James Bond. The Beatles and Bond, twin icons of early sixties British manhood, shared the same progenitor in 'Bud' Ornstein, and enjoyed the same prodigious success, 'Bondmania' matching 'Beatlemania' in national press coverage and box-office 'killings'. In a cosily incestuous move, studio executives were receptive to an affectionate take-off of the Bond phenomenon.

The entire plotline of *Help!* is reminiscent of the already formulaic narrative encountered in early Bond features with various attempts on the hero's life, meeting the girl who will become the principal heroine, villains with non-European evil ends and numerous chases through picturesque, overseas scenery. Bond aficionados already expected the high-definition Technicolor cinematography that added overseas tourism to treachery, and *Help!* shares Alpine locations with *Goldfinger*, while *Dr. No* (Terence Young, 1962) also included Jamaican colonial settings. Beyond equivalences, Bond parody abounds. The opening dialogic now coheres, moving from the elaborate – and evidently expensive – set-piece to the credit song, not with Bond aiming a gun out but Clang throwing his darts in to the group's title-track performance. Daubing Ringo in red house paint parodies the deathly gold spray applied to Shirley Eaton, while Bhuta unfurling his turban to use as a weapon recalls Oddjob's lethal metal-rimmed bowler hat. Professor Foot – a Bond-style mad scientist out to 'rule the world' – allows a parody of how *Goldfinger* foregrounds and fetishises technology and gadgetry, reappropriating its industrial laser to burn a way through his rival's flesh, if only he can find a British plug to make it work. Q presents Bond with all manner of communication devices and secret weapons; Clang talks into the wooden handle of his umbrella and later uses it as a flamethrower. These and other parodic procedures allow *Help!* both to satirise the Bond cycle while employing its narrative and visual formulae to assist its commercial potential. This no doubt pleased United Artists and filled its coffers, but in this instance generically 'having one's cake and eating it'[71] meant running the risk of getting ideologically 'stuffed', and I believe that this inheritance may largely account for the film's failure to remain in the popular consciousness to the same degree as *A Hard Day's Night*.[72] Tony Bennett sees Bond as underpinned by a set of narrative codes that regulate the relationships between characters: the 'sexist', the 'imperialist' and the 'phallic'.[73] These can all be discerned in *Help!*, none of them working strongly to the film's ideological advantage.

The 'sexist' code regulates the relationship between Bond and the 'girl'. She is usually wrongly positioned, either sexually in being initially resistant to Bond, or ideologically, being in the service of the villain: she may be both. Bond's seduction of the woman has an ideological function in that it 'repositions' her, returning her to her 'correct' place, subordinate in relation to men and supportive of his own mission. Eleanor Bron's Ahme, like Pussy Galore in *Goldfinger*, changes sides, abandoning her Goddess and her clan to act ostensibly through affection for Paul in the service of the (Western) male. Elsewhere in the film the women are only decorative commodities, reified to the point of being a bikini-clad guitar substitute for Paul to 'play on' as, on a Bahamian beach, he sings of using yet 'Another Girl'.

The sexist code was apparent in *A Hard Day's Night* but *Help!* is rendered doubly problematic by overlaying it with a colonial or 'imperialist' code, again absorbed from the Bond movies. This sees loyal colonials deferring to Bond, defender of the realm, committed to preserving the reactionary institutions and society of Britannia. In *Help!* this 'imperialist' code is largely mediated through the Goons, which places the Empire in a different perspective. As George Melly notes, this is largely down to ex-soldier Charles Wood, 'outside his range' with this script but 'a very serious writer, obsessed, like the Goons, with our Imperial past',[74] and the dual influence on *Help!* of Spike Milligan and spy movies problematises the film's attitude towards this code, at times openly satirical, at others ambivalent, but also in places covertly (and culpably) complicit.

The Bond world characterised Britain and its Secret Service as an efficient worldwide operation – a worthy target for a Soviet assault in *From Russia with Love* – and as an equal and often dominant partner in dealings with the United States. That is not a world view shared by *Help!*'s Goonish scientists Foot and Algernon. Foot's bomb fails because of what he sees as government underfunding: 'useless ex-Army rubbish! I can't get the equipment.' When he finally succeeds, with the slow-motion relativity cadenza, Foot knows why: 'it's from Harvard!' Wilson's 'white heat' of technology is hardly being realised by the British scientists on show.

It is, though, by its soldiers. If *It's Trad, Dad!* placed music against the military through allegory and association, the link is here rendered more explicit – and more ambivalent. As the Beatles perform 'I Need You' amidst manoeuvres on Salisbury Plain, Lester makes several visual parallels between the tools of the musician and the military. While George, left profile, sings into an angled microphone, its long metal shape is graphically matched by the gun of a tank screen right. An aerial shot, similar in spatial composition to the film's Kaili temple opening, surrounds the group with a circle of six tanks, before a close-up of the neck of George's guitar alters focus to show Stonehenge behind. Lester's play with pattern, size and focus – the frets of George's guitar are as large on-screen as the pillars of Stonehenge – intuits how the Beatles are the new focus of a nation's worship, and a new weapon in Imperial penetration. The replacement of the group's good-natured fans by the menacing cult members allegorise the frightening underbelly of Beatlemania (that so scared Gilbert Taylor) while the Stonehenge setting reminds that human sacrifices are not confined to the foreign, the 'other'.

However, a third trope to the code reveals clear racial undertones in the Bond films' representation of British imperialist ideology and here *Help!* is on less secure, self-deprecating ground. After George nonchalantly escapes from a cage on New Providence Island, an indigenous officer who touches the bars receives an electric shock and looks down at his hand close to tears. It exemplifies what Shohat and Stam term colonialism's 'infantilisation trope': an 'unthinking Eurocentrism' that leaves no doubt where the superiority lies.[75] Raymond Durgnat notes how, in *Dr. No*, 'the British Raj, reduced to its Caribbean enclave, lords it benevolently over jovial and trusting West Indians and faithful coloured police-sergeant, the Uncle Toms of Dock Green'.[76] Bond's intervention in Jamaica provides a reassertion of white, British hierarchy, just when in reality Britain was running away from Empire. An identical discourse, one that 'embodies, takes for granted and "normalises" the hierarchical power relations generated by colonialism and imperialism',[77] is evident in the concluding scenes of *Help!*, where a quick marching octet of native officers act as loyal colonists fighting those who have turned against their former rulers – the oppressed complicit in their own oppression. They might not have been so deferential had they seen the film's earlier depiction of Indians. With one standing on his head down a coal-hole while another rests on his bed of nails, *Help!* delivers a crudely stereotypical characterisation, a representation of 'the mystic East' that is as tastelessly reductive as is its depiction of Clang and his devotees. Worse still, it instances what Jim Pines terms 'one of the characteristics of colonial and mainstream race relations discourse' by ensuring that the colonised is 'silenced'. This is doubly so since 'the colonised subject does not have access to the means of self-representation':[78] in *Help!* white actors, notably Alfie Bass and Warren Mitchell, are chosen to play all the Asian parts, and to play them broadly, for laughs. In *A Hard Day's Night* Ornstein had rejected a shop scene because of its openly racist depiction of the Eastern customers: no such compunction was evident in the Beatles' Bond-fuelled second feature.

A Hard Day's Night was, overall, a forward-looking escape from 'tradition', but throughout *Help!* the Empire strikes back. In constant collision with the 'now' phenomenon of the Beatles and youth-oriented 'Swinging London' are an array of images from the Imperial past and the technological future. It is arguable which trend wins out. George first encountered the sitar while filming in a London Indian restaurant, and was given a copy of *The Illustrated Book of Yoga* when in the Bahamas.[79] These experiences would profoundly influence the Beatles' future musical soundscape and mental outlook, the *Moonstone* mockery leading directly to a search for the reality of Indian religion through the counsel of an Eastern patriarch in the Maharishi.

Where, though, in *Help!*, is such a father figure? Bennett's third narrative code of relationships, the 'phallic' code, regulates the relationship between Bond and his symbolic father figure, M, and also that between Bond and the villain who threatens him with castration through torture. There are no father figures in *Help!*, though over the closing credits John, lost in life and needing 'Help', improvises a clearly audible and vaguely Oedipal 'It's me, dad.' There are, however, constant plays on the notion of castration as images of knives – and lasers – attempt to sever the appendage on which Ringo's sacred ring is stuck. John makes explicit the

Freudian aspects in this sanitised fantasy as, taking a knife to Ringo, he explains that 'we're risking our lives to preserve a useless member!'

However, a move back from the film text to its immediate social context renders the phallic code more insidious. *Help!*'s lampooned images of Empire are somewhat compromised, not only by a royal premiere, but by the award to the Beatles, during filming, of the Membership of the British Empire, the MBE. This stirred up strong feelings: several outraged elderly recipients even returned their medals.[80] It was though, initially at least, a *victory* for the older generation, a vote-grabbing piece of self-publicity by a government and an avuncular if not patriarchal member for Liverpool keen to be seen as youth oriented: by such means Prime Minister Harold Wilson carefully crafted his part as the boys' own 'M'.

Wilson's award was ostensibly recognition of the Beatles' importance as the vanguard of a worldwide appreciation, and purchasing, of British products. Wherein lies the enduring ambivalence/doubleness of the Beatles' second film. The Empire of Army and India may have passed, but in its place had come the new Empire of Culture. Cultural imperialism is today largely synonymous with American penetration, but for a brief period in the sixties, with the Beatles personifying an ethos centred on 'Swinging London', the transmission of British products, fashion and styles to newly dependent markets including the United States led to the creation of patterns of demand and consumption underpinned by and endorsing the cultural values, ideals and practices of the United Kingdom. The Beatles were the most pervasive image of this 'British invasion', with *Help!* swamping indigenous product in countries as far apart as Argentina and Singapore, but behind them corporations such as EMI, becoming increasingly multinational, played the key role in this process. Finally, for all its lyrical introspection and Eastern imagery, and for all the daring Pop spirit evident in its editing, colour and camera movement, this product ultimately constituted the dissemination of ideologies consonant with the Western capitalist system. George's guitar and guns are not entirely antithetical, and the most successful sections of the film, the 'unspoilt Beatles' entering their private palace and enjoying the freedom to ski on foreign slopes, tellingly show the young rubber-soul rebels luxuriating in the fruits of capital.

The Chekhovian pop music film: *Catch Us If You Can* (1965)

Columbia had been severely jolted when Parlophone, formerly EMI's junior record label, swiftly rose to prime position by signing up most of Brian Epstein's Liverpool acts. They were determined to find 'the new Beatles' and invested heavily in a group from Tottenham, London, the Dave Clark Five. Their third Columbia release, written by drummer Clark and keyboardist Mike Smith, finally delivered: 'Glad All Over' reached number one in mid-January 1964. Conspiracy theorists could have construed from the saturation media coverage afforded 'the Tottenham Sound' a concerted effort to return control from upstart Merseyside to the top London-based entertainment agencies. But it never quite happened – at least not in Britain. The group did, though, enjoy phenomenal success in America where the publicity drive was completely opposite and they were promoted as if they were another Merseybeat band. Even replicating a breakthrough appearance on the *Ed Sullivan Show*, 1964 marked the beginning of a two-year American onslaught that would see the Dave Clark Five rival the Beatles in the US popularity stakes. Through his previous job as a stuntman, Clark had made over 40 film appearances, while his group had briefly featured in Katzman's musically eclectic *Get Yourself a College Girl* (Sidney Miller, 1964). Clark felt that his group was ripe and ready to match the Beatles by starring in their own film vehicle, and Clark was already getting what he wanted from record companies impressed by his hard-headed attitude towards shifting product: 'Music as an art form was not what he was about.'[81]

Perhaps it was an attraction of opposites, therefore, that led producer David Deutsch to entrust Anglo-Amalgamated's first pop venture since *Play it Cool* to debutant John Boorman. An emerging television director, Boorman had collaborated with Charles Wood, pre-*Help!*, on *The Newcomers* (1964), the party-set denouement to which was described by Alexander Walker as 'Antonioni-esque'.[82] This was followed by *The Quarry* (1964), the story of a sculptor whose name, Arthur King, signposted his Grail-like quest to find the final shape, the 'quarry' captured in his quarry-hewn marble block. While party-expressed communality and the legend of Camelot would become constants in Boorman's work, most explicitly manifested in *Excalibur* (1980), budding auteurist tropes scarcely concerned studio executives keen to replicate the template of *A Hard Day's Night* – get the hottest new band, pitch them in with a Young Turk of television, stand back and wait for money to roll in.

With UK and US distribution guaranteed, Deutsch promised an initially hesitant Boorman creative *carte blanche*. Boorman's friend the playwright Peter Nichols, who soon joined the project as scriptwriter, noted that 'As long as Dave and the other four appeared and some of their music was played on the soundtrack, the American distributors would be happy and the drive-in movie-houses would have something to show the kids.'[83] In a radical move, Boorman and Nichols eschewed a musical setting, mining instead Clark's backstory to create a loose plot centred on a group of stuntmen who run away with the latest top model. The Dave Clark Five composed nine new numbers that would serve as the film's musical score, while casting surrounded them with dependable screen professionals, notably David Lodge as Louis, Yootha Joyce and Robin Bailey as middle-aged couple Nan and Guy, and Barbara Ferris as Dinah.

Filming began in early February 1965. Shot chronologically with no initial idea of the film's ending, Boorman revisited notable settings from his documentary years, Bath, the Mendips and Salisbury Plain. To these were added a final scene shot at Bigbury Bay and the adjacent Burgh Island Hotel, a 1930s-designed fashionable retreat whose post-war decline suited Boorman's move towards a down-beat conclusion. This led to some late friction with Anglo-Amalgamated: Deutsch wanted a more traditional generic boy-gets-girl denouement but Boorman 'felt that that would betray the spirit of the film'.[84] To his artistic credit – and commercial folly – Deutsch kept to his initial promise and *Catch Us If You Can*, Boorman's self-professed calling-card for Hollywood, was released at the Rialto, Leicester Square on 6 July 1965. Retitled *Having a Wild Weekend*, it was released in the United States on 3 September.

The national press were, on the whole, impressed, at least with the director's contribution to the project. Kenneth Tynan commended 'a promising first feature by John Boorman that tries enormously hard to be more than just another film about a pop group'.[85] Most agreed with *The Times* reviewer who found the scenes with Bailey and Joyce's edgy couple 'the best in Mr Peter Nichols' thin and contrived script'.[86] The inevitable pop comparisons were not to the Dave Clark Five's advantage: *The Times* felt that 'this group do not have the sort of natural talent form putting themselves over as personalities that the Beatles have' while Cecil Wilson specified that 'it might be said of Mr Clark that as an actor he is a very good pop-group leader'.[87] Even that pop-group function was largely ignored, only Margaret Hinxman commenting on how the 'music provides a haunting, not too obtrusive backing'.[88]

The British trade press had warned how 'a picture that stars a pop group without showing a pop group takes a risk'[89] and this 'burial' of the group's primary function undoubtedly contributed to poor box-office returns. Indicative of cinema's power to sell related product, however, the film briefly relaunched the Dave Clark Five on home territory. 'Catch Us If You Can' was their only UK top five hit of 1965: that it became the group's eighth million-selling record was again due to its reception in America, where the film helped to cement their Beatles-level chart status, and further hits followed.

Over time, as Boorman's auteur stock has risen, so has the reputation of his feature-film debut. *Catch Us If You Can* is one of only two British pop music films included in Pauline Kael's collection of reviews *5001 Nights at the Movies* (the other, if seeking a yardstick of *New Yorker* critical respectability, is *Expresso Bongo*). Kael wrote that 'It's as if pop art had discovered Chekhov – the Three Sisters finally set off for Moscow and along the way discover there isn't any Moscow.' She also compared Guy and Nan to the Almans, the 'constantly bickering pair from *Wild Strawberries*' (1957).[90] For Ehrenstein and Reed, the film 'represented rock revisionism of the first rank, painting a bleak and Byronic picture of rock high times'.[91] Chekhov, Bergman and Byron: the trade press was right to label it 'interesting fare for thinking youngsters'.

The start to Boorman's first film, with its fast editing and slow-motion sequences, its visual emphasis on flags, faces and numbers, plus its placement of the motivating pop group in a communal living space, is incontestably indebted to the products and pacing of Lester's second Beatles movie. Nonetheless, the black-and-white insistence on signs and symbols gives credence to Kael's coupling: the opening shots of *Expresso Bongo* placed the semiotics of show business in a public domain; the opening of *Catch Us If You Can* brings these signs into a private, domestic space. A white arrow on a bedroom wall, in its centre a circle containing the single word 'Thrills', points down bottom left. On the second beat of fingers clicking, the camera pans down, following the arrow, alighting on the visual correlative of the written promise, the sleeping face of Dave Clark. The sixth click brings a switch to the bottom quarter of a white clock face, its long black hand on the number 5. The film thus visualises the name of its pop protagonists – 'Dave Clark' and 'Five': rather than meeting them individually, we have an initial indication that the power of images will predominate over intimate portrayals.

In the first 75 seconds, there are 37 cuts, eight pans, three tilts and six zooms in or out. It is a modish beginning, virtuosic, full of the 'razzle-dazzle' of the 'Lesteroid' Beatles' music films and their French *nouvelle vague* feel and flow. Two similar scenes quickly replicate this rush of sights and sounds. We first follow the boys on their way to work, bombarded with advertising billboards mainly featuring their current project – 'Meat for Go!!' (Figure 3.4). The next sequence follows Steve and Dinah's subsequent flight from the city, replete with the semiology

Figure 3.4 The Dave Clark Five and plastic pop – *Catch Us If You Can*

of transport: tunnel lights, road markings, a further arrow signalling (serendipitously) 'Ahead Only'. Here is a young British director
experimenting with the possibilities of *montage court*, a fragmentation
of the image to allow the perception of dramatic relationships and to
provide an aesthetic form for otherwise shapeless documentary material. As much as Godard, this mosaic of images recalls Alain Resnais'
Bordeaux-set *Muriel* (1963), a film which, for James Monaco, reveals
'an extraordinary montage of images and sounds which are not primarily meant to advance the storyline (although they do that too) but to
describe a precise milieu, an aura'.[92] This tension between the demands
of reality and the pull of abstraction creates what are among the film's
finest *cinematic* sequences. For the British pop film genre, though, this
is new terrain: abstraction and/or existential itinerary rather than (the
expected) adolescent escapism. As Andy Medhurst noted, 'Even *A Hard
Day's Night* had half a foot in kitchen-sink naturalism, but *Catch Us If
You Can,* especially in its first startling thirty minutes, goes all out for
the shiny plastic immediacy of the moment.'[93]

Unlike Medhurst, I would argue that *Help!* rather than Boorman's
debut is 'where the pop film becomes the Pop film'.[94] *Catch Us If You
Can* is, though, the first British pop film to privilege indigenous Pop Art

influences. If rock'n'roll was singularly American in origins, then Pop Art had its own separate British origins through the Independent Group centred at London's Institute of Contemporary Art. Boorman's opening half-hour is especially redolent of the work of a founder member of this Group, the painter Richard Hamilton, not only in the bright and polished signs and circles such as the 'Slip It to Me' badge of *Epiphany* (1964), but principally in the cinematic realisation of Hamilton's prophetic collage *Just what is that makes today's homes so different, so appealing?* (1956). This displays the (American-led) raw material that Pop Art would exploit: photography, cinema, television, advertising, comic-strips, pin-up and muscle men, food, consumer products and brand names. Re-viewing the start to *Catch Us If You Can*, it is almost as if Boorman and Nichols listed and enlisted Hamilton's aggressively commercial content: the pin-up posters above Mick's bed, Steve reading the newspaper, the cups of tea on the table, the stairs and arrows, Steve himself as the muscle man, the television and commercial work, the distinctive make of car, the logos just about everywhere, and all contained in the latest offspring of the Empire cinema's brightly advertised *The Jazz Singer* – its musical soundtrack separately available – with, slap bang in the middle, the all-motivating meat. The busy carpet is, Peter Conrad notes, a blown-up extract of a photograph of Coney Island beach, swarming, according to the photographer's caption, 'with over one million people':[95] thus even the crowded denouement on Bigbury Bay is paralleled in Hamilton's collage.

Marco Livingstone sees in Hamilton's collage, itself a poster for the Whitechapel Art Gallery's *This is Tomorrow* show, 'a knowing paraphrase of the seductive language of advertising'.[96] Such knowingness does not immunise against seduction, and Hamilton's poster, while ostensibly adopting a critical stance (the title is to be read as ironic), takes evident pleasure in the colour, brightness and vigour of the new consumer items. Boorman also, true to the dualism of the mature pop music film, has it both ways: Michel Ciment contends that the film's opening scenes, again foregrounding the machinery of mediation, 'might almost be said to endorse the advertising and television world of its heroine'.[97] This is not to condemn either artist or auteur. Hamilton's complicity with commercial practice forms part of his project: as Robert Hughes notes, Hamilton's collage fulfilled 'almost to the letter' his own wish-list for an art 'which did not yet exist except as uncoalesced subject matter'. Indeed, in a letter of January 1957 proposing an exhibition for this emerging mode of artistic expression, Hamilton declared that 'Pop Art is: "Popular (designed for a mass audience) / Transient (short term solution) / Expendable (easily forgotten) / Low cost / Mass produced / Young (aimed at youth) / Witty / Sexy / Gimmicky / Glamorous / Big Business".'[98] All these adjectives can be applied to *Catch Us If You Can*: even 'gimmickry' is repeatedly named and shamed, Steve dismissing Louis' western ranch as 'a gimmick on the moors', and Dinah ultimately rejecting her island quest as 'a gimmick in the sea'. The final epithet, though, is the most telling. Hamilton knew that this could never be a folk art, made by the people. Hughes summarises Hamilton's take: 'Pop art, far from being "popular" art, was made "by highly professionally trained experts for a mass audience." It was done TO the people.'[99]

This too is true of *Catch Us If You Can*. Intercut with the market shoot for Meat is a key scene revealing those that dictate public tastes from on high – literally on high, as we witness David De Keyser's advertising CEO Leon Zissell looking down from his penthouse office on London and the team of fashion-setting executives that he commands. The scene's knowingly ironic satire on programming and commodification chimes with Hamilton's take on changing Britain and has clear parallels with *A Hard Day's Night*, specifically George's stand-off with the style-guru Simon. Jon Savage, who discusses how 'both films make a connection between the sudden enfranchisement of youth and the sudden shift in political power from Conservative to Labour in 1964', pinpoints these two scenes of reactionary market manipulation to enter the caveat that 'this is a fragile freedom'.[100] This may be so, but the ultimate optimism of the advertising scene in *A Hard Day's Night* was fuelled by the understanding that Simon is an ineffectual *follower* of trends, looking to the street for signs of a changing cycle in fashion: the power lies with George and the young. Zissell, however, works on the (unchallenged) premise that the public wants what the public gets: the film even ends with Zissell, overseeing the moulding of 'Swinging London' lifestyles, repeating his strategy shift to a weary Dinah: the public *will* get gracious living, it is not their choice. This denotes an important and enduring shift, an explicit pronouncement of cultural recuperation that will echo repeatedly down the history of the pop music film, through *Privilege* to *Absolute Beginners* and beyond.

From Zissell's eyrie everything is mediated, even the notion of youth itself. 'That's why you chose her, wasn't it?' he is asked of campaign model Dinah. 'That's her image, rootless, classless, kooky, product of affluence, typical of modern youth.' It is an image that Boorman also captures well, especially in his musical set-pieces which demonstrate a cinematic correlation impressive both for visual flair and narrative development. When Steve brings Dinah home prior to leaving the city, the images accompanying 'Having a Wild Weekend' show a party is in full swing. Unlike past pop teenage events, though, these dancers all look in their twenties, an age confirmed when the camera cuts to their young children watching television. The fashions on display suggest moneyed middle-class bohemia – as might the abundance of alcohol on the table. It is a leisurely establishment of a relaxed community, with 13 cuts in 45 seconds. But as the harmonica solo leads into the second verse, the pace of editing accelerates in time to the music: as the lyrics now scream of 'reelin' and a-rockin'', we cut rapidly between the main protagonists with 34 edits in the final 25 seconds. The main play is a reiterated close-up interchange between a female blonde and brunette dancer, their hair tossing in abandon, the cutting so quick that it is hard to distinguish them apart: they 'lose themselves' and blur into a sweep of exhilaration. This will be the final 'set-piece' dance number in a major 1960s British pop music film: its community, transparency (the mature married couples argue 'honestly' and 'openly'), abundance, energy and, especially, intensity replay, in almost elegiac mode, the categories constituting Richard Dyer's utopian sensibility.

Elsewhere, the music's placement may be more unobtrusive, but it is far from redundant, its sound and sense always appropriate to narrative mood and meaning. Soon after their escape from London, as Steve and Dinah walk through the snow-covered lanes of the Mendips, side by side but not arm in arm, we hear in full the verse and chorus of 'When': 'When the world looks stark all around you, / All you need is love.' An instrumental version had earlier accompanied Steve leading Dinah by the arm in an underwater swimming session, an interaction promising romance. Now, though, even when the couple fall and roll in the snow, the scene is devoid of any erotic charge, at least from Steve. The chorus, 'Please come back to my arms, / I need your love,' establishes the growing but unreciprocated feelings of Dinah for her travelling companion. The song as deployed fulfils a narrative and nostalgic function, reminding us of a relationship that is failing to follow the expected generic development.

This is largely because the director has abandoned his commercial brief – and four members of the group – to pursue a more personal project. Boorman later pleaded guilty as charged: 'I was obliged to begin with them [the Dave Clark Five] as that was what the public expected. What I wanted was not to disappoint their fans, but gradually to engage them in something quite different.'[101] That 'something quite different' again reveals the duality prevalent in the mature British pop music film as at key moments *Catch Us If You Can* questions where the real ends and the illusory begins: as in *Help!* the epistemological imperative is writ large and quickly presented. The early TV commercial, seemingly a clear case of artifice, is shot in a meat hanger of stark authenticity: when Steve and Dinah escape in the E-type jag those in pursuit include those portrayed in the film as 'real' porters. The starkest example comes when Steve and Dinah's country walk is brutally disrupted by the sight of a burnt-out tank and a series of collapsed buildings. It triggers a sudden, bewildering switch from the rural bucolic to a post-atomic wasteland. In a still-standing structure Steve and Dinah meet a group of CND beatniks: soon a convoy of tanks places them under attack and places the film firmly in its mid-phase generic lineage. Where *It's Trad, Dad!* positioned trad jazz in a connotative relationship to warfare and protest, and *Help!* intercut musicianship with a military mise-en-scène, *Catch Us If You Can* provides a more mimetic, music-free presentation of the potential for annihilation in the age of the bomb. Here, instead of Clang's mild squibs and flares, a rocket destroys a chimney while another blast leaves the stolen E-type jag a smoking wreck. Steve heroically saves Dinah (Clark in his stuntman element) as a roof collapses ahead of them and soldiers lob grenades into the terrified beats' retreat. All seems brutally, life-threateningly real until, with a cry of 'cease fire' from the commander-in-chief, we realise that the grubby tanks and gutted houses are the background for 'mock' military manoeuvres. Even so, when the soldiers surround the protesting beatniks a mood of 'genuine' antipathy, of violence barely contained, rears up and swings the film back from the ludic to a 'real' antagonism. A telling coda links the meat porters and military personnel, returning us to Zissell's office where the beef barons applaud his marketing strategies: 'all's fair in love, war and advertising'. The Marxist explanation of warfare as the inevitable result of capitalist overproduction floats around the office like their cigar smoke. Even the bland inquiry into a large round mobile's provenance – Japan – is tainted through association with economic booms and atomic bombs.

Cinema is not blameless in this blurring. The critically commended Bath scenes with Guy and Nan explore this most explicitly, entering areas similar to Resnais' admittedly more structurally complex audio-visual explorations of time and memory. When invited to view Guy's collection of memorabilia – 'stereoscopic, stroposcopic, epidioscopic, kaleidoscopic, telephonic' – Dinah is shown in essence an Edwardian version of Richard Hamilton's collage: Guy himself ventures that 'I collect the Pop Art of history.' Later, when the couples attend a fancy-dress party, the main protagonists all disguise themselves as Hollywood film icons. Dave Clark is dressed as Groucho Marx, the same impersonation carried out by Cliff Richard the previous year in *Wonderful Life*. But where Cliff 'recreated' Groucho, wisecracks and all, Clark (stiffly) serves to present the Hollywood myths that Boorman is already, in his debut, aiming to deconstruct. Steve's one-time hero Louis, for example, will prove to be a deep disappointment, a seedy opportunist looking to turn his farm into a fake 'western' ranch. All are measuring out their lives in cinema spools, and driving the plot is one girl's refusal to lend her image to the factory of dreams – of lies. In the ultimate act of iconoclasm, she defaces her own image, drawing a pair of glasses and moustache onto one of the myriad posters of her face that cover inner London.

Above and beyond an epistemological imperative, though, Boorman's personal project is explored through the prism of his life-long interest in analytical psychology. As such, if the primitive pop music film was prone to Freudian melodrama, Boorman's contribution could be explored – if not retitled – as 'the Jung ones'. Michel Ciment, in his auteurist study of Boorman, labels Carl Jung 'a critical influence on the film maker',[102] though he quickly passes over *Catch Us If You Can* to explore the later 'major' works. Nonetheless, this debut film – financed for bobbysoxers but made while the director was reading Jung[103] – is laden with figures and actions that are symbolic for Ciment in Jungian terms. The 'omniscient individual', an amalgam of the Jungian archetype of the 'trickster' and 'wise old man', feeds out into Boorman's oeuvre – and future pop music films – from omnipotent advertising director Leon Zissell, while the Boorman hero, an archetypical 'heretic', again debuts with Steve and Dinah who fight the all-seeing advertising agency. Ciment notes that all Boorman's films 'are based on the notion of a quest' that leaves the hero 'radically transformed'[104] and uncovers a principal element of Boorman's personal cosmology in 'the image of the island' that 'becomes a prison for those who take shelter in it'.[105] This Arthurian search for a symbol, figurative or real, can be followed all the way back with Steve to Louis' farm and Dinah's hoped-for off-shore purchase.

Jung observed that 'every psychological extreme secretly contains its own opposite or stands in some sort of intimate and essential relation to it'.[106] This enantiodromia is at the centre of Boorman's work, where the interplay between Steve and Dinah, readable as Realism and Romanticism or 'the Social' versus 'the Mythic', constitutes oppositions that fail (literally) to marry. Finally, Ciment notes how Boorman repeatedly taps into mythic thought but roots his films in the present: thus *Deliverance* 'interweaves the most timeless of phantasms with the contemporary preoccupations of the ecological ideal, "that tranquil weekend of fear", as the film's Italian title has it'.[107] One could echo this transatlantic nomenclature: *Catch Us If You Can* juxtaposes the quest for *nature sauvage* with the swinging sixties ideal, 'having a wild weekend', as the film's American title has it.

'Swinging Sixties', an integral part of England's heritage and a defining point of reference in the shared repository of cultural experience, is here problematised through the dissatisfactions of its leading (unromantic) couple. Robert Murphy sees *Catch Us If You Can* as essentially optimistic, but possessing 'an aura of wistfulness, of melancholy, expressing a doubt whether – even with the challenges and opportunities open to young people in this interlude of full employment and expansion in education – one really can have a good time and not have to pay an awful price for it'.[108] It is an aura rather than open articulation since the setting is the locus for much of this questioning symbolism. Boorman asserted the importance of ending at the Burgh Island Hotel: 'I was struck by the lifelessness of a place that no longer fulfilled its function: it's what, in a sense, has happened to England. It's like those farms that are no longer farms but parks for strolling about in. They seem almost asleep, like waste lands.'[109] In the midst of the first wave of US rock'n'roll, *The Tommy Steele Story* was at pains to present an emerging indigenous popular culture. Almost a decade on, and with London seemingly the central repository of all that was culturally 'cool', Boorman insists on the persistent penetration of British life by American style and values. Enacting the trajectory of both Boorman's future career and previous pop music films, *Catch Us If You Can* begins with a fresh invigorating style that proclaims the novelty and opportunity of youth, before slipping to a slow and sleepy ending in England's coastal Wasteland. 'On Margate Sands / I can connect / Nothing with nothing', wrote T.S. Eliot. *Catch Us If You Can* ends, as Jon Savage terms it, with 'the final Felliniesque shot of a crowd of cameramen and journalists, caught where sea and sky meet in nothingness'.[110]

Coda

Catch Us If You Can signalled the sub-genre's (paradigm) shift to the marginal status that it would subsequently occupy. The sacrificing of narrative also meant the sacrificing of audiences – as even the Beatles found to their cost with the bemused and hostile response that greeted their television film *Magical Mystery Tour* (1967). Yet aesthetically, after this radical mid-1960s shift, there could be no return to the more accessible narrative naiveties of *The Golden Disc* or *Summer Holiday* if one hoped for any semblance of credibility. Billy Fury, a front-runner in *Play It Cool*, was now far off the pace in *I've Gotta Horse* (Kenneth Hume, 1965) where animal welfare vies with 'getting to the show on time'. Joe Brown, previously a monochrome reminder to the Beatles of dubious sexual politics, was now a Cliff colour epigone, chivalrously showing his favourite female film star around London in the unremarkable *Three Hats for Lisa* (Sidney Hayers, 1965). The plot for *Dateline Diamonds* (Jeremy Summers, 1965), with the Small Faces caught up in diamond smuggling via Kenny Everett's pirate radio ship, may have promised a proto-decadent synthesis of star and crime generic tropes, but 'neither element is in anyway distinguished, and the intervals for music merely slow down the detection'.[111] Then there was *Every Day's a Holiday* (James Hill, 1964), the misguided, mistimed vehicle for John Leyton and Freddie and the Dreamers which, though retitled for the States *Seaside Swingers*, ends with an even more depressing seaside spectacle than Boorman's beach break-up. In truth, as Medhurst notes, 'The British pop film, in all its endearing awkwardness, was pretty much dead.'[112]

Con- or co-textually, it was effectively killed by television. After the edgy, experimental but ephemeral incarnations of Jack Good, and the vanguard running *Ready, Steady, Go!*, the establishment of the 'tame' chart-led and long-lasting *Top of the Pops*, first aired on BBC on 1 January 1964, meant that the economic exploitation angle that had given birth to the genre was henceforth largely unviable, television providing a cheaper and significantly quicker fix for the latest teen craze.[113] The mature pop music film knew this, ambivalently playing with the enemy as it openly acknowledged its interdependence on – and imminent capitulation to – the small screen. What route remained for rock stars keen to 'branch out' into new artistic territory, and directors willing to take a chance on unproven acting talent? The only truly cinematic option, the performance-free Pop Art knowingness kick-started by *Catch Us If You Can*, leads inexorably into the final, decadent phase of the British pop music film, a shrinking maze (or Jungian mandala) of self-referentiality and psycho-political pretension, an art-house, gestural cinema that will finally implode in the Borgesian gunshot of Cammell and Roeg's *Performance*.

4
The Decadent Pop Music Film: Politics, Psychedelia and Performance

Introduction: *Blow Up* and the backlash

The year 1966 was the first of the lean years for British pop music films. In Hugh Gladwish's musical comedy *The Ghost Goes Gear*, the Spencer Davis Group's manager (Nicholas Parsons) holds a pop festival to finance his ancestral haunted house. The group were scared enough to disappear halfway through while the producers were so terrified they truncated the movie and released it as a supporting short to *One Million Years BC* (Don Chaffey, 1966): an apt pairing since critics found the 'embarrassingly artless affair ... uncomfortably reminiscent of the "quota quickie"'.[1] Of pop's prime movers only Cliff Richard and the Shadows turned in appearances. Cliff Richard Junior, 'the biggest star in the universe', made a cameo appearance in David Lane's *Thunderbirds Are Go*, described – a touch harshly – by Mark Kermode as Cliff's finest film performance.[2] However, oblivious to the advances of Lester, Boorman and Anderson (Gerry or Lindsay), Cliff again teamed up with Robert Morley to relive the innocent scheming of *The Young Ones* in Sidney Hayers' *Finders Keepers*. The film is generally seen as marking a low ebb in Cliff's filmography (as would Richard Lester's identically titled train-set comedy-thriller of 1984) but it still ranked as the year's top musical. At least it acknowledged the cold war context variously manifest in the genre's mature phase: an atomic bomb, lost off the coast of Spain, is found by Cliff and the boys who, after various cunning ploys and decoys, return it to its rightful American owners. Here, though, bomb culture is a pretext for Cliff not to save the world but to get the girl, a debutante Vivian Ventura, and for the Shadows to further their musical regression with a version of 'My Way'. The film only bears mention in Richard biographies since it was during filming in May

1966 that Cliff 'prayed the prayer that ended the search' for God.[3] One month on and Cliff would be on-stage with Billy Graham at Earls Court, going public on his discovery of the Christian faith. Peter Watkins, the director of *Privilege*, noted the phenomenon.

Elsewhere, the Dave Clark Five, forging ahead in America, preferred frequent appearances with Ed Sullivan to further archetypes with John Boorman. The Beatles, when not upsetting Imelda Marcos or middle America on unwanted world tours (exemplifying in the process the matrix of pop, politics and religion that would dominate the 'decadent' pop film phase), became engrossed in exploring new sounds through complex studio techniques. Their *Revolver* album transported pop music and its eager listeners to a new dimension, especially in numbers such as 'Tomorrow Never Knows' which was, for Ian MacDonald, 'one of the most socially influential records the Beatles ever made', introducing LSD and Timothy Leary's 'psychedelic revolution' to the young of the Western world.[4] If the primitive pop music film was fuelled by nothing more threatening than a frothy cappuccino, and its mature phase, most noticeably *Help!*, had the added impetus of the amphetamines known as 'speed', the later sixties saw a move to greater experimentation with cannabis and LSD, drugs that slow down thought and amplify feelings. Under the influence, everything was possible, nothing was real. For the privileged few with an established following, record (and film) companies were happy to join in the ride: they had little inclination or justification to force their contracted charges into shooting exploitation quickies. L.S.D. still meant £.s.d. and the creative longevity now accorded to the musical elite would be meticulously recorded in Jean-Luc Godard's diptych on the garlanded Rolling Stones and grassroots political action, *One Plus One/Sympathy for the Devil*.

Political engagement grew because, back in the 'real' world, all was not well: Wilson's strategy to modernise industry had failed to take off and earlier ideologies of affluence ceded to openly coercive and confrontational political programmes. To cap the growing discontent, all the talked-up drive of well-educated youth had disappeared into a druggy haze of introspective as Britain witnessed a further unwanted US influence, hippydom. This new alternative movement received little attention from the commercial film industry. At a push one could interpret James Coburn as living the hippy life in Donald Cammell's scripted *Duffy* (Robert Parrish, 1968), but narrative films about late 1960s youth culture – the obligatory squatting, the abundant drugs, the occasional sex – only surface after the event in low-budget efforts such as John Pearse's *Moviemakers* (1971) and Barney Platts-Mills *Private Road* (1971).

Yellow Submarine would give its culture of dissent a cartoon make-over, while Peter Whitehead made two documentaries: *Wholly Communion* (1966), a cinema-verité account of the June 1965 Poetry Conference at the Albert Hall; and *Tonite Let's All Make Love in London* (1967), where, through interviews with Julie Christie, David Hockney, Michael Caine, Andrew Loog Oldham and Mick Jagger, Whitehead tried to find out what it was that made London so different, so appealing.

Between those pieces, in the summer of 1966, with the Beatles at their creative peak (if performative low) and Alf Ramsey's 'revolutionary' wingless wonders winning the World Cup, the myth of a New Age London was a magnet for American studio subsidiaries and foreign film directors: for MGM Michelangelo Antonioni shot what many consider the quintessential 'Swinging Sixties' film, *Blow Up* (1966). Here David Hemmings, progressing from Lance Comfort's 'cheerful minor musicals' *Live It Up* and *Be My Guest* (1965),[5] plays the latest incarnation of the working-class hero, a bored and blasé David Bailey-esque fashion photographer who, on finding he may have photographed a murder, starts to care passionately. *Blow Up* is again largely predicated on the processes of mediation, with lengthy scenes dedicated to the shooting, not of a person in a park, but of photographs, and their subsequent developing, cropping and framing. Unlike the 'speed' generated in the Lester and Boorman movies, however, *Blow Up* is itself slowed down. The scene where model Sarah Miles expects Hemmings to declare his love for her is full of awkward silences, intercut with bursts of energy and intensity. It is the rhythm of the new drug culture, and reappears at the start of *Performance*. Tonally, from the cool, crisp black and white of *A Hard Day's Night*, through the bright, colour-supplement pot-ridden *Help!*, *Blow Up* collapses into the muddy, insipid tones of excessive self-examination – another prelude for *Performance*.

Musically, the exuberant, life-affirming soundtrack of earlier pop films now becomes an introspective, destructive medium. In a celebrated scene at the centre of *Blow Up* – one that 'blows up' the surrounding film's pretentious ennui – Hemmings wanders into the Ricky Tick club where (Who substitutes) the Yardbirds, then featuring Jeff Beck and Jimmy Page, are performing 'Stroll On'. If the Beatles and their pubescent fans shook the rafters of the Scala in communal hysteria, here the audience is silent, still and studentish. But when the band's equipment plays up and an annoyed Jeff Beck attacks the amplifiers with his guitar before flinging the broken instrument into the crowd, a near-riot breaks out as the crowd frantically fight for possession of the relic. Hemmings grabs the neck and dashes out of the club, but, once on Oxford Street, looks at his prize and – in a gesture recalling the existential Adam Faith in *Beat Girl* – throws it away. Possessions are not cool, they are not 'real', a point enacted in the film's conclusion when Hemmings encounters a jeep full of prime exponents of the counter-culture, who mime a tennis match with imaginary ball, a 'happening' to entrance the art-film circuit and infuriate the artisan.

The following year Columbia offered a more populist approach to Swinging London with James Clavell's *To Sir, with Love*. A throwback to the primitive pop music–social-problem melodrama format of *Serious Charge*, plot and casting effectively brought *The Blackboard Jungle* to London's East End. Sidney Poitier, in 1955 a JD giving Glenn Ford a hard time, was now a pedagogical 'poacher turned gamekeeper', teaching the kids self-respect and prompting appreciative 18-year-old Scottish pop star Lulu, backed by the Mindbenders, to sing him a stateside number one – the title track became Billboard's top selling single for 1967. Poitier's caring supply teacher Mark Thackeray marks an advance on *Help!*'s dismal representation of black characters, but the film removes the key theme of miscegenation from E.J. Braithwaite's source novel and, as Jim Pines points out, Thackeray's assimilation into a world of white middle-class values (foregoing his native patois to learn 'proper' English, for instance) constitutes a further strand of pop film 'emasculation'.[6] Though patronised by the press as 'good old-fashioned sentimental nonsense'[7] the film performed strongly in the UK. However, alongside Poitier's casting and tie-in single release, the overplayed shots of red London buses, colourful markets and miniskirts, together with the recuperative message that 'in the cinema at least, the young still know their place',[8] all indicate more than one eye on the American market where *To Sir, with Love* enjoyed a theatrical take of close to $20 million, making it, after *Thunderball* and *Goldfinger*, Britain's third best grossing film in the States of the entire 1960s.

While American studios continued to mine this rich seam, an indigenous backlash occurred in what Robert Murphy terms 'Anti-Swinging London films'.[9] These turned from the capital and its well-off anti-capitalists towards a working-class realism reminiscent of the northern British New Wave films of the late 1950s–early 1960s. Murphy focuses on Peter Collinson's *Up the Junction* and Ken Loach's *Poor Cow* (both 1967) but mentions Saul Swimmer's *Mrs Brown, You've Got a Lovely Daughter* (1968), the second feature film of Herman's Hermits and a first pop film venture for the Stones' and Beatles' manager, Allen Klein. Lead singer Peter Noone and company were the most lightweight of the British beat bands, but enjoyed American success comparable with the Dave

Clark Five. Here, the group spend the first and final thirds of the film in their northern home town, Herman (Peter Noone) reasserting regionalism with his motto, 'remember, you're not Britain, you're Manchester!' Aerial views of back-to-back houses, greyhound racing and knees-ups in the local pub establish a materially poor but enriching sense of community. When the group finally move south for national greyhound trials, they are followed around by a 'spaced out hippy chick', relieved of their money by a conman and refused accommodation by a landlady objecting to 'bloody foreigners'. When they get involved in a fight with paisley-patterned Chelsea 'floaters', a 'happening' is proclaimed, while the Hermits' first-night performance at a trendy nightclub highlights the vacuity displayed on the dance floor when intercut with the absent Herman desperately searching the streets for his missing greyhound. The divide as played out here is geographical, not generational. The finale retreads the values of Cliff Richard musicals, a split-screen giving equal space to Herman and his aged employer, Variety's own Stanley Holloway, who sings that, while 'the world is for the Young', they will need 'to explore / the strange new lands of Experience'. When Herman returns to the North and bicycle rides with the girl he left behind, he confesses to Holloway that they are 'no better than five hundred other groups', adding caustically that 'in London there are more groups than there are coppers'. With greater cultural capital, *Performance* also enlists this class unrest, the proletarian gangster dismissive of the 'long hair, beatniks, druggers, free love and foreigners' that he finds in Notting Hill, while strategies to contain this new unease are explored in the first 'decadent' pop music film, *Privilege*.

The pop music film as personal polemic: *Privilege* (1967)

The third phase of the British pop music film again begins with bombs. Cambridge-educated Peter Watkins had a spectacular but short career with the BBC. *The War Game* (1965), his exploration in a near-future setting of a nuclear attack on Rochester in Kent, continued from his debut *Culloden* (1964) in using non-professional actors and the techniques of cinema-verité – jerky hand-held camera, coarse editing, hands held out to stop filming – to create a world both self-reflexive and disturbingly 'real' in its foregrounded mediation. Fearing a television equivalent of Orson Welles' *War of the Worlds*, the BBC shelved the film indefinitely: instead it received a limited theatrical release – and a 1966 Oscar for best documentary. Watkins, particularly angered at the BBC's critique that he presented a 'biased and subjective' account to an audience seemingly unable to find alternative points of view, countered that 'objective' filmmaking was impossible: all newscasts, merely by editing material, created a subjective presentation of observed 'reality'. He resigned from the BBC, determined to problematise further the documentary form and expose the inherent dangers of media manipulation.

Watkins' opportunity came when producer John Heyman approached him to direct a project exploring the manipulation of popular taste by the movers and shakers of the pop world. With American novelist Norman Bogner, Watkins adapted Johnny Speight's original storyline to his preferred form and focus, yoking a metaphorical plotline to documentary-style interviews and broadening the attack to include government, Church and press, the full forces of hegemony feeding the populace the opiate of pop and diverting their attention from the real ills of society. Funding came from Universal, part of their (disastrously) late addition to the American invasion of the British film industry. With a budget of just $700,000 *Privilege* was the smallest of the 13 (unerringly unsuccessful) UK films the studio backed between 1967 and 1970. Even so, this would constitute by far the largest budget of Watkins' career, and his first venture into colour.

Though union regulations necessitated the employment of Equity-card actors, Watkins secured non-professionals for the lead roles of pop star Steve Shorter and his love interest, Vanessa Ritchie. For the latter Watkins cast the first photographic model to become an international superstar, David Bailey's protégée Jean Shrimpton. Early reports suggested that Eric Burdon of the Animals would take the pop star role, but the selection of Paul Jones for Shorter was shrewder, supplying artistic credibility – and compatible stature, an extra six inches in height to match the 5'10" Shrimpton.[10] Oxford-educated Jones had found fame as the lead singer with Manfred Mann, one of the most consistent hit makers of the 1960s. He had begun angling for solo challenges, however, and left the group in July 1966 to work on *Privilege*. Jones' casting again guaranteed the film plentiful pre-publicity and met with no opposition from Universal, who (naively) granted Watkins complete artistic freedom.

To gain an insight into the pop music business, Watkins studied at length *Lonely Boy*, Wolf Koenig and Roman Kroitor's influential 1962 cinema-verité documentary on Paul Anka, one of the first films to give an equal focus to the pop world backstage. The music itself was entrusted to Mike Leander who had previously scored Peter Whitehead's Rolling Stones' documentary *Charlie is My Darling* (1965) and arranged Lulu's 'To Sir, with Love', while former Stones stablemate George Bean was booked with his band the Runners to perform Leander's two rock-arranged hymns. With no pressure to produce an exploitation 'quickie', shooting began in Birmingham in August 1966, a full eight months before the scheduled opening date. Even so, an approach replicating Richard Lester's expedient use of chance events is evident in the final concert scenes. These had to be completed in a single night at St Andrew's, the home of Birmingham City Football Club. The two thousand spectators grew restless watching the filming process and rioted: this unscripted 'real' response found its way into the final edit, the crowd breaking just as Shorter runs towards the podium. However, studio executives grew equally restless on seeing the final cut, damning it as a prime example of 'the cult of the amateur'.[11] Universal was tied to Rank who, even more alarmed, refused to give the film a general circuit booking. Publicly, Universal voiced uncertainty over marketing strategies: 'this is an unusual film, interesting and problematic. We are not sure how to sell it.'[12] Privately, Watkins' work was again stifled because Rank thought his film 'mocked the Church, defied authority and encouraged youth in lewd practices'.[13] The final mix of the contingent and the un-Christian was at least premiered at the Warner Leicester Square cinema on 27 April 1967.

To compound its problems, *Privilege* was savaged by the British press. Alexander Walker led the attack, decrying 'a flailing, hysterical, misdirected film' for double standards: 'attacking the totalitarian trends it thinks it can spy in Britain, it uses the very rhetoric of Fascism, all the propaganda tricks of half-truths, shaky hypotheses, and distortions that range from the subtle to the crude'.[14] The inexperienced leads were not spared the critical mauling, though Dilys Powell deflected the blame onto Watkins, judging that 'Paul Jones is personable and may be gifted. But when he is not belting out a song he is being directed to the point of extinction.'[15] It was left to Nina Hibbin to defend Shrimpton's 'quiet, introverted performance' as 'entirely real and valid'.[16] Hibbin's strong (far-left) support for the film was only matched by *The Observer*'s Penelope Gilliatt, who lauded 'a hugely impressive feature film' with 'grasp, substance, aptness, human detail and social perspective' and 'an energy and concern that seem gouged out of its guts'. Gilliatt alone discussed the film's music: 'one of the most intelligent and liberated sound-tracks I've ever heard'.[17] It was certainly the most commercially successful aspect of the project. Jones' single 'I've Been a Bad Bad Boy' reached the UK top five in February 1967, spending nine weeks in the top 50. The attendant soundtrack album failed to chart, however.

Audiences able to find the film were also disappointed, indicative of the genre's new commercial difficulties. Just *who* was *Privilege* aimed at? Joseph Gomez surmised that 'the so-called youth audience felt somewhat cheated because the film was not like Richard Lester's films with the Beatles, nor was it even a pop musical in the Cliff Richard fashion, and it made no concessions to those expecting conventional narrative development'.[18] On the other hand, so-called adult audiences anticipating the intense 'experimental' experience granted by *Culloden* and *The War Game* found more traditional camera angles and editing, a slower pace and a more nebulous overall structure. The film certainly disappointed Shrimpton: her autobiography noted that, on first viewing the final print, 'I squirmed lower in my seat every time I appeared on-screen. I was a spectacular failure.'[19] With its leading lady reacting thus, it is not surprising that, unlike with *The War Game*, no groundswell of support rescued *Privilege* for exhibition or Oscars and, no doubt to Rank's relief, it soon faded from its non-circuit circulation (though it would later gain cult status in US college film clubs).

Watkins later bemoaned the fact that *Privilege* was eclipsed by events at the time of its release – he cites as an example Mick Jagger meeting in a walled garden by Canterbury Cathedral with the Dean and two dons for a televised colloquium.[20] However, a similar media move provided *Privilege* with one last infusion of publicity. The idea of a (once) threatening rock'n'roller switching gear to pedal religion chimed with Cliff Richard's Earls Court announcement that he had discovered the Christian faith. Planners at ABC television saw the parallel and, when Cliff accepted their invitation to appear opposite Paul Jones on the discussion programme *Looking for an Answer* on 16 July 1967, *Privilege*'s implied dialogue with Richard was explicitly enacted. The odds were stacked against Cliff from the start. Alexander Walker described the film's Christian Nationalist meet as a 'Billy Graham-type rally' and, as if to confirm Watkins' view that all editing establishes a bias, the programme opened with a scene from *Privilege*, showing the cynical exploitation of Shorter and his fans, before cutting to 'real-life' footage of Cliff singing at Graham's Earls Court rally. Interviewer Robert Kee then posed the key question: 'Is the Church exploiting Cliff Richard too?' Cliff strenuously denied the accusation, but was systematically out-argued by Jones. A difficult moment in his career, the interview is not mentioned in Cliff's evangelical autobiography *Which One's Cliff?*, while even quasi-official biographers concede that 'His genuine witness won him respect even if in the battle of words he did not win the final comment.'[21]

Cliff may, though, have had that final comment. The pop stars' discussions would continue and culminate in Jones' 1984 embrace of

Christianity – (ironically) after both attended an evangelical rally at Loftus Road football stadium. Furthermore, the implication in *Looking for an Answer*'s editing that Watkins' fictional film housed a greater truth than the Earls Court documentary footage was complicated by a later awareness that Cliff too had been playing a part at the rally, in preparation for his next film venture. *Two a Penny*, released in July 1968, had been set up and funded by Worldwide Films, part of Billy Graham's organisation. The script demanded the involvement of Cliff's character, Jamie Hopkins, in an authentic crusade scene, and this was clandestinely shot during the Earls Court rally, Cliff responding to cue cards given to him by director Jim Collier to sneer towards Graham or mock the audience's gullibility.[22] The filmed 'exploitation' of the masses was not just the province of media-savvy Watkins and ABC – Cliff too had a personal project to realise. Made for £150,000, Cliff's Equity-stipulated weekly minimum wage of £40 was devoted to charity, as were all proceeds from the film, predominantly shown in UK church halls. In a distinct character shift, *Two a Penny* depicted Cliff as the drug-trafficking seducer of an older woman, but one who eventually agrees to attend the Billy Graham rally. The film ends with Jamie, aware of the emptiness of his life, reflecting on Graham's words. The music for *Two a Penny* was composed and conducted by *Privilege*'s own Mike Leander – Cliff's tie-in single 'I'll Love You Forever Today' reached the top 30 – and the two films attained a further, final equivalence via their dismissive reviews: 'naïve propaganda' with 'the general air of Sunday School homily' wrote the *Monthly Film Bulletin* on the saving of pop's former saviour.[23]

The opening to *Privilege*, a clapperboard filling the screen and snapping shut for sound before Steve Shorter speaks to camera, thanking his fans after an American tour, announces it as the most heavily mediated pop film since *A Hard Day's Night*. We cut to scenes of the teenage, female adulation such media-fuelled globetrotting induces: Birmingham boy Steve is receiving, the voice-over tells us, 'the first ticker-tape welcome in the history of Britain'. The influences for these scenes reach back beyond Lester and *Lonely Boy*. Paul Jones recollects that, on first visiting Watkins' office, 'there were photographs pinned all over the walls, most of them stills from Leni Riefenstahl's *Triumph of the Will*' (1935).[24] The entire ticker-tape parade, with tracking shots of the crowd during the motorcade, the low-angle medium shots of Shorter in the front of the leading car, the close-up shots of the back of his upraised hand as he passes enthralled onlookers along New Street, effect quasi-exact matches for Riefenstahl's presentation of Hitler's entry into Nuremberg, a pastiche that will return in the finale's National Stadium rock concert sequences.

Before then, though, we see a significant shift in the genre's employ-ment of musical performance. Discrete from the scant storyline in Lester's movies and demoted to an ambient soundtrack in Boorman's more picaresque plot, here as in other final-phase pop films the musical numbers serve primarily to drive the narrative and its attendant, largely pessimistic ideological programme. Steve's street parade leads him to Birmingham Town Hall, where a screaming and expectant crowd view centre-stage a large metal cage protected by burly prison warders, trun-cheons in hand. The voice-over again explains: 'The reason given for the extreme violence of the stage act that you are about to see is that it provides the public with a necessary release from all the nervous ten-sion caused by the state of the world outside.' This is pop as purgation. Backstage preparations are revealed through a series of black-and-white stills: emphasising the scene's mediation, a security man has his hand raised to block the photo, though a heavily guarded Steve remains vis-ible in the distance. As further shots show Steve being handcuffed and stretching out his splayed hands to camera we hear that 'the perfor-mance for which Steve Shorter is now being prepared is based on the sentence he once served in prison'. With these calmly delivered words and swiftly edited visuals we reach the final synthesis of the British pop music film: the merging of the coffee bar tropes of music as a passport to success and an index of violence – 'youth-as-fun' and 'youth-as-trouble' are now inseparable. The switch to black and white thus signals not only an ersatz documentary veracity, but the redeployment of pop's brief heritage. The voice-over confirms the efficacy of this socialising synthesis: 'So successful has this violent act become that Steve Shorter now finds himself the most desperately loved entertainer in the world.'

The violent act that follows has Steve flung on-stage from a gallery and locked into the cage before he slowly rises to his feet and sings impassionedly to a solid rock backing and a baying crowd for some-body to 'Free Me'. An onrushing fan is slapped and dragged off-stage, the auditorium builds up its chant of 'free, free, free!' until, when Steve is led away by prison guards, the stage is stormed and a full-scale riot ensues. The composed voice-over contextualises: 'There is now a coali-tion government in Britain, which has recently asked all entertainment agencies to usefully divert the violence of youth, keep them happy, off the streets and out of politics.' Steve's performance, an unsubtle mould-ing of mass emotion, affects the required catharsis.

With a cut to Jean Shrimpton's Vanessa in her artist's studio, speak-ing to camera of her first sighting of Steve, the opening ten minutes confirm that *Privilege* will not present a conventional narrative: the development of Shorter's realising and rebelling against his manipulation is intercut with voice-overs, photomontages and interviews which stand outside the chronological progression. They function explicitly as Brechtian devices inviting an intellectual before emotional engagement – a dangerous ploy, perhaps, for the dynamics of musical performance. Here, Vanessa's *sotto voce* recollections grant us our first opportunity to reflect on the slick-paced, high-decibel number just witnessed and, while Watkins connotes Beatlemania with his reiterated inserts of Steve's ecstatic female fans – the focus on one screaming girl repeats Lester's 'white rabbit' in *A Hard Day's Night* – the context denotes the disconnectedness of Shorter's performance from their reaction. The overt theatricality precludes the communion between pop star and both internal and cinema audiences as attained by the Beatles' 'She Loves You', or even Cliff's 'We Say Yeah'.

Penelope Gilliatt termed the show as 'nothing better than a two-way ravening process between a resentful public mascot and an audience out of its mind. The teenagers are begging an emptied man to make them feel something; the singer is battering them for a response instead of addressing his music.'[25] This may have been Watkins' intention, but engagement is further undermined by an awareness that this is again a second-hand enactment, now borrowing heavily from *Lonely Boy*. The female fan lowered on-stage during 'Free Me' is no spontaneous display of devotion: it constitutes both a skilled diegetic manipulation and the precise recreation of an identical moment during Paul Anka's rendition of 'Put Your Head on My Shoulder'. Numerous parallels, if not straight purloinings, reappear as we meet Steve's entourage at the post-performance party. Max Bacon's publisher 'Uncle' Julie Jordan may recall Meier Tzelniker's persona from *Expresso Bongo* but is primarily modelled on 'Uncle' Jules Fidel, owner of the Copacabana nightclub where Anka performed. Press officer Alvin Kirsch's initials invoke impresario Allen Klein, but he bears a close resemblance to Irvin Feld, Anka's personal manager. Several of Feld's documentary pronouncements – 'Paul, you no longer belong to yourself: you belong to the world' – are adapted for Kirsch's interviews to camera. Character moments, as when Steve presents Jules with a large framed self-portrait, and mannerisms, as when 'fixer' Marcus Hooper massages Steve's neck during a boardroom meeting, are further liftings from Koenig and Kroitor's documentary. The cumulative effect is of imitation before investigation.

Building further on *Lonely Boy*, Watkins insists that the real pop-realm drama is off-stage, notably in the boardroom where the pop star is exposed as a replaceable commodity. With *A Hard Day's Night* Richard

Lester spoke of undermining 'a society that was based on privilege – privilege by schooling, privilege by birth, privilege by accent, privilege by speech'.[26] Such a target is embodied in Shorter Enterprises' manager and merchant banker Andrew Goddard Butler, orchestrating Steve's career with the plum tones of a private education and the sharp mind of economic success. Straight after Steve's exhausting Beatles-style American tour, Butler hawks him out to the Ministry of Agriculture for 35 adverts to avert an apple glut. It works: at Steve's behest the population will eat six apples a day for the entire summer. It works too as comedy, the apple ad director's declared indebtedness to 'the Moscow Arts theatre and certain of our modern philosophers' pointedly mocking the pretensions of those in the publicity industry.

The advert also illustrates the easy interchangeability of discourse, and the hegemonic function of pop stars and their harmonies remains *Privilege*'s underlying 'serious' issue. With a vision easier to accept in an age of transparently 'manufactured' boy bands and *The X Factor*, Watkins refutes the notion that talented individuals like Cliff or the Beatles can exist independently of the vertically integrated marketing system that delivers their image and their music. Here a George Harrison cannot walk out of a fashion meeting with a cocky self-assurance: Steve, 'the greatest star of all time', can only enter the board meeting of the company bearing his name long after his new outfit – and outlook – have been decided for him. The board's designation that 'the youth of the future' should display the 'swing towards respectability, social grace and, above all, a new found innocence' instead advances the discussions on 'gracious living' initiated in Zissell's penthouse office in *Catch Us If You Can*. The announcement that fashion style's 'restrictive line and penal motif' will disappear so that the young will be 'released' echoes the voice-over for Steve's stage violence and emphasises the totalising control over youth culture. At the declaration that 'in ten days' time we're going to make Steve Shorter repent' a close-up on Steve underlines his surprise at this ideological volte-face, though the rhythm of a non-diegetic drumbeat connotes the economic continuity. As the scene concludes with an 'advisory Professor' explaining that Steve will publicly declare his newfound 'respect for law and order' because 'we've always wanted the youth of Britain to say [these things] also', his statement represents the cynical nadir in the genre's representation of rebel rock. 'Britain in the future' exposes the entire pop phenomenon as a social safety valve allowed to teenagers but ultimately serving established societal aims and objectives, the preparation of an ever-manipulated younger generation for 'recuperation' into mainstream values and commercial norms.

Religion is here the chosen path as the rebel becomes the Rock on which the Church will found its new crusade. In *Privilege* the media-savvy clergy know how to put on a show and the Christian Nationalist rally is skilfully worked to a converting climax. A Salvation Army band's 'Abide with Me' allows us to take in the setting: a huge outdoor stage, red banners, cheer leaders and a giant illuminated cross up on the stage. The compere, Reverend Jeremy Tate, cajoles the crowd to shout back the three words of salvation 'we will conform!' before beckoning Steve across the field up to the stage. After George Bean and band provide a fascistic salute and a rock version of 'Jerusalem', Steve, alone on-stage, forsakes the violence of his prison-phase version of 'Free Me' for a new 'sincere' religious mode. As he confesses that 'A sweeping spirit moved me, a shining light was mine' the visual correlative for this oversee-ing deity is a mid-shot of a large eye behind him, Steve's own inflated image, an Orwellian power of persuasion (Figure 4.1). The scene ends as the bright colour photography of the rally dissolves into a series of black-and-white still photographs of the audience rejoicing as the voice-over informs us that 'In the one evening in the National Stadium 49,000 gave themselves to God and flag through Steve Shorter.' A new pop culture trinity is born.

Figure 4.1   Paul Jones at the Cliff's edge – *Privilege*

With its future setting, *Privilege* was always meant to serve as metaphor, not mimesis, and the prescience of its 'withering critique of the supposedly revolutionary nature of rock' has rescued its reputation to the extent that Garry Mulholland recently declared it 'the Greatest Rock'n'Roll Movie Ever Made'.[27] While greatly admiring the film, my dissent from Mulholland's ranking is primarily that the past inescapably shapes – and problematises – the film's *musical* vision with Watkins' cinematic correlation so markedly born of pastiche. Though for me closest in its faux-sentiment and church choirs to Cliff Richard in *Expresso Bongo* – the change from Beat to Ballad a generic microcosm of Cliff's career shift – contemporary critics striving to locate Shorter/Jones' stage persona in the pop pantheon looked elsewhere: in the UK Robin Bean labelled him 'the Beatles and Stones rolled into one',[28] whilst for *Time* magazine he combined 'the sequined splendor of an Elvis Presley with the sullen magnetism of a Bob Dylan'.[29] The prime failing of *Privilege* is musical: the narrative invites these lofty comparisons, but then makes Jones a hostage to fortune when he has to perform. He acts his songs well, but, as Andrew Sarris noted, 'the whole point of the characterisation is undercut by the credibility gap between what we are told about his fabulous career and what we see and hear on screen'.[30] For all his histrionics and spectacular entrances, Shorter/Jones is eclipsed as a performer by George Bean and his Runner Beans with their Beat-Blake 'Jerusalem'. Jones is physically – and generically – rather isolated on-stage as throughout the National Stadium's display of mass manipulation one again feels not an energising rock genealogy but the propagandising pressure of Leni Riefenstahl's record of the sixth Nazi congress at Nuremberg, a feeling confirmed by the closing switch from colour. Here the uplifting rock 'Jerusalem' replaces 'Horst Wessel Lied'; crucifixes and Shorter's cross-like arrow symbol stand in for swastikas; one can even read Tate and the Bishop of Essex reviewing the gathered faithful as new world versions of Rudolf Hess and Joseph Goebbels. However 'cleverly' intertextual, within the parameters of performance this diminishes: Watkins is trying to show that the public likes what the public gets, but it comes at the cost of the dislocation of the film audience's emotional engagement.

Privilege is paradoxically more effective in its investigation of the performative power of language. In the narrative denouement, Steve's 'rejection' speech at the Awards Dinner is limited to an almost inarticulate, strangulated cry: 'You worship me as if I was a ... god. But I'm someone ... I'm a person. I am nothing ... I hate you.' This stuttering rebuttal may lessen the dramatic climax, but it maintains character consistency and the film's contrast between Steve's lengthy silences and inarticulacy (Tate could not be more mistaken when he claims that Shorter has 'found God, has found the Word') and the endless verbal extemporisations of Kirsch, Butler and others surrounding and sucking the life-blood out of the rock star. When being tied in knots by Paul Jones during their television debate, Cliff had complained: 'No, no, no: again you're using words.'[31] It happens all the time in *Privilege*, more awash with words than any pop music film since *Expresso Bongo*. Yet for all their loquacity, Steve's personnel speak to little *personal* effect: theirs is the language of hype, the divisive marketing discourse of a society where all are judged on delivering the *mot juste*. The one exception is Vanessa Ritchie, with her sincere concern for Steve and her barely audible semi-utterances. Her lack of expertise in the ready rhetoric ever-audible around her becomes all the more laudatory simply because it sounds so unrehearsed and, amidst the new privileged elite of the media and its 'applied' arts, she registers as the ingénue, the 'real thing'. Of course such an interpretation raises the issue of casting: is Vanessa meant to be so muted or is Jean Shrimpton merely out of her depth? Contemporary critics thought the latter, and ended her acting career there and then. Yet, as S.M.J. Arrowsmith has argued, one of *Privilege*'s strengths resides in the 'utterly vacuous' relationship between its romantic stars. 'Scripting and performance are both so shallow and so determined to decline any possible narrative movement that these passages achieve a remarkably effective revelation of a peculiarly British application of the inertia factor in the manufacture of glamour as a commodity.'[32] Establishing this emptiness at the emotional centre of *Privilege* may disappoint fans in search of a trusted love story, but it offers a trenchant template for a society which lets itself become preoccupied by such manipulated – and hence manipulative – 'personalities'. (Posh and Becks, anyone?)

Penelope Gilliatt concluded that the central social point of *Privilege* concerns monolithism: 'The attack isn't on pop, on the Church but on the kind of souped-up communal sentiment that hinders audiences from making distinctions.'[33] Which raises a second caveat to Mulholland's primary ranking: is *Privilege* itself immune to such an accusation? Just *what* is *Privilege* aimed at? Ultimately Steve Shorter constellates and condenses too many issues: some worthy, such as artistic autonomy in a mediated industry; others trivial (if amusing), such as 'existential' adverts for Granny Smiths. This overloading occurs because Steve stands at the interface between consumer and cultural producer. As much as representing manipulated youth, Shorter merges with an aggrieved director and *Privilege*'s social effectiveness is compromised by Watkins' insufficiently filtered personal grievances, the expression of which first attracted him to the project. Watkins' empathy with his creation's position is most evident at the film's conclusion when we learn that, following the pop idol's haltering attempts at honesty, 'Steve Shorter is barred from this and any further appearance on television, just to ensure that he does not again misuse his position of privilege to disturb the public peace of mind.' Clearly this equally signifies Peter Watkins after *The War Game*. An auteur is creating a narrative of his experience as an index of media suppression but, perhaps too close to his material, jeopardises any ethical advantage with a distorted extrapolation. Regrettably *Privilege*'s ending all but affirms the Adorno-like condescension to the masses articulated by Steve's puppeteer Svengali, Andrew Butler. Even as a metaphor the immediate and total turning of the public against Shorter stretches credulity – and certainly did not happen to Watkins, who received plentiful public support. Over the final silent, black-and-white rerun of the film's opening images one notes, sadly, a touch of the double standards identified by Alexander Walker as Watkins shows himself to be as contemptuous of the public as the BBC governors he used the film to attack. The ending enacts Guy Debord's late 1960s regret at youth's mindless and passive consumption, their 'imprisonment in a flattened universe ... where they know only the fictional speakers who unilaterally surround them with their commodities and the politics of their commodities'.[34]

One of the enriching qualities of the mature British pop music film was its savouring the best of both worlds, its espousal of a fertile, questioning duality: even the early *Expresso Bongo* recognised its complicity with what it denounced. *Privilege,* prescient and powerful but born of a self-justifying rage, finally presents a poorer 'decadent' duality, having one's cake but choking on it.[35]

The pop music film as underground parable: *Yellow Submarine* (1968)

The Beatles might well have envied Steve Shorter having his image barred from television. Back in November 1964, Brian Epstein had sold the group's animated rights to Al Brodax's US-based King Features company, allowing for 52 half-hour shows and the use of two Beatle songs in each. The show premiered on ABC television in September 1965, immediately broke all US television ratings, and lasted as long as the Beatles themselves, only closing in September 1969. Far from being flattered by the project, however, it proved to be a constant irritant for the group who received little financial return and zero creative input – here they were the party denied the access to self-representation (see *Help!*). Epstein therefore faced a dilemma when Brodax, now working for United Artists, reminded the Beatles' manager of his promise that, should the series prove a success, he would ensure the group's cooperation in a feature-film project. The success of the previous Beatles efforts had left United Artists pushing for a quick start on the final installment of their three-film deal. The group, however, bored silly on the pot-marked *Help!* and retreating deeper into the LSD-fuelled fantasies that would produce the *Sgt. Pepper* album, had no desire to return to a movie set. Even so, having had their fingers – and finances – burned by the American TV series, the proposal for a full-length animated film seemed the last avenue to explore. Brodax, though, was determined and, armed with an original idea by Lee Minoff based on the Beatles' August 1966 number one 'Yellow Submarine', he visited Paul McCartney late that year to persuade him of the project's viability. As the most artistically aspirational – and self-styled financial expert – of the Fab Four, McCartney liked the idea of a film built around one of his compositions. Envisioning a 'wonderful Disneyesque adventure, only a little bit more far out',[36] McCartney readily agreed: the other Beatles rather reluctantly did not say no.

Much to the group's alarm, however, Brodax went straight to George Dunning and John Coates, whose Soho-centred unambiguously titled TV Cartoons company had, alongside lucrative animated commercials, churned out a number of episodes for the Beatles TV series – with a strenuous avoidance of Disneyesque animating techniques. Though previously less show than business, Dunning was determined to use the opportunity afforded by a million-dollar budget and longer schedule to make a more elaborate, experimental and 'artistic' film. TVC's antipathy to the Disney style fed into production practice: whereas Disney kept its artists all closely controlled and under one roof, Dunning's animators did not even work in the same country, remaining at their home bases with the freedom to explore the story and experiment as they saw fit. That such diversity did not lead to artistic anarchy is largely due to the strong original designs of Czech-born commercial artist Heinz Edelmann, who managed the overall visual style, developed the characters and, conscious of the need for conflict in the plot, initiated the Blue Meanies. 'Disnification' was also avoided by encouraging the use of brilliant, vibrant colours, unlike the more delicate pastel shades of recent 'enemy' features such as *The Jungle Book* (1967).

Starting in August 1967, *Yellow Submarine* was completed in just under a year, with a team of 40 animators and 140 technical artists turning Edelmann's first sketches into half a million completed pictures. This is far less artwork than demanded by Disney, and resulted, as much by design as expediency, in a jerky, stuttering movement far different from Disney's sleek, smooth 'realism'. Such lack of cohesion was proving less successful at a narrative level, however, and writing credits officially listing Brodax, Minoff, Jack Mendelsohn and *Love Story*'s Erich Segal indicate problems finding a sustaining screenplay. Dunning and production supervisor Coates had even considered abandoning the project until George Martin invited them to hear pre-release tapes of the Beatles' latest album, *Sgt. Pepper's Lonely Hearts Club Band*.[37] These tracks proved a revivifying creative catalyst. Brodax later stressed that: 'We derived a lot from the "Sgt. Pepper" album. We took the word "pepper", which is positive, spicy, and created a place called Pepperland which is full of colour and music. But in the hills around live Blue Meanies, who hate colour, who hate everything positive.'[38] The Beatles' new album also informed the movie soundtrack. Their film contract allowed King Features to use up to a dozen existing Beatles songs to accompany the animation and five songs from the *Sgt. Pepper* album were enlisted for the soundtrack. The group was also contractually bound to provide four original songs, a quota they fulfilled with little enthusiasm, offering up existing cast-offs from other projects.

No longer the main motivation for a Beatles movie, *Yellow Submarine*'s soundtrack album would provide a (relatively) indifferent financial return. It crucially lost the chance to tie in with the film's launch when its issue was held back for six months in Britain and three in America, largely because the Beatles did not want it to interfere with their *White Album* project, due for a November release, but also because George Martin, the major creative investor in the album, insisted on re-recording his underscore material. Eventually released in January 1969, *Yellow Submarine* reached number three in a ten-week stay in the UK chart. In America it lasted 24 weeks in the chart, with two weeks at number two (the *White Album* keeping it from the top spot), and going on to sell over one million copies. Nonetheless, it was not considered a notable intermediary between the *White Album* and *Abbey Road*.

While its 'new' musical numbers disappointed, the visual inventiveness of the *Yellow Submarine* animation marks the apogee of artistic influence in the British pop music genre. All together in *Yellow Submarine* are styles and imagery taken from a range of Pop Art paintings, prints and designs: contemporary reviews, seeking to convey the eclecticism on show, cited *inter alia* the ubiquitous Andy Warhol[39] (most notably in the early Charles Jenkins 'Eleanor Rigby' sequence), fellow Pop artists Claes Oldenburg and Robert Indiana,[40] 'the vibrating poster art of Peter Max',[41] 'everything that every colour supplement has done in the last two years',[42] and influences stretching back through Salvador Dalí[43] and *Alice in Wonderland*[44] to Hieronymus Bosch, 'that medieval chronicler of a bad trip'.[45]

Beyond these 'respectable' influences, however, *Yellow Submarine* in its most daring sequences looked to the graphic artists that were themselves a part of the drug-taking, counter-cultural underground – the psychedelic poster designers. Beginning on America's West coast, this style quickly crossed to the British underground, influencing in particular the work of Martin Sharp, designer of *Oz* magazine covers, and 'Hapshash and the Coloured Coat', the *nom de plume* of Nigel Weymouth and Michael English who, alongside contributions to *International Times*, advertised the activities of UFO (Unlimited Freak Out), a 'happening' that sought to create a totalising mind-expanding environment involving music, light and people. It is an aim entirely germane to *Yellow Submarine*, and the film's attempts to replicate the UFO experience are evident in the concluding 'It's All Too Much' sequence. Informing Hapshash, the shaping presence of *fin-de-siècle* and art-nouveau illustrator Aubrey Beardsley merits emphasis: his work featured in a hugely successful exhibition at London's V&A museum in the summer of 1966 which led to his immediate elevation to the status of guru of psychedelic style and design. The illustrations of the *Yellow Book*'s art editor pervades *Yellow Submarine*'s animation, a point noted by contemporary critic John Coleman who, bucking the general 'cuddly' reading of the Nowhere Man, Jeremy, was put in mind of 'that diseased dwarf who appears in a bottom corner of some Beardsley'.[46]

Beardsley features in the top left corner of the single most iconic example of sixties pop graphics, Peter Blake's album cover for *Sgt. Pepper's Lonely Hearts Club Band*. In *Yellow Submarine* the influence of Blake's cover is present at a narrative level, the Beatles using similar life-size cut-outs to creep up unseen to the music stand. It is present at a musical level if one accepts Tim Riley's description of the fade-out to 'All You Need is Love' as 'the aural equivalent' to Blake's montage.[47] Above all, it is present at a stylistic level. The album sleeve collects items indicative of the Beatles' past and present preoccupations, with an Indian goddess, a portable television and a row of (some say) marijuana plants; images (and sounds) of Eastern religion, mediation and hallucination equally pervade *Yellow Submarine*. Most importantly, though,

Figure 4.2   A film entitled *Yellow Submarine* but imbued with *Sgt. Pepper*

Yellow Submarine shares the album cover's – and most psychedelic art's – fascination with the Edwardian era. From the film's opening scenes, the inhabitants of Pepperland, grandfathers on penny-farthings, servants and maids, soldiers in colourful uniforms, are consistently Edwardian in appearance (Figure 4.2).

When the Beatles saw such sections of the film they were highly impressed by its imagination and re-evaluated it as an adjunct to rather than distraction from their new serious intellectual status. Hence they agreed to a brief live action appearance as a coda, where they invited an international audience to join them in musical unison: it was indeed 'all together now'. The belatedly group-endorsed movie was premiered on Wednesday, 17 July 1968 at the London Pavilion with a flood of marketing and ancillary merchandising.[48] The American premiere followed on 13 November.

Yellow Submarine was certainly a critical success. 'It is a fantastic achievement, not only a new kind of entertainment, but a new step forward in animation techniques,' wrote Nina Hibbin.[49] For Ian Christie it was 'an absolute joy ... the best film the Beatles never made'.[50] Alexander Walker was not alone in claiming that the film captured the *Zeitgeist*: '*Yellow Submarine* is the key film of the Beatles era. It's a trip through the contemporary mythology that the quartet from Merseyside have helped create ... a pop voyage that sails under the psychedelic colours of Carnaby Street to the turned-on music of "Sgt. Pepper's Lonely Hearts Club Band". It combines sensory stimulation with the art of the now in a way that will appeal to teenage ravers and Tate Gallery goers alike.'[51] The film was indeed reviewed in Nigel Gosling's *Observer* Art Column: he gave the work a new title, 'mop art, for it succeeds in soaking up acres of the fringe material thrown off by serious painting developments and putting them to such effective use that they are at the same time both valid and exhausted'.[52] That final caveat was picked up by several critics who saw the film as just too inventive for its own good: Cecil Wilson, for example, confessed that 'towards the end I began to lose concentration and sank back punch-drunk from the dazzling imagery'.[53]

In America the film was also a great commercial success, bettered only by *Funny Girl* (William Wyler, 1968) at the year's box office. Not so in England, however. Exactly three weeks after the London premiere, articles ran in most British daily newspapers that Rank was considering dropping the film due to disappointing attendances at its 12 selected pre-release theatres around the country.[54] This purely financial explanation does not stand up to investigation, however. United Artists and Apple vigorously contested this judgement and the published box-office receipts for the Pavilion – a capacity £7000 per week – proved they were right and Rank wrong.[55] So why the curtailed distribution and exhibition of the film? Was it a purely financial miscalculation on the part of Rank or, as with *Privilege*, did they baulk at the content, sensing something much more subversive than a simple kiddies cartoon? What *could* Rank object to?

Yellow Submarine works perfectly well, of course, as a family fantasy on the forces of good overcoming those of evil. But the film can, if desired, be seen as an allegorical play on late sixties states of consciousness and statesmanship: as Bob Neaverson describes it, 'an underground parable of how the psychedelic Beatles (symbols of the peaceful and apolitical forces of hippy counter-culture) overcome the forces of state power to establish a new regime of karmic awareness and universal goodwill'.[56] A cross-generational resonance of meaning is there in the extant title, for while the group have always claimed that 'Yellow Submarine' was only a children's song, a 'yellow submarine' was also (allegedly) the code-name of the popular yellow, submarine-shaped narcotic pill Nembutal. The narrative journey, sailing to sea, is easily interpretable as a simulated 'trip', a fuller recreation of the acid-inspired visions than had been possible with the use of real people and locations in the Beatles' self-directed *Magical Mystery Tour*.

Ian MacDonald labelled the sound of *Sgt. Pepper*, especially its use of echo and reverb, as 'the most authentic aural simulation of the psychedelic experience ever created'.[57] The songs employed in *Yellow Submarine* contain large amounts of drug-inspired imagery. *Primus inter pares*, 'Lucy in the Sky with Diamonds', in spite of Lennon's explanation of origins, is clearly readable as a hallucinatory trip: its visualisation is central to the film, described by creator George Dunning as 'the fantasy within the fantasy' of *Yellow Submarine*.[58] But the 'throwaway' songs given to the film are equally open to alternative interpretations. Indeed, the imagery accompanying 'Only a Northern Song' and 'It's All Too Much' only 'makes sense' when read as attempting an audio-visual recreation of the hallucinogenic state, while 'All Together Now', following the childlike line 'Black, White, Green, Red' by asking 'Can I take my friend to bed?' subverts infantilism with references to the free love so written about and so hard to find in the Summer of Love.

Yellow Submarine is open to a wealth of allegorical readings. The Blue Meanies in particular lend themselves to symbolic treatment, at a personal, industrial, social and political level. John Coates emphasised the internal and internecine: 'Al Brodax was the chief Blue Meanie and his sidekick was Abe Goodman – the assistant he sent to London to keep an eye on us.'[59] The Blue Meanies clearly bear Mickey Mouse ears, suggestive of Disney's aggressive monopoly on the animated genre – a prescient design since *Peter Pan* (1953) flew in to fill the breach when the Beatles film was quickly withdrawn from several London cinemas. Dilys Powell suggests that the Ferocious Flying Glove, who points a finger and then destroys, might be 'a dig at the censor',[60] though looking outwards and to the recent past, the Glove, the Apple-Stompers and the Blue Meanies, with their paranoid fear of music, together with the Hidden Persuaders, Jack the Nipper, the Butterfly Stomper et al. can also be 'read' as the various disconcerted bodies that united into the record-burning hordes from the group's final 1966 American tour – or even the unsympathetic critics from all sections of the media that blackened the Beatles' image by stonewalling *Magical Mystery Tour*.

Above all, though, these unfeeling hordes can be seen as wider symbols of state oppression. In appearance and *modus operandi* the Meanies resemble the British police – they wear blue uniforms, carry weapons for hitting people and use fierce dogs. American critics noted how the Chief Meanie wears cowboy boots, spurs and a robber mask, a further suggestion of American cultural imperialism: foreign populations are bled dry by the Big Apple, and the Pepperlanders' period costumes act as reminders of 'the good old days before the Americanisation of England'.[61] Most evidently, though, one can read the Blue Meanies as general forces of European fascism. As with *Privilege*, the Third Reich informs the third phase of the British pop music film: old newsreel footage of Adolf Hitler served Heinz Edelmann as a model for movements of the Chief Blue Meanie,[62] and from the film's opening scenes the Chief, arms resting in front of groin before shooting into the air, adopts Hitleresque stances as he switches from smooth cajoling to enraged imperatives. The Meanies enact a military subjugation of Pepperland, lightning bolts and apple drops turning citizens to colour-drained stone, razing flowers and shattering or sinking statues underground. A tear falls down the lens of a man's glasses and the cheek of a young girl before the glove rounds up a small group, forcing them into obedience by bashing its fist on the ground. Orwell's dystopian vision in *Nineteen Eighty-Four*, which also ends with two trickling tears, was to picture the future as 'a boot stamping on a human face – for ever'.[63] Here that future is a giant blue fist, stamping on the innocent, trailing behind it the stripes of Old Glory.

Nonetheless, on spying this tyranny, John, the socio-political conscience of the Beatles, makes no reference to police or military brutality, nor fascist ghettoisation or Vietnam bombings. Instead, combining childhood recollection and the forces of reaction, he notes how the chief Blue Meanie reminds him of a more personal figure of authority, his old English teacher. It is a comment that will lead forward to the generic reworkings of *Pink Floyd: The Wall* and leaps back to the pop music film's origins in *The Blackboard Jungle*, a reminder amidst adult messages in a childlike idiom of the perennial teenage need to rebel against the nearest representative of establishment authority: to sir, with love. David Robinson noted how '*Yellow Submarine* seems to express a sort of retreat into a nostalgia for forgotten innocence, for a time of childhood, for a (chimeric) world of certainty and self-confidence.'[64] This journey back in time fits perfectly with the film's musical soundscape since many Beatles' compositions were then rooted in historical pastiche. 'When I'm Sixty-Four', the eponymous 'Sgt. Pepper's Lonely Hearts Club Band' and even 'Lucy in the Sky with Diamonds' make fuller sense for Wilfrid Mellers as 'a revocation of a dream-world of childhood'.[65]

Nonetheless, amidst the idyllic Edwardian fantasy, the denouement of *Yellow Submarine* can clearly lend itself to a contemporary political – and counter-cultural – reading. The Beatles help to establish a new world order in Pepperland, but do so, as Bob Neaverson notes, 'more through the redemptive consciousness-raising powers of music and nature than by violent retribution'.[66] They bash a few apple-stompers but it is with 'instruments at the ready' that they fight most effectively. Their musical performance of 'Sgt. Pepper' reanimates the population, returning colour to their costumes, patterns to their hair and smiles to their faces: the song climaxes with the re-emergence, literally from the underground, of the Sgt. Pepper statue. Through Jeremy's final incantation which covers the Chief Blue Meanie in floral attire, we witness a winning enactment of the revolutionary force of 'flower power'.

This victory also completes the Beatles' voyage of discovery that began with the early use of the end of 'A Day in the Life', a glissando that for Ian MacDonald symbolises 'a spiritual ascent from fragmentation to wholeness, achieved in the resolving E major chord'.[67] Whatever flimsy narrative drive exists in *Yellow Submarine* comes from this search for wholeness, the sense of transformative Quest. The press release called the film a 'Modyssey', and Homeric allusions – John declares their adventures 'rather reminiscent of the late Mr Ulysses'; he sights a Cyclops in the Sea of Monsters – pepper their journey. This also links the film to its partner in trippy transcendence, Stanley Kubrick's *2001: A Space Odyssey* (1968), in particular the Sea of Holes segment which, as well as quoting the optical art of Bridget Riley, forms a 'parallel universe' to the 'cosmic ride' through the time corridor that enables Keir Dullea's progression from Everyman to Space Child.

While the myriad influences at play in *Yellow Submarine* could be catalogued *ad infinitum*, I have always considered the most revealing comparison to be with a contemporary television series, ITC's *The Prisoner* (1967–68).[68] Both had a troubled industrial reception, with the project of central star Patrick McGoohan being shunted out to the anonymity of 11.15pm when ITC executives baulked at 'escalating budgets and the show's too controversial drug references'.[69] Both have a comparable setting, with agent McGoohan transported to the surreal, psychedelic Village where deerstalkered Edwardian nostalgia is tempered by the fearsome flying 'Rover' whose peremptory strikes warn against escape. Both conclude with a lengthy fight against an armed enemy dressed in depersonalising blue uniforms. Above all, in each work the central protagonists pursue a quest, the solution to which proves to embody their own physical form. This is perhaps more evident, infamous even, in *The Prisoner*, where McGoohan as Number 6 pursues Number 1 until, in 'Fallout', he corners and unmasks his nemesis only to confront his own face, laughing back at him in manic glee: Number 6 is Number 1. This ending baffled many: for Leslie Halliwell, the final episode 'explained nothing and fell apart almost completely, the intention apparently being to make a statement about Vietnam'.[70] However, the revelation that the battle between the individual and conformity is an internal as much as a social struggle signifies also at an indigenous level. As Matthew de Abaitua offered, 'there is part of us that wants to fit in, but there's part of us that wants to be ourselves. We are both prisoners and jailors.'[71] Thus *The Prisoner* allegorises the very British – or rather English – sense of repression, revealing for Greg Rowland how the English 'excel at keeping the status quo intact, perhaps entertaining some whimsical ideas of rebellion for a short while, but in the end they will always love Big Brother'.[72] Orwell again, and again ideological links to *Privilege* with the concept of 'contained', simulated rebellion.

Yellow Submarine adopts a similar allegorical structure but to a diametrically opposed message. To help in their final battle against the forces of repression, the 'beautiful people' that Ringo releases from the large glass bubble are shown to be the Beatles' doubles, their musical roots and completions in the form of Sgt. Pepper's Lonely Hearts Club Band. This doubling is narratively centred on John: his double introduces himself as 'the alter ego man' and John's duality is most evident in the skirmish accompanying 'Hey Bulldog'. With the Blue Meanies' hound confused by the Beatles' constant calling and the pounding rhythm from a mechanical piano, the upper panels of the instrument open to reveal hidden Beatles. One panel opens as John sings 'You Can Talk to Me', a lyric that MacDonald reads as 'rather menacingly pointed (possibly at McCartney)'.[73] But here – and more psychologically interesting – the second panel opens to reveal a second John, the alter ego. The four-headed bulldog, clearly itself in two minds, backs off, backs down. A happier John, more 'at one' with himself, and exemplifying a further late-phase fusing of the genre's youth tropes as a tyranny-troubling 'fun' musician, can now help to bring a similar unity to all of Pepperland.

During the animation to 'Hey Bulldog' we witness the classic image of hippydom, with John pulling a gun which then sprouts a flower in its barrel. It evokes the 'Mobe', the mobilisation of 21 October 1967 when over 100,000 demonstrators marched on the Pentagon and several placed flowers into the barrels of the guns being held up by the soldiers of the 82nd Airborne Division. That image of guns and roses would endure – a core image of the Summer of Love. However, that same night, away from the cameras, the Pentagon soldiers would charge the protestors with their guns, causing several serious injuries. It was an act more in keeping with the spirit of '68 and provides the crucial point of comparison between *Yellow Submarine* and *The Prisoner*. In both works this 'finding of oneself' and the accompanying battle take place to the strains of the Beatles' composition 'All You Need is Love' but, whereas the cartoon union presents a karmic completion of self, *The Prisoner* has a much more ironic view, the 'Fallout' episode ending, as its title states, in apocalyptic chaos with rifles firing in front of the image of the bomb.

The Prisoner is, for de Abaitua, 'a sour British slant on the Sixties with Flower Power replaced by Fire Power'.[74] It is, in short, the difference between 1967 and 1968.

Like *Yellow Submarine*, *The Prisoner* was begun in 1967 and completed the next year. The difference, though obvious, is crucial: the live-action television series could react to changing times while a laboriously completed animated feature had to remain true to previously established storylines. The pop music film genre had begun with an imperative for immediacy: even *It's Trad, Dad!* could 'tune in' to political movements of the moment. Not so the lengthy gestations of this decadent-phase vehicle. Critics such as Alexander Walker were wrong to see *Yellow Submarine* as capturing the *Zeitgeist*: it missed it by a good year – and the Edwardian costumes by two years. While finding greater favour with the Great British public than McGoohan's series, the Beatles' animated film was pacifist but also *passé* as the combatants of May 1968 looked to more aggressive tactics, more Mobilisation. A few critics did sense this datedness: John Russell Taylor, for instance, noted 'a real document of the fleeting moment at which one can already see "now" becoming "period"'.[75] By the time *Yellow Submarine* was released, it was an historical document: the Summer of Love was over. Even in nostalgia-loving Albion, 1968 was messy and discordant: it was guns, not roses, and Prisoners, not Pepperland. It was time for street-fighting men – and Jean-Luc Godard.

The pop music film as political diptych: *One Plus One/Sympathy for the Devil* (1968)

The Rolling Stones constitute the blueprint for rebel rock, their career, until the corporate bombast of the eighties onwards, seemingly free of the charge of recuperation and 'castration'. While each generation seeks its own way to rebel, the tone of voice and body language of lead singer Mick Jagger and the defiant, grubby rudeness of the group, defined by Frith and McRobbie as 'cock-rock' performance,[76] have driven subsequent aggressive and boastful movements through punk to Oasis and beyond. Yet the role models that led to this archetypal image feed back to the earliest phase of the British pop music film, especially the pounding rhythms and curved lip snarl of that earlier white rhythm boy, Bongo Herbert.

The link between the Richards Cliff and Keith lies with Andrew Loog Oldham, the Stones' first manager and self-styled 'pimpresario'. Oldham's autobiography, *Stoned*, provides an excellent case study of the influence of genre on life, in particular the way that fictions mediate self-image and intentionality. Oldham relates how the cinema fed force-ful models of behaviour, with the French New Wave, notably Jean-Paul Belmondo from Godard's *A Bout de Souffle* (1959), providing icons of cool marginality. James Dean's *Rebel Without a Cause* established the attitude for the times while the detail and discourse came from the ambi-tious characters portrayed by Laurence Harvey in *Room at the Top* and, especially, *Expresso Bongo*. On first seeing Mankowitz's play, the Stones' future Svengali knew that 'it would become my liturgy: a scenario where the manager was equally important as the artist. And Johnny Jackson became my object of worship.'[77] The role model 'where Bongos begged me to be their Johnny'[78] was confirmed for Oldham when Harvey portrayed the fast-talking hustler in the 1959 film version. Oldham reports quoting from the film to explain to Jagger his notion of fame: one can conjecture which quotes. While Brian Epstein softened the Beatles' working-class(-ish) rough edges to make them more acceptable to the British public, Oldham moved in the opposite direction and, just as Johnny Jackson saw in Bongo Herbert 'a chip on your shoulder, an H-bomb in your pants – it's you against the world, baby, and the world loves you for hating it', so Oldham saw in the embryonic Stones the sexual aggressiveness simmering beneath the middle-class surface and encouraged them to rebel. One early Jacksonesque example: while the Fab Four joked with royalty at Royal Command Performances, the Stones committed the ultimate showbiz V-sign by refusing to join the end-of-show revolving platform on *Sunday Night at the London Palladium* – cue the desired Monday morning outrage in Middle England.

The Rolling Stones also maintained more threatening musical models than the Beatles. In opposition to Merseybeat's pristine pop, the rawer sound of American blues and Chicago R and B gave the Stones their early musical direction and, via Muddy Waters, their name. Still, in late 1963 it was the Lennon–McCartney composition 'I Wanna Be Your Man' that provided the Stones with their first top 20 hit. Thereafter the groups, close friends in spite of media depictions to the contrary, would work almost symbiotically, responding to the leads given by their supposed rivals. They followed Lennon and McCartney by abandoning covers of black artists to pen their own numbers and quickly forged a personalised musical identity, centred on male teenage revolt. The strategy worked as '(I Can't Get No) Satisfaction' established the group in America, topping the charts in July 1965. While young audiences screamed and danced away, their elders fumed at openly hypocritical criticisms of consumer exploitation.

The year 1967, however, would prove to be a turning point for the Rolling Stones. The February drug bust of Richard's home in West Wittering, Redlands, and the severe prison sentences awarded to Richard and Jagger became a national debate, mobilising the counter-culture and prompting William Rees-Mogg's famous *Times* leader 'Who Breaks a Butterfly on a Wheel?'[79] Though their sentences were quashed on appeal, the constant scrutiny by the drugs squad and the media forced the Stones off the road and into the relative safety of the recording studio. However, the lengthy, introspective experimentation that resulted in *Their Satanic Majesties Request*, complete with artistic cover design and psychedelic rock chants, was roundly criticised for its weak imitations of *Sgt. Pepper*: 'peace and love' would never be the Stones' strong selling point. The album's difficult gestation also led to Andrew Loog Oldham's resignation, the Johnny Jackson parabola completed by his loss of the Stones' respect and cooperation. In all, it had been an *annus horribilis* for Jagger and Co. Their next album needed to get back to basics and deliver: and this was what Jean-Luc Godard came to film.

It was, perhaps, inevitable that the *enfant terrible* of Continental Cinema would come to nail down the coffin lid on the Swinging Sixties. Godard's entry to the London pop scene was not entirely a surprise since, alongside his acknowledged influence on Lester and Boorman, he had shown an interest in musicals from as early as *Une Femme est une Femme/A Woman is a Woman* (1961), where characters briefly and incongruously dance as in a Stanley Donen film. Here Godard was not so much criticising traditional genre cinema as registering its passing. 'The musical is dead,' he said bluntly in interview. 'You have to do something different.'[80] By 1968 he was ready to do that something different in Britain: a final-phase demolition job on the music film, with the Rolling Stones as the agents of his destruction.

The Stones had plentiful experience of cinemas if not of film. Whereas the Beatles tightened their act in the bars of Hamburg, the Stones honed their sound by joining the bill of one of the numerous six-act, 20-minutes-a-set line-ups that toured up to 60 UK cinemas per month in the early 1960s. They were often seen in the Odeon, Gaumont and ABC houses, but had seldom appeared on the screen behind the cinema stage. Their first appearance concludes Steve Binder's recording of October 1964's Teenage American Music International awards show in California. *The TAMI Show* (1965) records the group during its early, tentative assaults on the States. Britain's *Monthly Film Bulletin*, far happier with the same week's release *Three Hats for Lisa*, felt of their 'astonishing demonstration of exhibitionism' that 'Nothing so sub-moronic can surely have been included in a revue film before.'[81] America's Ehrenstein and Reed noted the oppositional strategy, the Stones' image as 'harmless ruffians – an answer to the "nice lads" aura emanating from the Beatles'. They also saw in Jagger's skilful stage moves 'an intimation of quasi-messianic power to come'.[82] It was very much to come, though, for the Stones, Chuck Berry et al., even Brit invaders Gerry and the Pacemakers, are completely overshadowed by James Brown's stunning, crowd-manipulating rendition of 'Please, Please, Please'.

There followed Peter Whitehead's documentary of the group's two-date Irish tour in September 1965, *Charlie is My Darling* (so-named because of drummer Charlie Watts' un-Ringo-like reluctance to be filmed). This includes brief footage of a performance of 'This Could Be the Last Time' and 'It's Alright', but the film largely comprises interviews with fans and band members, plus shots of the group getting in and out of limos, going on and coming off stage, their actions accompanied by several of their songs on the soundtrack. Three versions of the film were cut, but various production difficulties delayed any release until the moment was lost, and it was decided that a *Hard Day's Night*-style documentary was *passé* and a potential interference with other imminent film projects.

These arose when Allen Klein took over the Stones' business affairs in August 1965, leaving Oldham to concentrate on creative initiatives. Rumours immediately flourished, including buying the rights to Anthony Burgess' *A Clockwork Orange*, but as it transpired the group's next film appearance was in another Peter Whitehead documentary, his look at LSD-fed Swinging London, *Tonite Let's All Make Love in London* (1967). Here, in a five-minute sequence, the group are preceded by Oldham, orchestrating a recording session and talking about his future plans, especially that belated entry into films. Then, between brief footage of the Stones performing 'Have You Seen Your Mother, Baby?' and 'Lady Jane', testimony to the manipulative hysteria the band could now generate, Jagger talks about revolution and the young as if citing *Privilege* – 'when they're violent against the police it's the only way they have of showing it, because they're not organised'.

When Godard came to call, the Stones were willing participants: the agreement was for them just to be filmed in the recording studio – and they were used to documentary cameras – while the college-educated Jagger seemed particularly struck by the artistic potential of the venture. To back the film, Michael Pearson, son of Lord Cowdray, and the actor Iain Quarrier formed Cupid Productions and raised £180,000. Roughly equal to the sum available to Richard Lester four years previously for

A Hard Day's Night, this was still a pittance compared to most full-length features. For Godard, though, it constituted a larger budget than usual, and the chance to work *carte blanche* with complete and compliant beginners. The first batch of filming took place on 4 and 5 June 1968, just one week after the deal was finalised, Godard recording the Stones in session at the Olympic Studios, London. Now, though, after so many false starts in the group's film career, their first full feature was beset by difficulties. Contracted actor Terence Stamp was arrested for possession of cannabis, leading Quarrier to step in to take his part. Then, on 10 June while the crew was filming the Stones in an all-night session, the Olympic Studios caught fire. A fortnight later Godard's footage of the Black Panthers, filmed at a car-wrecker's yard at Lombard Wharf, Battersea, had to be reshot due to sound difficulties. Godard also dashed off in the middle of filming to shoot scenes of student protest back in Paris.

None of these problems, however, matched the events preceding the film's premiere at London's National Film Theatre on 29 November 1968 – events that gained far greater press coverage than the film itself. At his press conference, Godard denounced Cupid Productions for ruining his film by changing its end without his permission. 'They want to make *One Plus One* equal two. I don't.' In Quarrier's own, separate conference, he stated that the film had been given 'a minuscule gloss so that the ten million teen boppers who were going to see the film in America would understand it better'. He explained that his company had 'merely' included a complete version of the Stones' song 'Sympathy for the Devil' at the end of the film.[83] To accompany the song a series of treated images of Eve, similar to the 'Lucy in the Sky' section from *Yellow Submarine*, were also added. Prior to the premiere, Godard came on to the NFT stage to ask the audience not to watch his film, to demand their entrance money back and contribute it to the Black Panther Defense Fund: his proposal was defeated on a show of hands. There followed a full five-minute argument between director and audience, Godard only leaving the stage after landing a punch on the jaw of producer/actor Quarrier. Simultaneously, outside the theatre a group of young filmmakers were preparing to show Godard's own version (his own print) free to all comers. Godard argued briefly with this audience too, before disappearing over the bridge, vowing never to return to England, never to make another commercial film, and only to shoot on 16mm for people to see in the streets.

When the film eventually surfaced at the Murray Hill cinema, New York on 11 March 1970, the programmers, heedful of the birth pangs in Britain, showed alternate versions on alternate days, Godard's own *One Plus One* on Monday, Wednesday, Friday and Sunday, the producer's renamed *Sympathy for the Devil* on the other days. With only arthouse distribution, it was never seen by those ten million teen boppers.

After the NFT brouhaha the press virtually ignored the supposed main feature. The only substantial review came from Alexander Walker, who stated that he was not surprised at the lack of coverage, finding the film, in spite of the Stones and plentiful swearing, 'hardly sensational'. Summarising it as 'a series of self-important charades masquerading as metaphors for the violence of the world and decadence of Western society', Walker was particularly critical of the 'endless interviews that might have sounded significant in French, but are intolerably pretentious in English'.[84] The music press constituted the film's severest critics, *Disc* calling it 'complete and utter rubbish' and 'a mind-boggling mixture of sex, music, black power and politics – and its entertainment value is less than nil'.[85] Equally polarised was the film's full, fulsome reviews in the film journals. For Philip Strick of *Films and Filming*, '*One Plus One*, a really superb piece of work, is far more coherent an expression of Godard's beliefs and feelings, both in their naivety and in their profound anguish, than the man himself trembling before a microphone.'[86]

The Stones themselves were happy at the results. Jagger commented: 'Godard happened to catch us on two very good nights ... One night he got us going over and over this song called "Sympathy for the Devil". It started out as a folky thing like "Jigsaw Puzzle" but that didn't make it so we kept going over it and changing it until it finally comes out as a samba. So Godard has the whole thing from beginning to end. That's something I've always wanted to do on film.'[87] As Jagger implies, the devil is in the detail, and *One Plus One* is historically significant in two ways. Firstly, it shows the slow crystallisation of a composition with seemingly unlimited studio time: here is the pop music film as process rather than, indeed – for Godard – vehemently opposed to, product. We witness a privileged group, without prior notions of arrangements, play, tape, jam, relax and busk until they get the feeling of a number. Secondly, it reveals the shifting dynamics of a major rock band. We see how Brian Jones, once the centre of the group, is now almost literally out of the picture, while Jagger, aided by 'Glimmer Twin' Richard, provides the musical direction (Figure 4.3). Philip Norman noted how, from roughly this time, living at Redlands under Richard's care, 'Brian had lost the will for anything beyond his own desultory, and somehow secretive, acoustic strumming.'[88] Godard's filming reveals this mood had equally spread to Jones' studio work.

Figure 4.3   The Stones rolling: Brian on the way out – *One Plus One/Sympathy for the Devil*

Raymond Durgnat saw *One Plus One* as 'the indispensable complementary movie to the hairy muddle of *If*....'[89] but, from a pop music
perspective, a more apposite comparison can be made with the Beatles'
final film, *Let It Be* (1970), recorded at the Apple and Twickenham Film
Studios in January–February 1969. There are points of contact: Godard's
cameraman, the informal Tony Richmond, becomes the producer and
proudly titled Anthony B. Richmond of *Let It Be*; the sound engineer
on both is Glyn Johns; the Beatles are filmed by Michael Lindsay-Hogg,
fresh from directing the Stones (shelved) television special *Rock'n'Roll
Circus*; Bill Wyman makes a cameo appearance at Abbey Road. Above
all, both films constitute the sole extensive 1960s footage of the respective groups in rehearsal and recording mode. Almost everything else
about *Let It Be*, however, serves as a stark contrast to the Rolling Stones'
studio experiences. United Artists had deemed the Beatles' last-minute
last-reel involvement in *Yellow Submarine* insufficient to fulfil their
contractual obligations to the corporation and so, the following year,
dispirited and divided by personal and business differences, the openly
Fractious Four dragged themselves one last time in front of the cameras. *Let It Be* is an unsettling and sad cinema-verité chronicle of the

decline and disintegration of a musical collective. The creative tensions are evident, especially between the ever-organising Paul and a newly assertive George, no longer willing to be ordered around on his guitar solos. Meanwhile John shows himself less interested in the music than in Yoko Ono, ever-present at his side, while Ringo's thoughts seem far away, perhaps on his new film career with Peter Sellers in *The Magic Christian* (Joseph McGrath, 1969). The Beatles too were attempting here to 'get back' to basics, eschewing the intricacies of studio multi-tracking for raw, live recordings, but even dusting down their early blues composition 'One after 909' and the Everly Brothers impersonations on 'Two of Us' failed to revive the relationship: it was time indeed to 'let it be'. *One Plus One* is the complete opposite, the record of a rebirth, a successful reversion to origins in a burst of creative energy. Another difference, of course, between the Beatles' and Stones' films is that, while *Let It Be* exists as a straight documentary, *One Plus One* combines studio footage with a fictional counterbalance. It juxtaposes the two tropes adopted by the earliest British pop music films, and still prevalent in the media and the metropolis of 1968, the glamour of stardom and the violent underbelly of society.

Yellow Submarine centred its psychedelic odyssey in that metropolis, the Beatles' submarine diving into the Thames just by Tower Bridge. Godard's political adventure, seen by David Sterritt as containing 'passages of mise-en-scene so spare and stylised that they're almost cartoonish',[90] also begins in the waters of the capital though less salubriously: 'I left Bolivia and came to London where I hid in a toilet to escape the police,' the unseen narrator explains. At the film's end, he emerges from his hiding-hole, declaring: 'Now I was on the beach, waiting for Uncle Mao's Yellow Submarine to come and get me.' In Godard's aural collage the Beatles' animated film functions as a touchstone for political and cultural movements. A music critic condemns the white Western appropriation of black music: 'Stealing music, stealing heritage, making it white music from any place, any time to "We all live in a Yellow Submarine"' – thus the escapist betrayal of a potentially subversive medium is pinpointed and pilloried. As Frankie Dymon Jr. denigrates the 'romantic' integrationist in favour of the 'realist' activist, we dimly hear the condemnation conclude: 'exclusive meaning, isolated from the rest of humanity, in a yellow submarine, shooting nuclear weapons'. This arming of the Beatles' submarine reiterates, as much as Dymon's diatribe, the new mid-1968 impatience with psychedelic pacifism.

Such references prompted Raymond Durgnat to see Godard's London as a Nowhere Land and its protagonists, lonely and bookish, as

Nowhere Men.[91] The political and popular icons recounted by the narrator form an aural equivalent to the cover of the *Sgt. Pepper* album (an effect visualised in the French advertising poster for *One Plus One*). More generally, these fragments place the film in its decadent phase by privileging words – words that add strong descriptions of sex and drugs and further evocations of the Third Reich into the mix, while also questioning the Stones and their 'appropriated' rock'n'roll. These themes can be explored through a focus on the film's contested ending. Looking back to that night by London's South Bank, just who deserves our sympathy?

The case *against* Quarrier's alternative ending rests primarily on the manner in which it undermines Godard's implied message equating the fragmentary nature of the recording session with the disparate characteristics of revolution. In *One Plus One*, Godard attempts to anarchise the pop musical genre, to deconstruct it much as *Weekend* had, in all senses, 'done for' the road movie. Godard's historical contextualisation of the musical was not in itself an innovation: *Tonite Let's All Make Love in London* intercut footage of Second World War fighter planes with the Animals' 'When We Were Young', while Tony Palmer's LWT history of popular music *All My Loving* (1968) cut performance footage of Jimi Hendrix with newsreels of the Vietnam war. Godard's *title* is significant though, since the precise arithmetical arrangement of the different sequences equates (and negates) the current socio-cultural position with any idealistic programme of reform. This gives all human activity, be it the monosyllabic judgements of the hippy Eve Democracy, the elaborate creation of the Stones, the desired societal reconstruction of the black militants – *and* the artistic self-destruction of Godard – a sense of equal futility. Thus, as in *Help!*, Godard's soundtrack constantly impedes communication: a passing aircraft and a ship's horn drown out the readings of the black militants; the narrator's next page or the Stones' rehearsal overrides the visible discourse. The rock group's efforts are prominent in this aural fragmentation, often grinding to a halt as more sound is needed on the cans, an amp needs changing, the rhythm section is too fuzzy, a line is ineffectually sung. This inconclusiveness is replicated at a structural level as – crucially – the recording sessions end *not* with the completed version of 'Sympathy for the Devil' but by taking us back to the start of the creative process, the group (minus Jones) strumming towards their next song, Richard keen that it should build like 'Jumping Jack Flash'.

Godard's violent objections to Quarrier's late addition indicate that, rather than creating a dynamic relationship between the film's halves, he sought to keep them discrete. Godard does not want his film to be aestheticised, hence the insistence on alienation devices. Alongside the familiar inter-titles, beginning with the disruptive 'The Stones Rolling', and the visible signs of filmmaking – a boom hanging over Jagger, a clapperboard for Eve – Godard denies his actors any semblance of spontaneous speech. Each section is deliberately lifeless, notably second-hand. The black militants read from pre-existing texts, while Frankie Dymon Jr. has the phrases of one of his speeches fed to him by a prompter: the bookseller becomes a mouthpiece for paragraphs from *Mein Kampf* on societies becoming decadent; even the Stones, shown in rehearsal rather than performance, with single lines repeated numerous times, seem largely to be quoting rather than creating. In *Privilege* this 'borrowing' ultimately proved an unwitting 'aesthetic' impediment: here it is the witting intent.

Richard Roud, taking his cue from the inter-title 'Hi Fiction Science', sees such delivery as akin to Hal's slow, patronising voice in *2001: A Space Odyssey*, and Godard as an astronaut of 'the inner space of a stream of consciousness lacking faith either in emotional drive or in objective correlatives'.[92] Godard's objection to Quarrier's pop music ending is not only that it attempts to provide an objective correlative to the Stones' song via the treated images of Eve, but also that it signals the final victory of commerce, making the film another in the long line of 'exploitation' pop movies. As Godard knew, the aesthetic object or work of art can all too easily be isolated, 'castrated' and reabsorbed by the society it is attacking, often through a concentration on issues of form before content. Godard seeks to replace the concept of spectators with participants who, with no aesthetic features to seduce or mystify them, enter on equal terms with the director to a discussion – the *essential* one plus one. The film is an analysis of the assumptions behind the mass media, rather than a product designed for them: as Jan Dawson notes: 'the audience must exploit the film, and not the other way about'.[93] In *One Plus One* the dynamic of the pop music film comes full circle.

However, as noted by Ginette Vincendeau, 'Godard's films have been a site of contradictions', amongst which she categorises a politically motivated cinema that merely alienated audiences.[94] Godard's first British venture was (initially) intended to reach large numbers through the drawing card of the Rolling Stones: it was envisaged as an attempt to exploit the commercial system to different ends. But as in *Tout Va Bien* (1972), where Godard tried again for accessibility via Jane Fonda and Yves Montand, the surrounding Brechtian devices left the viewer, as Jill Forbes commented, 'demobilised by the spectacle rather than inspired by the struggle'.[95] Does Quarrier cut through the director's contradictions and help him to find his sought-for larger audience?

The case *for* Quarrier's alternative ending begins with Godard's subsequent admission of a failure of intent: *'One Plus One* was my last bourgeois film. I was very arrogant to make that – just to take images thinking I knew what they meant.'[96] Ambivalence and antithesis – one *plus* one – characterise Godard's film, resulting in readings escaping his intentions but 'in tune' with 'Sympathy for the Devil': 'Just as every cop is a criminal / and all the sinners saints, / as heads is tails'. Godard's work is noted for his predictions for the 'end of cinema' while his films simultaneously betray 'a romantic cinephilia'[97] and this contradiction pervades *Sympathy for the Devil*. While Godard's dialogue may imply that nothing new can be said, his editing is innovative, his camerawork effective, his mise-en-scène evocative. A discrete methodology becomes instead a defining metaphor as in place of narrative dislocation one discovers a marrying motif amidst Godard's deconstruction of image and sound, a parallelism linking the musical and the militant. Thus visually the Stones are as isolated in their separate recording booths as the lone slogan writer on the streets of London. The long tracking shots move deliberately among musicians and machinery in the studio just as they pass from wreck to wreck and beyond the Black Power militants in their junkyard. Aurally, the black revolutionaries stumble with borrowed white language just as the British musicians stumble towards foreign rhythms.

The film is not so much structured on deadening repetition but by investigating addition, by alteration: one plus one join together and become something else. Out by the Thames, the Black Power revolutionaries pass not just rifles but slogans that change from 'Dance down the Street!' to 'Up against the wall!' and 'Shoot them! Kill them!' The graffiti artist juxtaposes words to make new combinations: 'Freudemocracy' and (the sought ideal?) 'Cinemarxism'. The inter-titles find new words in given combinations: 'LOVE' is picked out in red from the black letters of 'All About Eve'. These can all be interpreted as an underlying, irrepressible concern for putting things together, and the film as striving for an ultimate, overarching collectivism. This is clearest with the recording of 'Sympathy for the Devil'. The Stones build up their song over the day: not only are instruments added such as the maracas, or changed as with the piano, but the lyrics also shift. In an early version Jagger sings of how 'the SS raved' (linking with the bookstore content) before the line settles on 'when the Blitzkrieg raged'. Elsewhere Jagger's delivery constantly shifts in emphasis, rushing a line, or stressing a different syllable. Eric Rhode noted that, with its repetitions, Godard's film 'might have been made by Andy Warhol',[98] but this comparison sells short the *coup de théâtre* enacted in the final recording of 'Sympathy for the Devil'. Here the camera starts on Jagger, singing alone before two angled baffles: after a false start he quickly finds the rhythm. As his performance coheres, the camera moves slowly to the left and around, revealing behind the twin screens the rest of the group plus partners, ready to provide the vocal backing to Jagger's chorus. As they sing their owl-like 'whoo-whoo' chorus, for Nick Dagger 'simply one of the great pop music moments',[99] Godard's unhurried tracking transforms the *solitaire* into *solidaire*. The recording is successful, as is Godard's intuitive movement to capture the developing interest. Quarrier's concluding addition 'merely' *completes* the collective process.

Heretical as it may be to die-hard exponents of the auteur tradition, producer Quarrier has a cinematic (as well as a self-evident commercial) case to dwell on. The final frames of this diptychal pop music film, its image-play with depth and colour and the Stones' song playing over it, all centred on Godard's wife playing Eve, are entirely coherent with the film's commitment to visual and audio experimentation and the discovery of new forms of narrative. It also coheres with the genre's synthesis of music and violence, a 'merger' completed in Jagger's subsequent solo film venture, *Performance*.

The pop music film as finale: *Performance* (1970)

Westminster-educated Donald Cammell's entry to film had been co-writing the script for 1967's *Duffy* where tie-dyed beatniks quoted 'daddy-o' and 'groovy happening, man' as if the cast of *Beat Girl* had aged ten years but enjoyed no lexical progression. Later that year Cammell discovered the updated reality, immersing himself in the brave new world based around Brian Jones' Earls Court flat, various country piles and holidays in the dope-drenched Maghreb where congregated *inter alia* Mick Jagger and Marianne Faithfull, 'hippy' designer Christopher Gibbs and underground filmmaker Kenneth Anger. It was this milieu of languid hedonism mixing rock, sex and crime that planted the seed for Cammell's next film script. It also gave him the necessary personal introductions, notably to Sandy Lieberson, an American agent who represented the film and television interests of the Rolling Stones – he arranged their collaboration with Godard – before setting up his own production company, Goodtimes. Lieberson offered to represent Cammell for both men's efforts to break into filmmaking and, after a failed approach to

Marlon Brando, they agreed that Cammell would write a treatment for his friend, rising star James Fox, and also direct. Since Cammell knew little of the practical aspects of cinema he brought in another old friend, cinematographer Nicolas Roeg, as a collaborator. A respected director of photography and about to direct *Walkabout*, Roeg also had experience of (an admittedly very different) pop film world, having shot *Just for Fun* and *Every Day's a Holiday*. Cammell completed an outline screenplay, with Fox playing runaway gangster Chas Devlin, Jagger earmarked as reclusive rock star Turner, and a topical drug bust providing the centrepiece of its second section. Lieberson then approached Kenneth Hyman, another personal friend who happened to be Warner Bros.' head of production in London. Although only Fox and Roeg had any sustained filmmaking experience, the promised participation of Jagger as star and soundtrack writer – there was a rough agreement he would do eight numbers – plus a publicity-generating Redlands recreation were enough for the immediate agreement to a $1.5 million budget.

And so, in a genre predominantly known for studio exploitation of audience and artist, we finally encounter the process contextually working in reverse as Warner Bros. unwittingly underwrote a home movie for Cammell and his – admittedly well-heeled and well-connected – friends. All the major participants in *Performance* already knew each other – with music their common connection. Christopher Gibbs, accredited as 'Turner's House design consultant', would largely recreate the look and feel of Brian Jones' apartment. Cammell's girlfriend Deborah Dixon became set designer, as well as living in separate threesomes with the film's two female leads, the Stones' serial girlfriend Anita Pallenberg and 16-year-old Michèle Breton, recently picked up by Cammell in Saint-Tropez. Since meeting at a 1967 Christmas party, a strong friendship had developed between Jagger, the rock star with aristocratic pretensions, and Fox, the upper-class actor dabbling in the hippy ideal. Cammell felt this friendship blossomed into 'a sort of romance',[100] though others would see Jagger's relentless on-set one-upmanship as toppling Fox over the edge and out of filmmaking.

To attempt a broad division of labour, Roeg took over at the call of 'action' and coordinated the look of the film, while Cammell 'prepped' his actor-friends prior to shooting, drawing on his knowledge of their public image and private idiosyncrasies to cast them either with or against the grain, in the process forcing some further than they cared to venture. The on-set 'happenings' that Cammell orchestrated have become the stuff of legend, a blurring of acting out a text and presenting true-life relationships. Central here was Pallenberg, cultivating her role as a rolling Stones' partner and muse. Allegedly an adept at black magic, she was unquestionably an expert at male manipulation and, alongside Jagger, her on-set mocking of the too 'straight' Fox reinforced their on-screen personas. Rumours that the film's sex scenes were authentic so unsettled Pallenberg's current boyfriend Keith Richard that any idea of a Stones soundtrack was quickly put to bed. Richard did, though, recommend another old friend, Hollywood composer and arranger Jack Nitzsche. The LA session musicians that Nitzsche recruited were just as close as the film cast and crew, including his wife Buffy Sainte-Marie and friends Randy Newman, Ry Cooder and Merry Clayton – all would later work on the Stones' *Let It Bleed* album. One song not entrusted to Nitzsche was Jagger's diegetic number, 'Memo from Turner': an initial version penned by Cammell sounded so inert, largely due to Richard's active antagonism, that Jagger himself put pen to paper. Even then, the song had to be re-recorded for release with a session group including Steve Winwood and Jim Capaldi from Traffic, which left *Performance* bereft of any music by the Rolling Stones. Warner Bros. would soon wish there had been no involvement from the group at all.

Filming had begun on 22 July 1968 in the Surrey countryside before moving to London's West End for the gangster scenes. The early shoot was trouble-free if profligate, with two cameras churning out over two hours of rushes daily. Two weeks in, Warner's objected to the lack of shape and demanded more concise extracts to view. Jagger started filming on 12 September and very quickly all hell broke loose. Alerted probably when the doped-up bathroom footage was first seen, initial aficionado Hyman came to visit the set and was horrified at what he saw: the film was 'dirty', even the bath water was dirty; it was, in Alexander Walker's phrase, 'a representation of British decadence coming into full flower'.[101] Even the audience-grabbing drug bust had been dropped from the improvised farrago – Chas' doorstep sighting of a couple of Mars Bars the only remaining recondite reference to Redlands' confectionary-fuelled debauchery. The set was closed for a week, until Hyman was persuaded, largely by Roeg's professionalism, to allow filming to continue, and *Performance* was completed in 12 weeks, one week over schedule and $150,000 over budget, both 'acceptable' business excesses.

The same could not be said of the film's final content. The initial preview, held in Santa Monica in July 1969, was disastrous. Shown to a provincial audience as an add-on to John Schlesinger's long-running *Midnight Cowboy*, the early scenes caused uproar and most of the general public walked out: it was reported that the wife of a studio executive threw up. Warner's insisted on a recut with their choice of editor.

A telegram, jointly signed by Jagger and Cammell, was sent to Warner's chairman, explaining (?) that 'the film is about the perverted love affair between *Homo sapiens* and Lady Violence' and objecting to the studio's desire 'to emasculate the most savage and the most affectionate scenes in our movie. If *Performance* does not upset audiences it is nothing.' There was no reply: Warner's preferred it to be nothing.

The fight to save *Performance* fell solely to Cammell since Roeg and Jagger left for Australia to direct *Walkabout* and star in *Ned Kelly* respectively while Lieberson returned to England to produce *Mary Queen of Scots* (Charles Jarrott, 1971). Cammell persuaded Warner's to entrust the re-edit to Frank Mazzola, an experienced Hollywood editor: with Mazzola's help Cammell spent a year recutting the film. This studio stipulation was not just to protect the public's morals: as much as the violence, Warner's were concerned that half the film passed before their star attraction, Mick Jagger, made an appearance, two-thirds before he sang. They were somewhat appeased by the recut version which toned down Chas' sado-masochism and presented a brief early shot of Jagger spray-painting his wall. The product that had lain on their hands for 18 months was accorded its world premiere in New York on 30 July 1970, right in the middle of the high-summer low-season for cinema attendances – August is traditionally the skip for Hollywood debris – and hot on the heels of Jagger's critically panned *Ned Kelly* (Tony Richardson, 1970). In Britain the official censors could now get to work, the BBFC insisting on 16 additional cuts before granting the film a certificate. *Performance* finally received its British premiere at the Odeon Leicester Square on 4 January 1971, Warner's explaining the delay as resulting from their desire to have it open their new West End showcase theatre.[102]

Performance immediately polarised critical opinion. In America the *New York Times* ran contrasting reviews on consecutive weeks. Peter Schjeldahl's piece was headed 'The Most Beautiful Film of All?'[103] while John Simon responded with the less interrogatively titled 'The Most Loathsome Film of All'.[104] Andrew Sarris of *Village Voice* saw the film as 'the most deliberately decadent movie I have ever seen'[105] while *Rolling Stone*'s Michael Goodwin emphasised its pop provenance, being 'particularly reminded of Richard Lester's one-line jokes in *Hard Day's Night* – the first (or gangster) section of *Performance* is peppered with gag lines that would be funny if we had time to think about them'.[106]

British criticism closely mirrored this pattern. Derek Malcolm judged *Performance* as 'richly original, resourceful and imaginative, a real live movie'[107] while Michael Wood termed it 'heavy-handed, ludicrously over-directed, and stylistically about as subtle as a Fu Manchu story'.[108]

Alexander Walker was as scathing as he had been for *Privilege*, criticising the way 'the film appears doubly violent because it transmits shock without a conscience'.[109] This time he found new allies, Nina Hibbin finding the sex and drugs and gangster scenes 'overblown and self-indulgent because they are forcing a parallel that, although honestly proposed, is only superficially valid'.[110] Hibbin thought the link 'too facile', the same phrase used by John Coleman for the film's 'equating the enacted violence of, say, a jeans-splitting Proby or guitar-smashing Hendrix with the real foulness of "putting the frighteners on" someone in Kray or Richardson style'. For Coleman 'the undoubted central failure of *Performance* is that it insists on the parallel'.[111]

John Russell Taylor noted a more successful 'merging' behind the camera, finding the film 'extraordinarily consistent in style, remarkably controlled: the points are made equally by words and visuals, the writer and the photographer as equal partners being, as it were, subsumed into the joint direction'.[112] On-screen Gavin Millar thought that 'James Fox is, on this showing, simply the best we have',[113] while for David Robinson 'Jagger is of a different quality' since 'the acting is secondary to the personality, which is mesmeric with his strange, fascinating features, his easy confidence, his range from extreme calm to the violence of his musical performance: he is a star in the old grand manner'.[114] Cecil Wilson found his features particularly fascinating, writing that 'for most of the film – in which Jagger plays the part of a decadent pop star – he looks remarkably like Brigitte Bardot'.[115] Ann Pacey, seeking greater generic purity, complained that Jagger 'not only slows the film up, he keeps trying to turn it into a musical'.[116]

Warner's must have decided he did not try hard enough since the film was shown in the States for just two weeks before being withdrawn. In Britain it fared little better, quickly disappearing from cinemas to enter the pantheon of 'cult' movies – and pornography: *Performance Trims*, containing the alleged real-sex footage, was awarded Amsterdam's 1970 Wet Dream Festival's Hung Jury Award, the only prize ever given to *Performance*. The initially coveted soundtrack album was reduced to 'Memo for Turner': released as a single in November 1970, it 'peaked' at number 32 in the British charts.

Of all the films discussed in this volume, *Performance* has received the fullest critical attention, consistently growing in stature to the point where, in his 1998 monograph, Colin MacCabe judged it 'the greatest film ever made'.[117] Again to attempt a broad division, most academic exegesis has focused on *Performance*'s dismantling of the gangster genre[118] but there is little on it as a self-conscious reworking of motifs from the British pop music film.[119] Yes, on its release reviewers saw Turner and Pallenberg's Pherber 'dress Chas in the 1930s gangster rig that came and went again with *Bonnie and Clyde*',[120] but he was also thought to be made up 'like a cross between the late Beethoven and Jim Morrison of The Doors',[121] and these latter frames of reference have subsequently receded from critical perspective. Much is made of the links with and echoes of the Krays and Richardsons, but *Performance* is narratively rooted in the pop music world, a context authenticated not only by Mick Jagger's casting but by the Powis Square Notting Hill setting which finally places a British pop film in the cradle area of 'Napoli' meticulously recorded in Colin MacInnes' *Absolute Beginners*. Appraised from a socio-musical perspective, *Performance*'s 'merging' of the pop music film with a gangster movie comments on the overtaking of a hippy pastoral by impatient violence; in doing so, it conclusively brings together the two strands of the genre's primitive phase, the pop star vehicle and the social-problem film. *Performance*'s references to the Old Man of the Mountain in his Persian fortress unite the superannuated rock star and cosh boy in the common etymological root of dropout and murderer, the *hashishin* and assassin. Here, a dozen years on, is 'youth-as-fun' and 'youth-as-trouble' in 'real-time' adult disillusion.

Performance also acts as the summation of a variety of incidents and investigations from previous British pop music films. There are coincidental details: Dana's first words to Chas in the morning are about her nightclub singing, an echo of Maisie and Johnny Jackson in *Expresso Bongo*; Lucy (Michèle Breton) views the mountains of Persia through an old card viewer, the Pop Art of the past as collected by Guy in *Catch Us If You Can*; when Lorraine, another of Turner's entourage, first visits Chas in his new flat she sings 'Onward Christian Soldiers', like an extra from *Privilege*. More generally, in *Performance* the genre's central themes are resumed, or rather ripped apart – all to more explicit and extreme effect. The opening oscillation between Chas and gangland boss Harry Flowers (Johnny Shannon), enacting the 'mergers' of 'healthy capitalism', extrapolates Hamilton Black exercising his legal and financial muscle to buy up the 'hooligans" youth club in *The Young Ones*. The modernist environment of Jennifer's father in *Beat Girl* is shown again, in Chas' pristine flat, to be an emotionless cradle for social violence. The attempt to incorporate racial minorities while denying them physical representation duplicates the processes of colonial discourse most openly manifest in *Help!* When Pherber uses a blonde wig to dress Chas in her own image, the subsequent mix of Lacanian mirrored self-examination and bisexual attraction works through the gendered undercurrents of Cliff

Richard and Lauri Peters' shower-room meeting in *Summer Holiday*. The film's ending, as in John Boorman's debut, invites a Jungian analysis: as the fragments of Turner's being are shattered while Chas enters the Rolls-Royce and his own extinction, John Izod notes how 'In death the walls between the two men break, and they merge in the collective unconscious.'[122]

The narrative of *Performance* may emphasise the body before the politic, but the residual political relevance is explicitly attended to in the film's sound and setting. Just as Godard used the Rolling Stones and a riverside wreckers' yard to illustrate the white appropriation of black music in *One Plus One*, the soundtrack and geography of *Performance* present the racial transformation of 'white' society. In Godard's film an activist recites the origins of rock; in *Performance* Mick Jagger performs it. While Pherber tends Chas' wounds, Turner sings extracts of two songs by Delta blues singer Robert Johnson, arguably the ur-text for popular music in the second half of the twentieth century. Here Turner/Jagger sings from 'Come on in my Kitchen' and from 'Me and the Devil Blues'. The latter references Johnson's supposed selling of his soul for his prodigious musical gift; here, in his own kitchen, Turner senses the opportunity to recover his demon by tapping into Chas' underworld psyche. (Jagger was also thought to espouse sympathy for the devil and as part of a return to roots Johnson's 'Love in Vain' would appear on *Let it Bleed*.) *Performance*, one of the first films to set up an assembled soundtrack, raids more widely the musical stock of other cultures: Cooder's American slide guitar alternates with an Indian sitar; an electronic synthesiser gives way to Eastern santur music. This quoting from a broad range of musical discourses adds an aural eclecticism to match the décor of Christopher Gibbs. It also articulates the notion of cultural blending: depending on one's outlook, the enrichment by or the encroachment of foreign cultural influences, most evident and audible in hippy culture.

The late sixties, though, increasingly forsook the hippy vibe for violence, and the influence of Black Power on London's racial centres is conveyed in *Performance* through Cammell's later soundtrack additions, steeped in the Los Angeles of the period. As Lorraine leads Chas upstairs the film foregrounds 'Wake Up Niggers' performed by the Last Poets, Islamic converts whose proto-rap performances reappropriated their heritage, 'spreading the news by way of the blues'. Their employment here makes textually explicit the link between black liberation and the other freedoms explored in the film. Intratextually, with its use on the soundtrack serving as an enduring influence on eighties rap, Jon Savage notes that 'the film parallels only *A Hard Day's Night* in the way it has fed back into popular culture'.[123]

This musical collage functions textually like the soundtrack to *Catch Us If You Can*, commenting on but not shaping the dramatic action. One number, though, structures *Performance*'s visual action and constitutes the film's narrative fulcrum. As such, it moves carefully from the real to the fantastical, eschewing the blunt audio dissolve – the sudden bursting into song – for a more psychologically credible 'merging' of narrative and musical discourses. It again constitutes a summation of the whole, but now moribund, pop music film genre.

With his mind rearranged by a mix of mushrooms and Pherber's sexual play, Chas is directed to 'go and tell Turner' in his music room. There, as Lucy dances, her image presciently doubled in the ceiling mirror, Turner further softens up Chas from his mixing desk, initially with the strong rhythmic pulse first encountered in the merger-advocating courtroom scenes and then, by playing Cooder and Clayton's 'Poor White Hound Dog', getting Chas to dance and smile, his first open manifestation of pleasure since arriving in the house. For Turner this is the moment to attack: waving a fluorescent strip-light as in a tribal ritual dance, we now see Turner in complete control, his demon refound, the Number One Artist reportedly so spellbinding on-stage suddenly re-energised. The effect is illustrated by Turner's scream, held in a freeze-frame and intercut with the hallway's psychedelic poster: old glories are here revived. Turner's attack refutes all previous strategies to 'castrate' the British rock'n'roller: emphasising his new priapic position, Turner now torments Chas, making as if to stab him with the 'phallic' length of light. Turner's stated intent to get inside Chas' head is achieved through sex, drugs and finally rock'n'roll, with the camera's move along the light and in through Chas' eardrum enacting this shift inside Chas' consciousness. We enter Chas' 'revolution in the head' as Turner replaces his old boss Harry Flowers in the replayed office scene. Cue music.

Though carefully established as Chas' druggy rock reverie, Jagger's performance has repeatedly been assessed through the prism of gangster precedents. For Alexander Walker Jagger 'imagines himself a modern Scarface',[124] while Gordon Gow described him (erroneously) as having 'a Little Caesar brilliantine-stick'.[125] The generic connotations have strengthened, Martin Scorsese using the track in *Goodfellas* (1990) when Ray Liotta's Henry is on a cocaine binge. Just as plausibly, though, Turner has here transformed himself from proto-glam rocker to primitive hard rocker, a fifties Ted with long shaped sideburns and slicked-back hair who takes the film confidently into a full-blown pop musical number (Figure 4.4).

Figure 4.4   Mick the Ted finishing off the pop music film – *Performance*

What follows is less a gangster's interrogation than a compendium of the British pop music genre in its primitive, mature and decadent phases. The temporal parameters are immediately established: 'I remember you in Hemlock Road in 1956.' Here is the early, rough and ready cinema-seat slashing rock'n'roller – 'you were a faggy little leather boy / with a smaller piece of stick', Turner reminds us. The next verse rehearses the more mediated middle period: 'Weren't you at the Coke convention / Back in 1965? / And you're the mis-bred greying executive / I've seen so heavily advertised.' Finally, Turner's ironically intoned pacification, 'come now, gentlemen, your love is all I crave', conjures up the Summer of Love, the Beatles and their cartoon conclusion to *Yellow Submarine*.

More than this broad-stroked, eclectic equivalence to the development of pop, or more accurately the pop business, the androgyny that sur-reptitiously threads through the genre is here brought centre-stage as, in another change from the scene's earlier 'serious' run-through, Turner, now back in his current pop persona and dancing round in a sleeveless black top, long black hair, lipstick and mascara, tells those in the office not to get out but to 'take 'em off!' As they strip, Turner makes a parting toast to 'Old England', exposing tradition's recourse, not to a Pepperland whimsy, but to economic and sexual corruption. When he returns, again in sober suit and slicked-back hair, the three members of the firm are lying naked and exhausted on the red-carpeted office floor – their intertwined limbs and the use of light and colour a clear reference to the work of Francis Bacon. Here, though, as Turner places a protective hand on the still-dressed Chas and announces in the song's final line how 'You gentlemen, why, you all work for me,' one is reminded not only of the gay influence in the underworld but also, and especially in this musical setting, of the 'ownership' of young stable stars by their gay managers. All of which leads the genre full circle to the issue of pop biography.

As Chas discusses Turner's career with Lorraine, she recalls: 'He was a chart-buster ... I fancied him myself, old rubber lips. He had three number ones and two number twos and a number four.' Chas curtly closes the retrospective: 'Didn't last long though, did it, his success?' The pop genre had begun with a series of films charting the overnight success of the new phenomenon, the pop star. A dozen years on and Cammell had many examples to choose from for the flipside to this story, the slow, debilitating potentiality of rock stardom. Adam Faith, with two number ones, one number two and two number fours, the last in October 1961, possessed the requisite blend of antiquity and androgyny. More internationally, Mick Brown notes that the Beach Boys' Brian Wilson was reportedly close to break-down and producer Phil Spector was increasingly reclusive in Bel Air.[126] Less dramatically, the Beatles had stopped performing, as had the Rolling Stones. But Turner is clearly not Jagger, in spite of Lorraine's use of the common sobriquet 'old rubber lips' and the cock-rock stance of the psychedelic poster. Apart from that momentary, neon-supported strutting, there is little of Jagger's swaggering self-confidence in the withdrawn character portrayed.

Instead Turner is readable as the first Stone to be stoned, the one who took the dandy's path all the way to self-destruction while Jagger took the secure route to pop aristocracy and a knighthood: Turner is Cammell's close friend and the group's own washout, Brian Jones. Scarcely seen in *One Plus One*, Jones, the founding member of the Rolling Stones and arguably its most accomplished musician, was rapidly disintegrating under the influence of drugs, his decline exacerbated by the defection of Pallenberg which symbolised his precarious position within the group's 'pecking order'. During *Performance*'s lengthy post-production period, he would be removed from the group and on 3 June 1969 join the '27 club' when found dead in his Cotchford Farm swimming pool. (Cue murder theories, as dramatised in *Stoned* (Stephen Woolley, 2005).)

Jones' collapse was acknowledged raw material for the film. 'Spanish Tony' Sanchez, the group's occasional drug dealer, witnessed Marianne Faithfull's instructions to Jagger, at a loss as to how to approach the role of Turner: 'Whatever you do, don't try to play yourself. You're much too together, too straight, too strong. You've got to imagine you're Brian: poor, freaked-out, deluded, androgynous, druggie Brian. But you also need just a bit of Keith in it: his tough, self-destructive, beautiful lawlessness.'[127] With dyed black hair there is the look of Richard about Turner, but the essence of the character and central aspects of the voice remain with Jones. Turner's record collection, with American blues and rock resting next to Indian ragas and Moorish music, is a perfect summation of Jones' shifting musical interests. As well as dictating the look of his apartment – the model for Turner's house – Morocco was a crucial late influence musically and emotionally on Jones. Philip Norman noted how 'in Morocco, Brian found a country whose daily life, both spiritual and secular, is indivisible from music'.[128] Sadly it would contribute to his emotional undoing. It was during a 'Chelsea set' visit to Morocco in March 1967 that Pallenberg switched her affections to Keith Richard. That the party all left while Jones was out recording indigenous music – he had developed a deep interest in the pipe sounds of the Master Musicians of Joujouka – further corroded his relationship with the rest of the band. Disconsolate, Jones could only think of one place to go: Cammell's apartment in Paris. Cammell, though, knew of another side to his friend's personality, and equal and opposite aspects of Jones are presented in *Performance* through the character of Chas. One could argue that Richard leaving Marrakech with Pallenberg was a charitable act since Jones had earlier expressed his suspicions by beating up Anita in their hotel suite. This had, apparently, become a common occurrence: like Chas with Dana, Jones' relationship with Pallenberg reputedly consisted of serial frantic sado-masochistic encounters, some with Pallenberg more willing than others. For *Stern* magazine, Pallenberg had suggested Jones pose as an SS officer, crushing a doll beneath the heel of his jackboot. The pictures, rejected, caused a furore in the British press, but constituted a fair reflection of Jones' darker, brutal, woman-beating side. In *Performance* the way that Turner and Pherber make over Chas re-enacts the way that Pallenberg would make over Jones to look like Françoise Hardy, or like herself. Their play with his image is matched by the film, superimposing Turner's face on a large close-up of Chas as he echoes the gangster's words, 'Time for a change'. Brian Jones, as Cammell knew better than most, was no straightforward, wronged romantic hero. Rather, his crumbling persona can best be understood through that overlaid image, a blend of the fragile Turner and the fascistic Chas, the pop star and the hoodlum. Unlike the commercial whitewash that began the genre, *Performance* effectively ends it by offering the complex 'artistic' biographical truth.

Coda

For John Walker '*Performance* put a hole through the head of the 1960s.'[129] It did the same for the British pop music film, marking a conclusive synthesis of the (sub-)genre's twin tropes and revealing the retired rock'n'roll star and the grown-up JD as 'different facets of the same male rebel archetype: the demon-lover, the son of a gun'.[130] The demon 'love' had one last thrust via a cluster of 'sexploitation' quickies apeing the antics of high-profile groupies like the GTOs and the Plaster Casters. Derek Ford's *Groupie Girl* (1970) delivered on a Redlands drugbust recreation while Lindsay Shonteff's assured but decidedly downbeat *Permissive* (1970) provided an authentic-feeling study of ingénue Maggie Stride's grubby 'progress' through the groupie subculture while giving exposure to hirsute loon-panted prog rock minnows Forever More and Titus Groan and adding a score by the (briefly seen) acid-folk band Comus. Much more the shape of things to come was Stanley Long's *Bread* (1971), which uncomfortably yoked British blues rockers Juicy Lucy and Crazy Mabel to a mildly saucy comic romp: Marjorie Bilbow fingered it as 'far too recognisably a Cliff Richard musical with nudes and swearing'.[131] By contrast, the son-of-a-gun violence would manifest itself for real in the beating to death of an armed fan at the Stones' Altamont Free concert in December 1969, an event filmed, with a savage symmetry, by the same team that had recorded the Beatles jubilant, first tour of America back in 1964. The Maysles brothers' snuff-rockumentary *Gimme Shelter* (1970), released in the United States just as *Performance* received its UK premiere, almost demanded critical comparison, and in its exploration of the destructive authority that Turner drew from Chas, plus its concluding breakdown in rock's cathartic ritualisation of violence (see *Privilege*), *Performance* was seen as eerily prophetic: for Michael Goodwin 'the Maysles aside, this is *the* Altamont movie'.[132] Television may have provided the genre's commercial *coup de grâce*, but this (filmed) finality left it ideologically bereft. The seventies, if it tried at all, could only start again. And again. And again.

5
Afterlife: The Historical Pop Music Film

The grit and the glam

If the 'long sixties' were the decade when the British had discovered the consumer society, the 1970s were when they discovered it had to be paid for. It would prove a fragmented, fractious decade, a time of ignominious economic decline. Following a 70 per cent hike in the price of oil, a country that had once ruled an empire faced the reality that it was a small link in a vast economic chain. People's expectations had run ahead of their incomes, credit cards were becoming a way of life, and as inflation spiralled out of control, mass strikes led to a three-day week.

None of this impacted on Cliff Richard, who continued on his merry way with *Take Me High* (David Askey, 1973), again produced by Kenneth Harper. After his dalliance with drug pushing in *Two a Penny* the title may have suggested a sequel in pop decadence: but no, here Cliff is a thrusting young banker who, posted to Birmingham, wanders its redeveloped centre, falls in love with Debbie Watling and becomes a fast-food entrepreneur with his invention of the Brumburger, so good that the city holds an open-topped parade in its honour (an intertextual payback for *Privilege*?). Though garnished with shots of Spaghetti Junction, crushed velvet and flared trousers, the film is almost bold in its refusal to move with the times, its one 'innovation' being Harper's intent 'to prove that we could do a musical film without dances'.[1] The first 'primitive' pop star vehicle since the mid-sixties, Cliff's musical musings singularly failed to repeat the success of his Technicolor trilogy, and proved a critical and commercial failure. Even the title single just crept into the December top 30.

If only inadvertently, Cliff's final film venture fits with the major trend of 1970s (and subsequent) pop music films, a nostalgic review of when British society seemed less divisive, and/or when the new generation of directors and commissioning producers had themselves grown up. This revisionist trend is evident from two films starring teen idol David Essex, *That'll Be the Day* (Claude Whatham, 1973) and its sequel *Stardust* (Michael Apted, 1974). The first is not, by the criteria of this study to date, formally a pop music film as its star aspires to the world of rock stardom, but does not perform: John Mundy terms it a 'proto-musical'.[2] A coming-of-age film, *That'll Be the Day* tells the story of young Jim MacLaine's rejection of A Levels and the path to university respectability, and his immersion instead in the 'grassroots' of the entertainment industry, working in fairgrounds, holiday camps and discovering the easy availability of sex. Reviving the 'youth-as-trouble' paradigm, rock'n'roll is seen as a major component in leading Jim from normative behaviour: he listens to records on coffee bar jukeboxes and in his bedroom rather than studying; when he goes to the cinema prominent is a poster for *The Duke Wore Jeans*; Jim's journey ends where Tommy Steele's began, with the purchase of his first guitar. The film has a strong pop pedigree in being co-produced by Sandy Lieberson, producer of *Performance*, and in its casting – Ringo Starr in a straight acting role as Jim's fairground mentor, and Billy Fury and Keith Moon as early rockers. Knowingly referencing pop history, Fury performs as Stormy Tempest, a play on his first renaming by Larry Parnes, but also a conscious mining of the early Beatles story – Rory Storm and the Hurricanes being the group in which Starr played prior to unseating Pete Best. The film has few performance sequences, however, and these function narratively to further Jim's desire to be a rock star rather than privileging the performance itself. Indeed, they strike the one false note in the film, Stormy and band performing the Who's unmistakably 1970s 'Long Live Rock' at a late 1950s jive competition. Instead period music saturates the film via the ambient diegetic soundtrack, featuring songs from Bobby Vee, Little Richard, Dion and others, with the Buddy Holly eponymous hit appearing over the end credits. Aesthetically this enveloping soundtrack is adjudged as making *That'll Be the Day* the British pop nostalgia equivalent to *American Graffiti*, George Lucas' film of the same year. But in the UK film the music was integral: not only did it cast a pop star and place him in the burgeoning pop world, but the soundtrack constituted the driving economic motivation for the film. As such, *That'll Be the Day* is a British pop music film financially, returning fully to the sub-genre's baldly commercial roots. Having secured only partial funding from EMI, co-producer David Puttnam struck a deal with the American Ronco record company whereby, if they would fund the film, it would feature a number of rock classics that Ronco could then exploit via a television advertised tie-in soundtrack double album. The deal struck, Puttnam and writer Ray Connolly revised the script, making regular incisions to add a radio or record player to the scene. Puttnam recalled how 'Characters took to walking along beaches and through fairgrounds, *anything* to squeeze in the necessary tracks.'[3] This was financially expedient but generically innovative. Until then pop music films had urgently sought contemporaneity; this was the first 'retro' rock movie, a music film capitalising on a pre-existent pop-heritage soundtrack both as a cheap means to evoke a period setting, and for a commercially synergistic compilation album release – which reached number one in a two-month chart stay. It would prove, aesthetically and economically, a lasting template.

The sequel *Stardust*, again based on a Ray Connolly script, reprises its pop icon casting by keeping Keith Moon, adding Marty Wilde as an influential music publisher, and replacing Starr with Adam Faith, now playing Jim's increasingly hardened manager Mike Menary. Repeating the Ronco soundtrack tie-in and enjoying fuller NFFC (National Film Finance Corporation) funding, the film expanded its location shooting to Los Angeles and Andalucía, and employed more performance numbers – the music of Jim's band, the Stray Cats, produced and arranged by Dave Edmunds. If *That'll Be the Day* preceded primitive pop beginnings, *Stardust* extrapolates its decadent demise, passing, via a paraphrase of mid-phase Beatles, from the grit and grime of Fury's Tempest to the detached and druggy world of Jagger's Turner. Moving the story into the 1960s, Menary's remoulding of the group as a vehicle for Jim MacLaine pays off: Jim and the Stray Cats find stardom, tour the United States, give television interviews and enjoy an endless supply of groupies. Jim's apogee is an inflated rock opera, *Dea Sancta et Gloria*, broadcast globally on satellite television. Extolling the virtues of womanhood, MacLaine's *magnum opus* not only pricks the pompousness of 1960s concept albums, but also completes the two films' Oedipal trajectory. *That'll Be the Day* begins with Jim's father walking out on mother and child, just as Jim will at the film's conclusion. The sequel shows how his misogynistic rise to fame leads to physical and emotional isolation, the loss of his mother prompting his (artistically deficient) atonement for his treatment of women. Male 'bonding' is equally troubled as *Stardust* does not shirk from showing the strident divisions within a successful band – Paul Nicholas pertly jealous as 'Knee-Tremble Johnny' – nor its remorseless exploitation by managers and agents. Here the accomplished Faith 'steals' the film from Essex, taking even more than the

Figure 5.1 Phoney Beatlemania – *Stardust*

manager he plays, who claims, in Johnny Jackson style, that 'I own half of you ...!' Jim's acrimonious split from the band does not end in rock reclusion since, unlike Turner, the revelation that he is close to insolvency impels a comeback interview, during which, as he recounts the sordid reality of his glamorous existence, he collapses from a drug overdose: his management have worked him (literally) to death.

One can read *Stardust* as a riposte to the Lesteroid lifestyle portrayed in *A Hard Day's Night*, as a cod-Beatles biography advocating that a grubby rock decadence was there from the beginning. The Stray Cats' fashion trappings and stage movements pastiche the Fab Four's public display (Figure 5.1), while the backstage parallels can be regularly ticked off: the early exclusion of a band member, the homosexual inclinations of a first manager, the post-Pepper entropy of drug-inspired musical 'masterpieces'. The accelerating malaise of the 'long sixties' is simultaneously amplified with contextualising references to political decline: the Kennedy assassination, Chappaquiddick, the Nixon years. Adjudged by *Sight and Sound* 'A jaundiced, insider's view of the pop explosion, meshing awkwardly with slabs of instant nostalgia,'[4] this was not a film aimed at the bobbysoxers, though Essex scored a top ten hit with the title song.

For Alexander Walker, the David Essex double-bill heralded 'the start of a revisionist view of the Sixties'.[5] Their cynical appraisal of the music business, generically more redolent of *Expresso Bongo* than any 1960s fare, is repeated in the backstage music film *Flame* (Richard Loncraine,

1974). Featuring Slade, a Wolverhampton quartet who, under the management of ex-Animals bassist Chas Chandler, had mutated from skinheads to prime Glam Rockers, *Flame* repeats the Essex diptych's narrative of the rise and fall of a rock act, condensing its pop parabola into a hard-hitting *Permissive*-style purview of late 1960s terraced houses and steel foundries, working men's clubs and pirate radio stations. The four band members largely play themselves, with singer Noddy Holder and flamboyant guitarist Dave Hill keen for success, bassist Jim Lea sardonic and resistant to their glam make-over, drummer Don Powell the comic relief. Around them pop film perennial Johnnie Shannon offered a variation on his Harry Flowers persona from *Performance* as the group's early psychotic manager, while Tom Conti made his big-screen debut as a Zissell-like London executive grooming the (renamed) provincial ingénus who then fail to cope with the pressures of fame. Termed by Ben Thompson 'The mother of all nuts-and-bolts portrayals',[6] *Flame*'s feeling of accuracy is born of director Loncraine and writer Andrew Birkin replicating the *modus operandi* of Alun Owen with *A Hard Day's Night* and accompanying the group for several weeks on their (unsuccessful) American tour, learning about their backgrounds and amalgamating the stories they told of their own and other groups' formative experiences into a semi-biographical slice of Black Country naturalism. Nonetheless, intertextual echoes of Owen appear in the quartet's characterisation, their train confrontation with toffs and in Don Powell's solo scene on a canal tow-path. Similarly, Lea's complaint at his commodification, 'I'm not a fish finger!', recalls Bongo Herbert bemoaning his manager: 'I'm just something he sells, like rat poison or fish and chips.' While similarities with the later *This Is Spinal Tap* (Rob Reiner, 1984) – a singer trapped on-stage in a coffin – may add a retrospective parodic air, *Flame* convinces as a carnivalesque but cuttingly accurate lesson in rock'n'roll history – such an event did befall Screaming Lord Sutch. *Flame* remains a pertinent exploration of pop exploitation – though one that comes, of course, with a tie-in album and novelisation.

While Tony Rayns found it 'virtually identical to *Stardust* in its hoary "social realist" conventions and melodrama',[7] *Flame* met with broad critical approval, though replicating the genre's inherent dilemma – add earthy realism and alienate the early teenagers – it was not a commercial success. As Noddy Holder admitted, 'the fans were a bit baffled because we didn't give them the glamour'.[8] *Flame* again exemplifies the genre's need for precise timing: filmed just as Slade's popularity was waning, the weeks the group spent on set removed them from beneficial stage and television-screen exposure. The second single release from the film, the melodic brass-inflected 'How Does It Feel', did not feel so good, breaking a straight run of 12 top five hits by only reaching number 15 in February 1975. A tie-in album, *Slade in Flame*, did chart, but its disappointing number six position confirmed a band slipping from the spotlight.

Nonetheless, its narrative formula was a distinct advance on concurrent Glam Rock movies that returned to the quasi-plotless revue or limp comic format of early 1960s fare. *Side by Side* (Bruce Beresford, 1975) used the rivalry between neighbouring club owners, traditionalists Terry-Thomas and Barry Humphries of The Golden Nugget Variety club versus 'with it' Billy Boyle and (Mud drummer) Dave Mount of the Sound City disco, as an excuse to feature a roster of Glam acts including Mud, the Rubettes, Fox and Kenny, all filmed in performance mode with no discernible difference to a Thursday night episode of *Top of the Pops*. The same year's *Never Too Young to Rock* (Dennis Abey) was implausibly predicated on an anti-*Privilege* near future where, with television threatening to stop showing pop music, Peter Denyer's young talent scout must scour the country for new acts. The misdirecting of his tracking van onto an army assault course once more referenced Beatles' film fare, while the acts he found again included, in (badly lip-synched) performance mode, the Rubettes and Mud, now joined by the Glitter Band and Slick. At least the film attempted a self-deprecating parodic literalisation of Glam's 'brickies-in-lippy' sobriquet with location shots of the Rubettes singing on the back of a lorry and Mud entertaining football fans in a transport caff. For Geoff Brown, 'once the silly plot is tucked away' the finale delivers as, 'in a kitsch wonderland of shimmering fronds, balloons and decorated flowers, the glittering bands pound out their recent hits'.[9] Both features were funded by the film arm of Laurence Myers' GTO Records, the latter in particular the pretext for a soundtrack album before any formal innovation of the genre.

The pop music film as rock opera: *Tommy* (1975)

This strain (sic) of platform-soled, silver-laméd visual excess culminated in *Tommy* (1975), a belated pop film entry for the Who, arguably rock's most cinematic group by origin, image and ambition. From the moment in March 1964 when drummer Keith Moon, in ginger-coloured clothing with hair dyed to match, marched on-stage in Greenford and insisted on performing, singer Roger Daltrey, bassist John Entwistle and their Acton County Grammar school friend Pete Townshend had their definitive line-up and an introduction to the benefits of visual shock tactics. That summer a management partnership with a propitious provenance, Kit Lambert, son of composer Constant, and Chris Stamp, brother of actor Terence, signed the band: inspired by *A Hard Day's Night*, they had been scouting for their own (unrealised) pop film, to be based on the West London Mod scene. Thereafter, the group honed their powerful, encompassing visual image on *Ready, Steady, Go!* and *Top of the Pops*, Moon gurning and toppling over his drum kit, Townshend leaping in the air and windmilling guitar chords, while Entwistle's still centre equally drew the eye: Daltrey, to get any attention, had to twirl his microphone and strut around the stage with evident 'cock-rock' menace. They nearly made it to the big screen when Antonioni, scouting for his concert scene in *Blow Up*, witnessed Townshend's ritual finale with a ruined Rickenbacker in December 1965, but negotiations failed, the tempestuous Italian and rock-sure Townshend disagreeing over how the scene should be shot: enter instead the more compliant Yardbirds. Meanwhile Townshend's compositions were becoming increasingly cinematic in scope and structure. Their second album concluded with the mini-opera 'A Quick One While He's Away', a trend to extended composition that continued with the pseudo-concept album format of 1967's *The Who Sell Out*, its pastiche broadcast from a pirate radio station proving both an elegy and epitaph for the medium that had brought Who music to much of their early audience. Around this time Townshend turned to the teachings of Indian mystic Meher Baba: from Baba's tenet that those who perceive earthly things cannot then perceive God, Pete worked up the story of a boy who, deaf, dumb and blind after witnessing a childhood family murder, finds salvation and becomes a new religious leader. When released in May 1969 the double album *Tommy* was a global hit topping ten million sales and bringing the Who international stardom and financial security. It was also, from the outset, a project with evident cinematic potential. Universal, Decca's film partner, were immediately interested but Lambert's management strategies were proving increasingly erratic and his two-year bureaucratic wrangle led to the studio's withdrawal. A brief cinematic outing came in Michael Wadleigh's 1970 *Woodstock* rockumentary with the Who performing the album's finale, 'See Me, Feel Me', just as the sun rose over the festival – a light show that no-one could have invented or afforded. *Tommy* then found theatrical incarnations as a concert and stage production (with Merry Clayton and Bette Midler respective Acid Queens) before, with Bill Curbishley replacing Lambert as the group's manager, a film deal finally came to fruition. Australian music mogul Robert Stigwood produced while the chosen director was British cinema's *enfant terrible* Ken Russell.

Russell is another pop film director with an apprenticeship in television, though his BBC *Monitor* commissions from the outset set image with music in intense, inventive biopics. From *Elgar* (1962) to his Delius piece *Song of Summer* (1968), his visual correlations of classical music continued into cinema with *The Music Lovers* (1969) and *Mahler* (1974): after rejecting the chance to direct Cliff's *Summer Holiday* (sic), a treatment of more popular musical idioms finally came with *The Boy Friend* (1971) before the invite to tackle Townshend's rock opera. Russell's screenplay fleshed out the album's characterisation, notably strengthening the motivation for Tommy's trauma by having him witness his father, RAF hero Captain Walker (Robert Powell), being killed by 'Uncle' Frank (Oliver Reed): the album had Walker killing Frank. Overall, though, Townshend's spiritual quest was rather subsumed under Russell's broader auteurist preoccupations such as gender performativity and the corruptions of religion, advertising and material culture. In a jointly beneficial adjustment, condensing the narrative to post-World War Two allowed for more contemporary images and settings, but also a more rock-inflected soundtrack – it had been agreed from the outset that the Who's libretto would be the only means of dramatic communication. Therefore, as there would be no non-musical dialogue, Townshend wrote four further songs and modified existing material to fit in with Russell's expanded narrative trajectory. The uniquely musical medium for the message is formally important for, as Justin Smith notes, 'There is an important sense in which *Tommy* is not a musical film, but a filmed performance of a song cycle' and 'its particular brand of stylisation marks a departure from the characteristic approach of prior pop film vehicles'.[10] This 'uncharacteristic' musical prioritising was embodied in the production process which began with a complete recording of the soundtrack before filming began. The cast then performed to camera to the playback of their recording. Columbia, who put up most of the $3.5 million budget, had insisted on American stars: hence the casting of Ann-Margret as Nora, Tommy's mother, Jack Nicholson as the doctor, and Tina Turner as the LSD-wielding Acid Queen. In a reversal of traditional pop film practice, the acting talent – of variable singing quality – had to be surrounded by dependable (box-office) music performers. Roger Daltrey was cast as Tommy, with roles for Keith Moon as his abusive Uncle Ernie, Paul Nicholas as sadistic Cousin Kevin, Elton John as the Pinball Wizard and Eric Clapton as the Preacher. Townshend and Entwistle made brief appearances, lip-synching in the Clapton and John numbers, the latter piece allowing the band finally to bring their auto-destructive stage act to the British pop music film. The music's primacy is also evident in production timing: the film was shot mostly on location in and around Portsmouth in three months, while the subsequent soundtrack dubbing and editing took four months, a task exacerbated by the need to produce various mixes for differing cinema sound systems, in particular a new – and in the event unreliable – multichannel hi-fi 'quintaphonic' system that placed a fifth speaker directly behind the cinema screen to locate the vocal tracks more closely to the singers, a further index of aural exaggeration.

Premiered in New York on 19 March 1975 and one week later in London, *Tommy* proved a huge box-office success, earning $16 million in the US alone, where it was placed number ten for the 1975 ratings. For the first time since *A Hard Day's Night*, a British pop music film found favour with the Oscars: Ann-Margret earned an Academy Award nomination for best actress whilst, to go with the royalty cheques, Townshend's scoring of the incidental music earned him a nomination for Best Score Adaptation. The *Tommy* phenomenon, including the ancillary merchandising and a revived Who 'Tommy' tour, was undoubtedly at its fullest in America. The soundtrack album, for instance, reached number two in the US charts but only number 30 in the UK, though Elton John's 'Pinball Wizard' was a UK top ten single. Critical reaction to Russell's film was mostly positive. For Alexander Walker *Tommy* was 'undoubtedly his best film of the decade',[11] while Dilys Powell admired Daltrey's performance, 'astonishingly ranging from silent vacancy to bawling confidence'.[12] Then, as now, though, most considered *Tommy* a cinematic curate's egg: for David Wilson of *Sight and Sound* the film, 'as nearly always in Russell's cinema, is bits and showpieces'.[13]

The bits can be seen in the film's 'primitive' topography and narrative trajectory. Russell himself said 'It was set in the fifties, so already we were doing an historical reappraisal of an era.'[14] Like other 1970s music films, the 1950s 'nostalgia' is visible in the early miserablist mise-en-scène with Teddy boys, terraced houses and spartan holiday camps. Narratively, the simplicity of Bernie's festive locale contrasts with the later overt economic imperatives of Tommy's Cult Holiday Camp, a pointed synecdoche of the 'merger' of the divine and the commercial. Like late-1950s pop melodramas, *Tommy* also plays out an Oedipal trajectory: especially with Russell's reversal of murderers, the idolised dead father becomes Tommy's 'mystical' master, the focus of his spiritual quest. Challenged as much by his mother's openly sexual behaviour with his stepfather as by his covertly abusive relatives, it is only when

Tommy learns to disavow the roles that others try to impose on him, notably his rejection of what society constructs as the masculine, that he can achieve independent manhood.

The film's visual style replays in more explicit mode the Pop Art influences of the genre's mature phase. Where Richard Lester would reference Warhol screen-prints, Russell steals them wholesale. Important here are the set designs of pop artist Paul Dufficey: alongside the direct use of Warhol's Marilyn silkscreens, taken from a publicity still for *Niagara* (Henry Hathaway, 1953), fields of oversized pinballs and Ann-Margret's extended bolster suggest (alongside an auteurist phallic frenzy) the enlarged plastics of Claes Oldenburg, while the bright colour palette and flattened picture frame recall the cartoon-strip artwork of Roy Lichtenstein. Their employment, as throughout the pop genre's middle phase, enables *Tommy*'s double, Janus-faced effect. That a film imbued by the teachings of Meher Baba concurrently critiques spiritual leaders is evident in the 'Eyesight to the Blind' sequence, where Eric Clapton's (rather underwhelming) rendition of the film's only non-Who number, Sonny Boy Williamson's 1951 12-bar blues, is redeemed by its cinematic correlation, an overlaying of religion and celebrity in the form of the Church of our Lady Marilyn Monroe. The Pop Art-impregnated 'service' proves both alarming and alluring as the song sequence narratively exposes the essential (and literal) vacuity of idolatry – the giant statue of the Marilyn Madonna, cast in the skirt-billowing pose from *The Seven Year Itch* (Billy Wilder, 1955), is smashed by Tommy to hollow pieces – yet stylistically relishes in the semi-synaesthetic rock-religious display of bells, smells and decibels (Figure 5.2). If Tommy's iconoclasm is here readable as an involuntary action, it is climactically deliberately employed – and against himself. Jon Lewis discerns a clear link with *Privilege*: 'At the end, Tommy, like Steve Shorter is rejected by his fans as capriciously and passionately as they had first embraced him.'[15] Exposing, as had Watkins, the equivalence of performance to the gullible masses, Tommy's final self-destructive behaviour is a call to rock rebellion that (at least temporarily) drives his followers away from their commercial exploitation. The subsequent mise-en-scène contests closure, however, as Tommy, half-naked on a cliff top, both registers as an image of liberation from the ties that bind, social or religious, *and* is redolent of Christian iconography, the golden sunrise haloing his well-toned ('classically' masculine) frame.

While *Tommy* proved itself supremely successful in bringing a new, non-rock-oriented audience to Townshend's work, Russell's film version was, for many rock aficionados, a betrayal. Andrew Sarris spoke for the latter when

Figure 5.2   Rock gods and goddesses – *Tommy*

he noted that 'we fans like what we see in *Tommy* because it confirms our belief that Rock has entered its mindlessly decadent phase, all noise and glitter and self-congratulation'.[16] That noise and glitter (and Glam) are most discernible in the film's musical 'showpieces' which, while evoking a recent historical setting, display a generically radical yet deeply 'classical' cross-media grammar of cinematic correlation. As *Tommy* employs a grand-opera format, there is, unlike in previous pop films, no 'audio dissolve' to these character-cameo song sequences. For example, following on from Nora and Frank's recitative, Keith Moon's 'Fiddle About' number emerges rather than erupts from the narrative world: for all its performative excess it remains formally anchored to the continuous soundtrack. Elsewhere song sequences can suggest diegetic performance, as with Eric Clapton sporting a signature guitar and Elton John pounding a piano that doubles as his giant pinball machine, but *Tommy* strives to provide a cinematic correlative for the singers rather than seeking to validate their musical performance. These showpieces constitute the most achieved segments of the film, their discrete nature a premonition of the MTV pop promo and recipient of the earliest critical paeans. David Wilson singled out the 'Pinball Wizard' scene where Elton John's enlarged performance, both for delivery and costume, become 'a genuine merger of method and material'.[17] Similarly upheld is the 'Acid Queen' sequence, where Tommy is encased in an iron maiden through which a plethora of drug-injecting syringes work to 'turn him on' to full consciousness. Largely dependent on the voice and movement of Tina Turner which allows Russell a commensurate surge of flashing lights, primary colours and blatant symbolism – VE poppies turning into blood – Jonathan Rosenbaum considered it 'a mini-masterpiece of visual inventiveness and dramatic cohesion'.[18]

Wherein lies Russell's problem, the micro-successes coming at the expense of any macro-fulfilment. *Tommy* is, as Sarris claimed, '*mindlessly* decadent' in that, contrary to *Privilege* where Peter Watkins' palpable design overcame its musical content, here any social critique or overarching dramatic cohesion is swamped by the visual pleasure and excess of individual musical sequences. The film's stylising of the diegetic world by making rock music the only means for verbal communication may, as Justin Smith notes, achieve 'an immense, visceral, emotional charge'[19] but only intermittently and at the expense of the method overall obliterating the material. There are no 'retired flowers' in Russell's world and, ultimately, we cannot 'hear' *Tommy*. The Who knew that they needed a substitute.

Quadrophenia (1979)

By the time the original concept made it to the cinema screen *Tommy* was close to six years old – a dinosaur in the chronology of popular culture: Jon Landau in *Rolling Stone* curtly headlined his review 'Too Big, Too Late'.[20] Four years on and the Who were at it again, encouraging a film treatment of their 1973 modyssey *Quadrophenia*. With the money gained from the film *Tommy*, the group could now make the films they wanted when they wanted – and they wanted to redress *Tommy*'s many wrongs. Aware of its 'Americanisation' they used the royalties to move back to realism from tinsel, ensuring that 'their next cinematic foray should remain as British as possible, with no concessions to the overseas market'.[21]

To that end, it is hard to locate a more British foray than the early 1960s Mod movement and now, in the late 1970s post-punk era it had a new topicality, thanks largely to Paul Weller and the Jam. Townshend entrusted the cinematic realisation of *Quadrophenia* to 30-year-old television documentarist Franc Roddam, with the altruistic brief that the double album's music should contribute to and support the narrative, but not, as with *Tommy*, take over. Roddam was pivotal to the creation of a *critical* space: an observer rather than practitioner of Mod, he took the ideas Townshend had invested in the album and expanded them in line with his own hinterland in social realism. His addition of a backstory, a layer of London social context, was important, as was the introduction of further characters, since the young cast this necessitated brought a fresh, punk-inflected sensibility to bear on their interpretations. These differing agencies all helped *Quadrophenia*'s tale of Mod teenager Jimmy (Phil Daniels) who fights the Rockers at Brighton, gets and loses the girl (Leslie Ash) and, increasingly disillusioned, walks away from it all, to house competing modes of understanding. *Quadrophenia*'s enduring appeal lies largely in opening a hermetic subculture to its social realist context: as such it is a cult film that dares to explore the dangers in being part of a cult; it is a Mod film that points out the potential mind-lessness of Mod.

As with *That'll Be the Day*, *Quadrophenia* exemplifies a new revisionist generic trope in its exploration of music's importance to the identity of young working-class people, but again scarcely features star-performed musical numbers. Apart from a few seconds of Jimmy admiring his heroes on *Ready, Steady, Go!*, the Who, while its executive producers and musical directors, do not appear in the film. Instead their music is heard diegetically at numerous parties, coffee bars, dance halls and bedrooms, an evocation of the period and an index of the depth of fan allegiance. It also functions, especially in the film's final third, as a non-diegetic discourse, its 'melodramatic' employment a 'siphoned-off' expression of Jimmy's increasingly fragile emotional states. For instance, when thrown out of the Brighton dance hall, Jimmy spends the night on the beach, staring out at the pounding waves. With a long shot dwarfing him against the pier and shoreline, visually the scene all but eliminates the insignificant human presence; it is the music, the instrumental section from 'Love Reign O'er Me', that centres, low key through synthesiser and lead guitar, the brooding sentiment of Jimmy's psyche.

That combination of cosmic indifference and experiential adolescent angst has made *Rebel Without a Cause* the enduring, even obligatory comparison for *Quadrophenia*. But the dialogics of social class, absent for Jim Stark and his bourgeois college cohorts, allow a more indigenous and informing genealogy to be traced. Though never cited as an influence by Townshend, there is a marked resemblance between several photos in the LP's booklet and scenes from *Bronco Bullfrog*, Barney Platts-Mills' 1970 depiction of working-class teen life in East London. Alongside a shared New Wave aesthetic, several plot turns, images such as Del with Irene riding pillion, and even snippets of dialogue – 'bit flash, inee?' – echo Roddam's later treatment. Ever influential, Jimmy's Brighton return resonates with the 1964 of *A Hard Day's Night*. Throwing his possessions out of the train corridor window wins the admiring glances of two schoolgirls, much as the Beatles' antics had attracted the attention of Patty Boyd and classmates. As well as referencing a photo from the album's artwork, Jimmy's attitude as he sits in a first-class carriage between two bowler-hatted commuters silently encapsulates the class warfare previously articulated between the obstreperous commuter and Ringo.

This generational divide was borne out in the film's critical reception. Young bucks were enraptured: for Richard Barkley 'the film is a magnificent achievement in current British cinema, shatteringly honest in intent and stunningly photographed'.[22] Felix Barker, though, who 15 years earlier had been swept up by the 'teenage enthusiasm', 'charm' and 'innocence' of the Beatles' films, now wrote that 'Just about everything I dislike is to be found in *Quadrophenia*. The music is so loud and raucous that there should be a free issue of ear-plugs with every ticket. The film reeks with mindless violence.'[23] *Films and Filming*'s end-of-year honours list (best film Terrence Malick's *Days of Heaven*) awarded *Quadrophenia* the accolade of 'most distasteful film of the year'.[24] While never more than a midnight-movie-circuit cult hit in the States, *Quadrophenia* was the eighth most successful picture of 1979 at the UK box office, grossing over £36,000 in its first week in the capital. As much an atonement by the Who as an exploitation of the Mod revival, there were no tie-in single releases. Indicative again of a reversal to *Tommy*'s transatlantic appeal, the soundtrack album peaked at number 23 in the British and 46 in the American album charts. For the Who at least, the Grit was less exportable than the Glam.

The punk and the Pink

Pierre Sorlin has argued that 'we can only understand characters and events in historical films by referring to the years in which those films were produced'.[25] *Quadrophenia* is no exception, readable as a punk film in (dubious) Mod clothing. The punk inflection is there in the casting: Toyah Willcox and Sting, if not directly punk, were prominent post-punk or 'new wave' personalities while Mark Wingett was a raw, full-on punk. (It is there also in the backstory to casting with the unsuccessful auditions by Johnny Rotten/Lydon and Jimmy Pursey.) It is there in the film's grim London locations, and in its dance-hall moves: Jimmy's balcony dive into the audience was a feature of punk gigs but far too gauche for Mod.

It is certainly there in the film's language. Never mind the bollocks? The continued use of that particular expletive contributed to a cuss-laden soundscape far more in keeping with a late 1970s punk aesthetic. Above all it is there in *Quadrophenia*'s very existence, punk's infusion of the music industry leading to a (belated) flourish of British music films, with *Quadrophenia* forming part of the slipstream that created *Jubilee* (Derek Jarman, 1978), *The Great Rock'n'Roll Swindle* (Julien Temple, 1980), *Rude Boy* (Jack Hazan and David Mingay, 1980), and carried through to post-punk manifestations such as *Breaking Glass* (Brian Gibson, 1980) and the Madness story *Take It or Leave It* (Dave Robinson, 1981).

This is the one pop film period to receive sustained academic treatment (with many former followers now tenured in universities), though investigations remain predominantly synchronic, situating the films within punk's broad cultural aesthetic rather than presenting a diachronic exploration of their referencing or reproducing previous pop film product.[26] Stretching from the release of the Sex Pistols' 'Anarchy in the UK' in December 1976 until Sid Vicious' death in March 1979, musically punk constituted a reaction to the pretensions of prog rock compositions, bloated stadium acts and cinematic self-indulgence such as Led Zeppelin's *The Song Remains the Same* (Peter Clifton/Joe Massot, 1976) which intercut full rockumentary coverage of the heavy-metal super-b(r)and's July 1973 (under-par) Madison Square concerts with wish-fulfilment fantasy sequences including Arthurian chivalry and mountain-top hermits. Punk's more 'grounded' DIY aesthetic would also prove a vibrant influence on fashion and publishing, but its impact on film arrived late. It was not so much the anti-authoritarian stance, but rather the in-built ephemerality of so many punk bands that, as with rock'n'roll, made mainstream commercial studios fight shy of a film exploitation vehicle until a band had demonstrated relative longevity.

The brief cycle of fiction films that eventually emerged differed in tone and technique, but all sought to convey, through a bricolaged punk stylistics, their troubled social context. The music scene of the late seventies saw increased pockets of political violence with the National Front opposing left-wing/Red Wedge followers and punk films invariably reference this mood of national division. Jimmy and his Mod mates beating up Kevin the Rocker in *Quadrophenia* is a 'staple' of the punk film grammar: scenes of sudden violence occur with outriders in *Jubilee*, fascists in *Breaking Glass* and Teds in *The Great Rock'n'Roll Swindle*, while scrapping skinheads even briefly upset the happy-go-lucky feel of the Two Tone *Take It or Leave It*. Steve Jenkins queried the Madness movie's 'celebration of an all-male working-class-lads-together attitude which is as dubious as it is here unquestioned',[27] and while punk opened up a subcultural space for female participation, most of its group vehicles present if not necessarily celebrate a masculine disposition of peer bonding and martial grouping with sex taken where and when it is offered: Steve Jones' cinema aisle 'quickie' with Mary Millington in *The Great Rock'n'Roll Swindle* and a toilet blow-job in *Rude Boy* are reminiscent of Jimmy's knee-trembler with Steph up a Brighton twitten. However, a British movement up a Sussex alleyway offers scant cultural translation and these are, above all, exclusively *British* pop music films, UK punk being, as the Clash sang, so bored with the USA.

Derek Jarman's independent 'art-house' *Jubilee* was the quickest onto screen, a less testosterone-charged film (cf. the Slits trashing a Ford Anglia) that was made for just £50,000 and applied punk's torn-up, Xeroxed aesthetic to an exploration of late-1970s social decay rather than any 'ballsy' celebration of anarchy. It cast 'punk' figures such as Jordan, Toyah Willcox and Gene October while 'introducing Adam Ant', and featured diegetic punk performances such as Siouxsie Sioux singing 'Love in a Void' and Jordan miming to Suzi Pinns' Hendrix-like desecration of 'Rule Britannia'. Jon Savage thought that 'With its persistent air of disillusion and warning, *Jubilee* captured the mood of Punk England better than anyone could have predicted, not least in its locations: it remains one of the few films where you can see the 1977 London landscape.'[28] However, at its Gate 2 Cinema London premiere, several of the punk musicians involved walked out in apparent disgust: *Jubilee*'s art-school input led Jordan to note disparagingly that the filmmakers 'all wanted to be extras in *Blow Up*, rolling around with David Hemmings',[29] while the outcome led Vivienne Westwood to print a t-shirt on which she asked if Jarman 'had a cock between his legs' and decried 'the most boring and therefore disgusting film' that she had ever seen.[30]

Why such vituperative responses from the punk sorority? Westwood demanded 'something here and now of absolute relevance to anyone in England' and, for all its social record and girl-gang sexual subversion, classical music accompaniments to Jordan ballet dancing and Adam Ant contemplating the Albert Memorial frieze to Mozart, Haydn, etc. implicitly support non-punk hierarchies of taste (and indict Jarman of 'exploiting' the subculture). Equally *Jubilee*'s copious collage of cultural referents – Madame Mao phones up for a film role, Jordan reads Lenin, Adolf Hitler reminisces in a country retreat, an *Evening Standard* hoarding decries Denis Healey's budget strategy – thrown together as a mash-up metaphor for England, explicitly applies the 'intellectual' strategies of Godard. Generically *Jubilee* also redeploys several long-standing pop film tropes. For instance, monopolising London's post-apocalyptic wasteland is media-mogul Borgia Ginz (Orlando) who has turned Westminster Cathedral into a throbbing discotheque where, to a rock version of 'Jerusalem', semi-naked apostles gyrate around a bloodied Christ (mime artist Lindsay Kemp). The scene's musical arrangement replays *Privilege*, as does the film's future-tense setting, while the outlandish sexualisation of religion reveals Jarman's early 1970s film apprenticeship with Ken Russell. Far closer to the 'here and now', however, is Jarman's indication that there would be no future in England's dreaming. *Pace* Westwood (later Dame), when Ginz proclaims with cynical satisfaction that 'They all sign up in the end one way or another!' he rearticulates George Melly's original 'castration' complaint that rock'n'rollers will inevitably reform: here is yet another Zissell-like puppeteer impresario, recuperating rebellion, packaging punk. Narratively realised as the girl punks join Ginz at his country retreat, the accusation is also formally supported: in *Jubilee*, as in an early social-problem pop music film such as *Serious Charge*, musical performance repeatedly concedes to narrative discourse – Adam Ant's televised 'Plastic Surgery' is largely ignored by the warehouse squat's inhabitants, while even Jordan's 'Rule Britannia' set-piece is disturbed by the sounds of an air-raid. For Claire Monk this indirect, constricted musical presentation 'itself becomes a comment on punk's predicted commodification and neutralisation'.[31] Punk's anarchists fashionably disapproved, but as Jarman later noted, they too buried their muzzle in the golden mash: 'Dr Dee's vision came true – the streets burned in Brixton and Toxteth, Adam [Ant] was on *Top of the Pops* and signed up with Margaret Thatcher to sing at the Falklands Ball. They all sign up in one way or another.'[32]

The pop music film as piss-take: *The Great Rock'n' Roll Swindle* (1980)

This subcultural appropriation – and concurrent raucous self-vindicating – were evident in punk's first baldly commercial film venture, *The Great Rock'n'Roll Swindle*. After the Sex Pistols' lucrative record sales, Virgin Films was formed expressly to distribute their first 'cross-over' commodity, a dramatised biopic of the group's – and manager Malcolm McLaren's – punk pioneering rise to infamy. With a £250,000 budget, *The Swindle* had a troubled gestation, with original director and exploitation maestro Russ Meyer fired by McLaren and replaced by Julien Temple, the group's documenter since his film-school days. A reworked narrative, centring on Steve Jones' comic turn as a trenchcoat-wearing gumshoe seeking his share of the spoils, employed the tried and trusted Beatles' film strategy of using the group's best actor as its narrative focus. Generic reflexivity abounds. There is again a Godardian as much as punk shock value in Jones' Brazil trip with drummer Paul Cook to record 'Belsen Was a Gas' alongside Ronald Biggs and on-the-run Nazi 'Martin Bormann'. The film makes conscious references to *Performance* as, alongside the *de rigueur* appearance of Johnny Shannon (billed as 'Man in Prison Cage'), a shot of McLaren disguised in the back seat of a black limo echoes the closing merger of James Fox and Mick Jagger, while the murder sequence on the train, kept over from the aborted Roger Ebert/Meyer script, called for the Sex Pistols to murder rock star 'M. J.' – another Jagger reference. Jagger is dismissed as a 'white nigger' in Eddie Tenpole Tudor's title-song diatribe against rock oldies and punk newbies ('Sid Vicious: rock'n'roll cli-ché!'). The song serves as a microcosm of the film's musical strategy which, moving from Sex Pistols' numbers ('Anarchy in the UK' sung in French to an accordion accompaniment), through burlesqued rock'n'roll classics such as 'Rock Around the Clock' and back to Sinatra's 'My Way' and Max Bygraves' 'You Need Hands', is itself a punk cut-up undercutting. And yet, while providing an historical overview and last rites on the punk movement, much as *Performance* had for rock, *The Swindle* is also readable as punk's version of and variant on *The Tommy Steele Story* (sic). Rock'n'roll's first exploitation biopic had sought to bring the new, mistrusted musical idiom to a broad public, but occluded investigations of historical veracity via its flashback structure. Punk's first commissioned biopic again seeks maximum exposure, but formally aspires to an opposite effect. With its 'bricolage' of cinema-verité footage, dramatic reconstructions of key group events and even – for scenes necessitating the differently departed Johnny Rotten and Sid Vicious – animated reconstructions (by a team including *Yellow Submarine* artist Gil Potter), *The Swindle* openly foregrounds the processes of making 'history', exposing how disparate sources are forged into the Sex Pistols' public 'story'. The film's very beginning, an anachronistic reconstruction of the 1778 Gordon Riots where Sex Pistols effigies are burned, immediately places the group in a tradition of insurrection *and* dispels any notion of 'historical' realism. Robert Rosenstone discusses anachronisms as a 'strategy' that 'cast into doubt notions of historical distance and objectivity, and insist that the questions we take to the past always arise from our current concerns'.[33] Here, though, the context complicates such seemingly 'honest' transparency, especially with regard to completions. After an

Figure 5.3 Director James Ferman (BBFC) betters director Julien Temple (Virgin) – *The Great Rock'n'Roll Swindle*

entire film tonally set at the ludic trivialisation of anarchy in the UK, appending a montage of newspaper cuttings detailing the recent deaths of Nancy Spungen and Sid Vicious could strike as the film's one act of genuine audacity – until we learn that it was a moral pill applied at the insistence of the BBFC, intended to function as a dire warning of the consequences of sex, drugs and rock'n'roll (Figure 5.3).[34] The 'swindle' which the film recounts, how the band, or more particularly McLaren (cast as 'the Embezzler'), manipulated the media and big business out of a fortune rather than the other way round, is in itself a doubtful premise – Temple's later documentary *The Filth and the Fury* (2000) atones for his own manipulation by McLaren in allowing antiphonal versions of events – and was undermined when internal legal struggles between Rotten and McLaren (who lost) led to the soundtrack double album being released a full year before the film and the loss for all parties of lucrative cross-media synergy. (A repackaged single LP soundtrack peaked at number 16 in June 1980.)

Beating *The Swindle* into British cinemas – though again two years in the making – was *Rude Boy*, the film entry for punk's other pioneer group, the Clash. Residing at the more 'intellectual' end of the punk spectrum, their film is loosely threaded with the narrative of a politically confused Clash roadie (Ray Gange), but formally replays a Godardian diptych of pop and politics. *Rude Boy* features plentiful footage of the Clash performing live, the minimal editing itself reminiscent of Godard's methodology when filming the Rolling Stones. This documentary strand is intercut with on-screen discussions on the rise of the National Front, Margaret Thatcher and police corruption, a social commentary illustrated by a fictional subplot concerning four black youths arrested by the police and charged with conspiracy. In essence the *One Plus One* of punk, for K.J. Donnelly *Rude Boy* 'validated' the Clash 'as still retaining their vocal social criticism, despite their increasingly corporate status' and he cites as supportive evidence the absence of a soundtrack album.[35] However, the film's 'strident editorialising' means that, as John Pym noted, 'the effect, finally, is only of strained special pleading',[36] while its UK distribution via exploitation specialists Tigon rather compromises any anti-capitalist credentials.

The 'blending' (or gelding) of punk into more mainstream idioms advanced swiftly into 'post-punk' or 'new wave' music – one could label it 'punk-pop' – and brought with it willing participants (such as Rotten – now Lydon – with his new band PiL), keen for the life-prolonging *Top of the Pops* much as early rockers had strategised the Variety circuit. Here again though, the first cinematic outing was exploratory, low-cost and art-house, Chris Petit's *Radio On* (1979). A 'cool' depiction of Britain on the edge of ruin (and thus a pre-apocalyptic partner to *Jubilee*), Petit's film follows a factory's night-shift disc jockey (David Beames) on his picaresque journey from London to Bristol after learning of his brother's death. While consciously referencing associate producer Wim Wenders' road-movie trilogy (a German girl, Ingrid, is searching In the Cities for a daughter called Alice), comparisons are again germane with *Quadrophenia*: with the evocative non-diegetic soundtrack, here running from Wreckless Eric and his Stiff Records stablemates to Berlin-phase David Bowie and Kraftwerk (pinned in the dead brother's flat is the band's declaration that 'We are the children of Fritz Lang and Wernher von Braun … Our reality is an electronic reality'); with the casting – Sting again, now a petrol-pump attendant, briefly sings Eddie Cochran's 'Three Steps to Heaven' to acoustic guitar; and with the journey itself, once more away from the capital and back into the past, revealing the hero's inability to communicate with those he meets en route (Bowie's opening 'Heroes/Helden' foretells the language barriers he will encounter with Ingrid), and ending with him stalled in his battered old Rover at a quarry edge, his questions still unanswered, forced to turn around or end it all.

New wave's 'mainstream' outing came with the distaff dystopia of *Breaking Glass*, distributed by the Glam-surviving GTO. With musical direction by Bowie's producer Tony Visconti and co-starring *Quadrophenia*'s Phil Daniels (and Mark Wingett) alongside the then-unknown Hazel O'Connor, it tells (yet again) the Bongo Herbert, Jim MacLaine, Slade-in-*Flame* backstage musical tale of innocent talent and exploitative management – one record boss, a generation on from Meyer in *Expresso Bongo*, wearily announces that he cannot understand this new music and longs for John Lennon. The depersonalising nature of stardom is formally conveyed through the film's 'robot' leitmotiv, climaxing at the drugged-up O'Connor's solo concert where she resembles another child of Fritz Lang, the Iron Maiden from *Metropolis* (1927). Though lacking pre-existent pop stars, the film succeeds as a history of punk's recuperation; it knowingly traces the softening of the band Breaking Glass and its lead singer Kate's anarchic sound and image; it inhabits the terrain of London's late-1970s alternative music venues, progressing from pub rock hovels to Camden's Music Machine and concluding at the Rainbow in Finsbury Park; it extrapolates recent social history, bringing a surface-level seediness to James Callaghan's winter of discontent – a key concert is stopped by a power cut; and it can (just about) be read as a metaphor for burgeoning Thatcherite corporate greed. To that end, *Breaking Glass* was the first 'punk' film with an accessible AA certificate, while its punk-pop soundtrack album reached number five in a 28-week LP chart residency and spawned two top ten singles, 'Eighth Day' and 'Will You', for its newly manufactured 'star' O'Connor.

The pop music film as primal scream: *Pink Floyd: The Wall* (1982)

This reiterated recuperation culminated in conflating punk with its prog rock anathema in *Pink Floyd: The Wall* (1982). Pink Floyd were another rock 'behemoth' late to fiction film, though they had been seen and heard before on celluloid documentaries. Their initial blues-based psychedelic incarnation, led by Syd Barrett alongside Roger Waters, Nick Mason and Richard Wright, was evident in Peter Whitehead's *Tonite Let's All Make Love in London*,[37] while their later prog rock stadium-arena line-up, with David Gilmour in for Barrett, filled Adrian Maben's concert movie *Pink Floyd: Live at Pompeii* (1973). They were heard in their ambient art-house soundtracks for Antonioni's *Zabriskie Point* (1970) and Barbet Schroeder's *More* (1969) and *La Vallée/The Valley Obscured* (1972) before the 1973 LP *Dark Side of the Moon* brought the group international superstardom and set their imprint for grandiose concept albums supported by highly theatrical, multimedia world tours. After further success with 'Wish You Were Here' and 'Animals', Roger Waters presented a disparate demo tape for a potential double album named *The Wall*: its cinematic potential was clear as, to give the demo shape, producer Bob Ezrin decided to 'write a script for an imaginary Wall movie'.[38] Articulating the growing sense of alienation Roger Waters had experienced through the late-1970s around the band's bloated concerts and increasing disconnection from their fans (a distance that in part had prompted punk), *The Wall* topped the American album chart for 15 weeks and reached number three in the UK. It proved an equally popular (though expensive) stage show, complete with 160×35ft 'wall' constructed and demolished on-stage, but when, in late 1980, Waters approached the film division of EMI they were unconvinced of its cinematic potential and passed.

Waters was so determined to realise the project that Pink Floyd stood initial surety for $2 million – their entire earnings from *The Wall* album. Thus, far from an industry-led exploitation vehicle, this was the pop music film as personal therapy/vanity project. Knowing he needed the assistance of an industry insider, Waters enlisted writer-director and Pink Floyd fan Alan Parker (later Sir). The protean Parker had progressed from high-production television commercials to a film-directing debut with the self-scripted child-cast musical *Bugsy Malone* (1976), and on to critical and commercial success in America with the thriller *Midnight Express* (1978) and the musical *Fame* (1980). Here his profile again swiftly shifted, from Waters' production mentor to script advisor and finally nominated director. This led to satirical cartoonist and illustrator Gerald Scarfe, designer of the album's artwork and the stage show's set and animated sections, being 'reassigned' to similar functions for the film version. Waters was also persuaded to give up ideas of taking the lead role as rock star Pink – which accelerated the dropping of planned Pink Floyd concert footage. Instead, the casting of Bob Geldof (later Sir), the Jagger-lite frontman of Irish post-punk band the Boomtown Rats, helped Parker to secure a $12 million production deal with MGM, the backers of his previous two films. The novice Geldof was, as ever, surrounded by experience, notably Bob Hoskins as Rock and Roll Manager and Christine Hargreaves as Pink's mother, while Gillian Gregory, following work on *Tommy* and *Quadrophenia*, was brought in as choreographer. Scarfe worked with key animator Mike Stuart, who cut his cartooning teeth on *The Beatles* television series, while Waters and the rest of Pink Floyd remixed, re-recorded or added new songs for the soundtrack, 'In the Flesh/?', now housing Geldof on vocals.

Filming, in autumn 1981, was conducted at Pinewood Studios and on location largely in and around London with war scenes shot at Saunton Sands in Devon. It was a troubled shoot, the billing of 'An Alan Parker Film ... by Roger Waters' indicating the power struggles at play. Waters and Scarfe had worked harmoniously on the album's previous visualisations, but Parker brought his own populist, stylised approach to the film set and the trio's 'creative differences' led to Parker forcing Waters to leave the shoot for six weeks. In that period Parker estimated that 'I was allowed to develop my vision' and 'I really made that film with a free hand.'[39] The arguments resumed in post-production where the 60 hours of filming were eventually edited down to 95 minutes. As irreconcilable as Iain Quarrier and Jean-Luc Godard on *One Plus One*, Waters' feelings can be deduced from the lyrics to 'Not Now John', released on Pink Floyd's 1983 album *The Final Cut*: 'we've gotta get on with the film show. / Hollywood waits at the end of the rainbow. / Who cares what it's about, as long as the kids go?' Parker later termed it 'the most expensive student film ever made' and admitted it was 'one of the most miserable experiences of my life'.[40] Finally constructed, *The Wall* premiered at the Empire, Leicester Square on 14 July 1982: three weeks later it opened in the still rock-opera-receptive US where it grossed a healthy $22 million. Though a soundtrack album was listed on the film's end credits, none materialised: instead, new film songs transmogrified into *The Final Cut* album, Waters' further reflections on his father's death at Anzio now coupled with the recent Falklands war with Argentina.

While garnering mostly positive reviews in America – Roger Ebert later considered it 'without question the best of all serious fiction films devoted to rock'[41] – many British critics sided with Parker and judged it one of their most miserable experiences. Steve Jenkins found it 'A vacuous, bombastic and humourless piece of self-indulgence'[42] while Paul Taylor expressed his surprise at off-camera contretemps, seeing the film as an example of 'stunning literalism ... little more than kinetic sleeve art keyed slavishly to a slim concept-album narrative'. Taylor warned (with a humour lacking from the film) of the dangers inherent in intra-generic hybridity: 'Crossing *Privilege* with *Tommy* couldn't result in anything shallower. All in all, it's just another flick to appal.'[43]

Tommy's stamp resides primarily in *The Wall*'s formal rearticulation of a rock-opera format: with almost no dialogue, narrative progression is provided by the songs which mostly appear as non-diegetic music. There are directorial flourishes – a swinging pendulum shot of Pink in his pool borrowed from *Napoléon vu par Abel Gance*; war scenes modelled on the D-Day photos of Robert Capa; Kubrick-style slow tracking shots – but Parker's grammar of cinematic correlation overwhelmingly confirms and consolidates song meaning. For example, as we hear in 'Mother' how Pink is 'always a baby to me' Geldof folds up into the foetal position on his lonely bed; to 'Is There Anybody Out There?' Pink bashes himself against a large brick wall. The trade press considered it no more than 'an illustrated album'.[44]

The Wall's depiction of the miserable life of an exploited and exhausted rock star marked a further reprise of the *Privilege/Performance/ Stardust* narrative paradigm. The film opens with Pink sitting in his locked LA hotel suite, and his review of where it all went wrong also takes us back to generic beginnings. As seen with *The Tommy Steele Story*, the flashback device evaluates the past through a subjective framing, and the film's first hour centres on the building of 'the wall', a metaphor for Pink's psychological isolation. We immediately learn that the origins of this dysfunctionality, as with *Tommy*, lie in the wartime loss of a father – *The Wall* as 'Floydian' analysis. This leaves Pink prey to (s)mother-love and a repressive education regime (he fantasises a *Blackboard Jungle* riot) and seeking a father figure in park playgrounds and pop managers. Music initially brings to Pink freedom and female adoration, but the wall continues to grow as he is trapped by fame and abandoned by his wife. So far, so literal: the wall metaphorically crude, the unhappy rock-god a 'decadent' semi-autobiographical conceit. Indeed, much as *Performance* can be read as a coded depiction of Brian Jones before Mick Jagger, so *The Wall*, while ostensibly Waters' cathartic self-analysis, his primal scream after spitting at a boisterous fan from stage in 1977, more fully draws on, especially in its cinematic version, the fragility and drug-induced decline of former band member Syd Barrett. The childhood may be Waters' but Barrett is explicitly referenced in Pink's shaving of his body hair, and his obsessive arrangement of the record shards, discarded drugs and smashed guitars into attractive patterns, the latter action doubling as a metaphor for the film's *modus operandi* (Figure 5.4).

The flashback's nostalgic desire for patterns of repetition fosters generic atavism and *The Wall* revisits enduring pop film tropes, ranging visually from Pink's Warhol portraits and Scarfe's Union Jacks collapsing into blood-stained crosses up to the *Privilege*-cribbed finale, and reaching narratively from the thrill of music itself to easy groupie sex and (uneasy) gender relationships, on to CND rallies and trench warfare, all informed by childhood feelings of abandonment. Here, though, the flashback's 'naturalising' subjectivity means that *The Wall* singularly fails to negotiate the distance it supposedly

Figure 5.4   Pink in his Barrett home – *Pink Floyd: The Wall*

investigates. Everything in the film is seen to conspire against the innocent 'artist', and every other character's sole motivation (even the absent father) is as a contributor to poor Pink's psychological problems. This creates both a repetitive structure of debilitating obstacles, regular summative montage sections and, even in the context of a largely male-gendered genre, serious issues with female characterisation. The mother, so grief-stricken by her soldier husband's death, becomes domineering towards her son; the wife, alienated by Pink's increasingly comatose removal from life, leaves him for an anti-war lecturer, a man who cares passionately and is left-wing. Even the teachers' cruelty is passed down from their treatment by 'fat and psychopathic wives'. As Marjorie Bilbow noted, 'behind all the sound and fury, the only cry to be heard is the whingeing of a self-pitying Adam blaming it all on Eve'.[45] Not even the male scrapping of the punk films matched this misogynistic myopia.

It is here, though, that Gerald Scarfe's interpolations, structurally reminiscent of *The Great Rock'n'Roll Swindle*, can be seen to register the unreliable nature of Pink's memories – and, perhaps, Parker's moviemaking. The animated sections where a bloom, vaginal in Georgia O'Keeffe style, seduces, envelops and finally devours a male flower, and where the silhouette of his wife transforms into a praying mantis, allow some perspective on Pink's self-immolating terror of castration. When Pink decides to tear down the wall in the concluding, self-interrogating 'The Trial', 'hammed up by Waters in the style of a Gilbert and Sullivan operetta',[46] Scarfe's periwigged judge initially harmonises with the musical pastiche but then distorts into a grotesque Dickensian variant on the Law as an Arse. Though a noted political cartoonist, Scarfe's animated torments, as when a dove becomes a screaming fascist eagle and warplane, here signify successfully because they are placed as discrete sketches of a singular state of mind rather than extended satires on the state of the nation.

They thus contrast with Parker's more ponderous interpretations. Scarfe's promo video had helped 'Another Brick in the Wall (Part 2)' to become the last number one single of the 1970s with a succinct combination of live-action shots of children at play, the stage show's puppet pedagogue, and animated sections showing pupils being fed into a meat grinder and becoming, like their teacher, goose-stepping hammers. This cartoon-stroke anti-authoritarianism, a more vigorous variant on *Yellow Submarine*, would be reassigned in *The Wall*, ceding to Parker's visualisation of the 'set-piece' song where the pupils lose their faces behind blank masks that are later worn over the faces of Pink the fascist's followers. This extended metaphor on education producing mindless fodder for cannons or charismatic dictators is again blunt as a brick wall, just as Parker's early intercutting of charging combat soldiers with fans rushing into a concert hammers home the decadent-phase trope on the equivalence of performance to undiscerning masses, but does so without the thought-inducing hinterland of *Privilege* or, sadly, the self-deflating humour that mitigates for *Tommy*.

As a desperate, deranged Pink, drugged up to go on stage like Kate in *Breaking Glass*, fantasises of taking his revenge on the world that wronged him, pop and psychosis blur and he performs 'In the Flesh' to what can be read as both/either the skinhead fans that idolise him (a contemporary subcultural phenomenon untouched in Madness' *Take It or Leave It*) and/ or their neo-Nazi uniformed wish-fulfilment extrapolation. For all the film's literalisation, this climax with flashback ceding to fascism is where Waters must most have differed from Parker's direction, and not just for the addition of a final scene in which a child (symbol of hope) pouring the petrol from a Molotov cocktail undercuts Waters' dystopian determinism. Rage against the Thatcherite machine may have appeared to be late punk's monopoly but, while rock's ageing statesmen largely stayed aloof or became obliquely complicit (Jagger's 1987 'Let's Work' strikes as an unironic Norman Tebbit-like call to 'get on your bike'), Waters shared punk's politicised outrage, even if filtered through a millionaire's 'comfortably numb' prog rock ruminations. As well as being a mental wall, Waters' script referred to 'the wall of post war reindustrialisation';[47] it was animated by Scarfe as a 'Pop Art' wall made of consumer goods, and by 1982 was a construct extendable to the start of post-industrial alienation.

There is a danger, though, in sharing a punk ethos with a major commercial budget – and uncooperative director. *The Wall's* set-piece fascist rally and accompanying violence – perpetrated by the uniformed skinheads on Pink's command against 'queers', 'coons', Jews and (again) women – reruns the ubiquitous NF risings of punk cinema, but where the latter's low-resolution enactments kept mimesis at bay (cf. the paucity of policemen at the Notting Hill demo in *Breaking Glass*), Parker's high production values and punchy editing, redolent of his television commercials, flirt with a complicit excitement. Problematically, the progression from punk to Pink sees an undermanned, over-stagey DIY cede to a fulsome fascist aesthetic as Parker codifies and contextualises his meaning in an 'authentic' authoritative structure.

In 'Fascinating Fascism', Susan Sontag explores fascism's 'utopian aesthetics', noting how 'The fascist dramaturgy centers on the orgiastic transactions between mighty forces and their puppets, uniformly garbed and shown in ever swelling numbers. Its choreography alternates between ceaseless motion and a congealed static, "virile" posing.'[48] This is unnervingly applicable to the musical genre ('entertainment as utopia'), and Sontag herself cites *The Gang's All Here* (Busby Berkeley, 1943) as exemplifying 'certain formal structures and themes of fascist art'. Sontag posits that the *telos* of fascist drama is not to purge our emotions through pity and fear; rather fascist pageants are 'epics of achieved community, in which everyday reality is transcended through ecstatic self-control and submission; they are about the triumph of power'.[49] This citation does not imply that Parker, having wrestled control of the film's direction, is revelling in the triumph of his will/wall, much as Pink lords it over his acolytes. Like Peter Watkins in *Privilege*, Parker aims to pastiche the fascist aesthetic, and Pink's encomium that their enemies go 'up against the wall', exactly paralleling the call from Godard's black revolutionaries in *One Plus One*, reminds us, as Sontag did explicitly, that such incitements are not restricted to the far right.[50] But whereas Watkins' future-tensed voice-over worked as an effective alienation device, in *The Wall* the distance again is just not there. The pastiche is so precise in its Nuremberg lighting, its uniformed masses and its Fritz Lang choreography that the realisation is potentially *enjoyable*, and in that enjoyment, even if only at the aesthetic level, Parker's style betrays Waters' content. Key to Waters' outline was enlightenment: 'As the rally reaches its climax, Pink suddenly realises he has become an ally to the very forces of tyranny which killed his own father. This proves too much for the core of human feeling within him and he rebels.'[51] As staged by Parker, the point is completely lost: in *The Wall* there is no rebel rock.

The postmodern and Plan B

The late 1970s had seen a wide fragmentation of popular music styles as, alongside punk and prog rock, disco and reggae enjoyed large sub-cultural followings – and each earned a mainstream pop music film outing.[52] Their production histories differed: the international success of *Saturday Night Fever* (John Badham, 1977) prompted the habitual British low-rent rushed response, this time in Camden's new answer to Studio 54, *The Music Machine* (Ian Sharp, 1979); conversely, the success of *Quadrophenia* helped writer Martin Stellman to conclude a five-year hunt for funding (largely from the NFFC) for his earlier co-written tale of Deptford depression, *Babylon* (Franco Rosso, 1980). Textually, however, the films have several (perennial) parallels. As with *That'll Be the Day*, music provides each film's central character with the means to potential salvation: Gerry (Gerry Sundquist) sees an escape from his tower-block home life by dancing his way into the affections of the gang and the girl (Patti Boulaye), while Blue (Aswad frontman Brinsley Forde) targets a way out of his dead-end garage job and constant police harassment through his night-time work as a toasting DJ. Both films employ the established getting-to-the-show-on-time plot: Gerry's participation in the disco dancing final – metatextual first prize to feature in a disco movie – is jeopardised by maulings and misinformation from the crooked disco owner who favours his Travolta-posing rival; local racists smash up Blue's new equipment the night before his Ital Lion's sound-system final against toasting nemesis Jah Shaka. Each succeeds and, though Blue's victory seems more provisional, each narrative brings an equivalent ideological charge. Both films' 'social realist' credentials were praised: the trade press liked *The Music Machine*'s 'basic realism of detail and character delineation',[53] while *Time Out* lauded *Babylon*'s 'sharp use of location, the meticulous detailing of black culture' and, not least, Dennis Bovell's 'stimulating soundtrack'.[54] However, it was suggested on *The Music Machine*'s release that 'one might take exception to the film's racial stereotypes, whereby the "naturally rhythmic" black weans his protégés off "that honky hustle shit"'.[55] Similarly, with a non-black production team, *Babylon* reverses *Quadrophenia*'s gang composition with David Essex's old mucker Karl Howman now the token white – a decent guy and a key entry for the white liberal perspective. Seeking to 'chant down Babylonian oppression' but employing Babylonian forms,

Steve Jenkins found that 'the film's inability to present its characters as other than likeable rogues, villains or victims limits it to being merely another depressing, but easily consumable, slice of life'.[56]

The primitive postmodern pop music film:
Absolute Beginners (1986)

After Paul McCartney's less easily consumable *Give My Regards to Broad Street* (Peter Webb, 1984), an unadventurous exercise in self-referencing nostalgia to match the most solipsistic of Pink's fantasies – though one lacking the fanatical (box-office) following – fashion and fascism returned to the British pop music film in *Absolute Beginners*, Julien Temple's promotion from punk chronicler/video-maker to big-budget feature-film director. The reprint of MacInnes' novel at the end of the 1970s fed, like *Quadrophenia*, into a revision of youth culture origins: Temple picked up the film rights in 1981 when working on a (finally abandoned) *Teenage* documentary for Granada Television. Eventually co-produced by the supposedly trend-savvy Virgin and Palace Pictures, *Absolute Beginners* was financed by Goldcrest Films, strongly identified with the early 1980s 'renaissance' of British cinema since its (modest) investment in *Chariots of Fire* (Hugh Hudson, 1981). This was a time for 'heritage films' which, depending on one's political viewpoint, either investigated the causes for shifting national identities, or retreated into aesthetic and ideological conservatism, termed by Richard Dyer a 'museum aesthetic'.[57] By the mid-1980s Goldcrest had severely over-reached by simultaneously investing £20 million in the historical epics *Revolution* (Hugh Hudson, 1984) and *The Mission* (Roland Joffé, 1985), with a further £6 million pledged to the first big-production British musical since the Cliff Richard era, the 'alternative', 'remembered' or 'youth heritage' *Absolute Beginners*.

A huge financial gamble from the outset, elaborate outdoor sets were constructed at Shepperton Studios to re-present MacInnes' Soho, Notting Hill and Pimlico through the hyper-real Technicolor prism of 1950s Hollywood musicals. Initial tabloid press reaction was optimistic, snowballing as further cast names, a Who's Who of British music talent past and present, were released. Here, they trumpeted, was a sumptuous feast to save the beleaguered British film industry. It was, alas, but pride before a fall for a project plagued by unceasing production difficulties: a wet summer expensively delayed on-set shooting, two cast members caught pneumonia and Temple demanded numerous reshoots in pursuit of visualising a ramshackle script that had already been through five writers. Tensions rose further as, following the disastrous box-office performance of *Revolution*, it became evident that Goldcrest could ill afford a second failure. With costs soaring, press coverage changed tack and *Absolute Beginners* was now portrayed as British cinema's last-chance saloon, with numerous jobs depending on its commercial returns. When Temple felt constrained to run a trade advertisement asking for people not to think of the film as an industrial panacea, the press considered it an *a priori* admission of failure: in *Time Out* Julie Birchill created 'Ten reasons why nobody should bother going to see *Absolute Beginners*',[58] while even ITV's puppet satire *Spitting Image* stuck the boot in – all before a frame of film footage had been seen. Thus *Absolute Beginners* (now a gift title to copy editors) became a self-fulfilling prophecy as pre-release publicity of its prodigal production fed the need to make the film's consumption conspicuous. A full, perhaps frantic saturation marketing campaign by Palace costing £500,000 again proved counter-productive. For Goldcrest founder Jake Eberts, '*Absolute Beginners*, which had been a textbook case of how not to make a movie, now proved a textbook case of how not to market one.' Countering Temple's strategy, 'the expectations of the audience were raised to such heights that the picture could only suffer by comparison'.[59] Whoever was to blame for the debacle – Alexander Walker implies a nostalgic boardroom loss of perspective, the source novel having been 'a talismanic part of teenage culture' for the company's now-middle-aged executives[60] – *Absolute Beginners* finally came in at £8.4 million, 30 per cent over budget. It received a royal premiere on 2 April 1986 and awaited the nation's verdict.

The sheer weight of critical opprobrium, especially in Britain, instantly crushed any chance of saving the film, and its financiers. There were pockets of praise for the spectacular cinematography and ambitious scope – 'No doubt about it,' proclaimed *The Sun*, 'THE film of 1986'[61] – but the mix of tone and styles was deemed too loose and its teenage stars – Eddie O'Connell as Colin Young and Patsy Kensit as Crepe Suzette – too slight to carry the narrative. The storyline had double weight since for the first time a British pop music film also had to contend with the potential antagonisms of novelistic adaptation. They were plentiful: for Kim Newman the film 'undermines its explo-sive energies by being a travesty of an outstanding novel',[62] while for Marjorie Bilbow 'the spirit of the late Fifties which Colin MacInnes cap-tured so vividly' had been betrayed: 'The demands of internationalism have operated like a retrospective vasectomy denying the existence of Teddy boys and gyrating guitar-strummers.'[63] American critics proved more accepting of an 'exotic' product, *Variety* not alone in judging it 'a terrifically inventive musical for the screen'.[64] Nonetheless, *Absolute Beginners* took less than $1 million in the States: disastrously it clawed back just £1.8 million from UK cinemas.

Goldcrest's supposed youth guru partners had employed a succession of tie-in singles to market the film: Bowie's title track reached number two in the UK, his last top ten hit of the decade – but it failed to break the top 50 in the States. With diminishing returns, the Style Council's 'Have You Ever Had it Blue?', released three weeks after Bowie, peaked at number 14; Ray Davies' 'Quiet Life', issued in May, failed to chart. The soundtrack album, released concurrently with the film, was more favourably reviewed but only reached number 19 in the UK chart. Thus with its ancillary products also bombing, *Absolute Beginners* 'contributed' fully to the collapse of Goldcrest, the winding up of Virgin Films – and the simultaneous rise and fall of the high-scale British musical.

Critical opinion has largely failed to mellow. Writing in 2004, Alexander Walker felt that *Absolute Beginners* could only claim 'a museum value for the sight of Pop stars of the 1980s who played the roles' while aesthetically the film was 'absolutely all over the place, wasteful of its effects and huge sets, dazzling but confused, with the restlessness of an extended pop video, not the rhythm of a movie musical'.[65] It is an unrelenting view, perhaps, but the criteria employed in Walker's retrospective provide a helpful context for *Absolute Beginners'* cinematic correlations and critical reception. The launch in August 1981 of the dedicated music video channel MTV quickly brought to cinema an 'MTV aesthetic', discernible by the frequent use of pop songs on a film's soundtrack, the privileging of gloss, atmospherics and camerawork, and a conspicuous rapid-fire presentation where editing submitted to the customary tempi of pop music.[66] Temple's disparate visual accompaniments to an eclectic roster of current stars, running from the jazz-revivalist Sade and Working Week, to Two Tone Jerry Dammers and reggae Smiley Culture, facilitated the critique that the film was overinflected with the music video aesthetic: for Chris Peacock in *Time Out*, 'The whole film is an example of the strange influence of pop promo mentality on cinema. All that noise, all that energy, so little governing thought.'[67]

However, the pop video boom was indispensable to the genesis and not just the generic shape of *Absolute Beginners*. MTV had enabled a second 'British invasion' of the US through 'new pop' bands such as Duran Duran and Culture Club: British pop star involvement in a blockbuster musical now made it possible to finance what otherwise would have been considered too parochial a project. It was also thought that international audiences were again attuned to song and dance narratives; 'new pop', as Andrew Goodwin argues, 'openly acknowledged pop performance as a visual medium with a sound track'.[68] Nonetheless, with a longer format (and seemingly limitless finance), Temple sought to overlay his 'youth heritage' product with traditional generic codes. This allowed a different perspective: as Caryn James noted, Bowie's 'That's Motivation' is 'an excerptable rock video that in old musicals would have been called a production number'[69] and 'old' Hollywood musicals permeate *Absolute Beginners*. Bowie's dazzling cynical guided tour of adland, dancing with Colin on the keys of an oversized typewriter and gigantic globe, has all the scale and panache of a Busby Berkeley number (even if, in MTV terms, one could judge it a 'nice video, shame about the song') (Figure 5.5). The film's colour schemes, lush surfaces and camera styles are as redolent of Vincente Minnelli as MTV, its pop playfulness reminiscent of Frank Tashlin. The leads are a Soho variant on *West Side Story*'s Tony and Maria, while its gang warfare is choreographed like the Sharks and Jets. There are numerous incidental echoes: Jon Lewis notes references to *Love Me Tonight* (Rouben Mamoulian, 1932),[70] while for John Mundy, gossip columnist Dido Lament's party alludes to Bob Fosse's *Sweet Charity* (1969).[71] Behind it all, though, is an indigenous imperative: as Kim Newman remarked, the

Figure 5.5 'That's Motivation': Bowie does Busby Berkeley does Big Brother – *Absolute Beginners*

film's overindulgence is reminiscent of 'those opulent spectaculars put out by MGM (*Ziegfeld Follies*) or Warner Bros. (*Thank Your Lucky Stars*) to emphasise their greatness and, in a roundabout contributing-to-the-war-effort way, their patriotism'.[72] Here again, the British were coming.

Or so they desperately hoped. *Absolute Beginners* has been seen as failing because generically it fell between these two stools of 'emergent' MTV and the 'residual' Hollywood musical. That gap is bridged, however, if the film is understood as reworking its British pop music film heritage. Its casting, by appearance or association, takes in all four phases of the (sub-)genre. Patsy Kensit, frequently described as 'Bardot-like', is a 1980s Gillian Hills Beat Girl; Alan Freeman, a genial BBC disc jockey in *It's Trad, Dad!* is now the older, clueless TV trend spotter Call-Me-Cobber, a mix of Gilbert Harding and George Harrison's nemesis Simon; *Performance* provides both James Fox, now Henley of Mayfair, Dressmaker to the Queen and sugar daddy to Crepe Suzette, and the obligatory Johnny Shannon as bullying slum landlord Sartzsman; even *The Great Rock'n'Roll Swindle*'s Tenpole Tudor returns as Ed the Ted.

More precisely, in its return to the origins of UK rock'n'roll, *Absolute Beginners* is an historicised coffee bar musical: it is *Expresso Bongo* revisited. This is evident from Temple opening not with an MTV montage but a lengthy tracking shot along Old Compton Street: most reviewers' frames of reference made this 'a fully worthy homage to the opening shot of Orson Welles' *Touch of Evil*' (1958),[73] but its ambition, design and topography clearly replay the *tour de force* credit sequence to *Expresso Bongo*. Exploitative Harold Charms, a role based on Tommy Steele's manager Larry Parnes, is here seen through the prism of Laurence Harvey's (admittedly more virile) version as Johnny Jackson; Colin's television appearance with Call-Me-Cobber reworks *Cosmorama*'s investigation of the teenage phenomenon; even Maisie, Sylvia Syms, reappears 25 years older as Cynthia Eve. The film is criticised for a clash of tone, but it redeploys the twin tropes of the primitive phase that housed *Expresso Bongo*. Colin and Crepe are 'professional teenagers', incarnations of 'youth-as-fun' as they rise through the neon-lit sound-stage coffee bars, clubs and *haute couture* salons of London. This is juxtaposed with Colin's run-down Notting Hill neighbourhood, crawling with counter-examples of 'youth-as-trouble': Jess Conrad, Cliff's chain-wielding partner from *Serious Charge*, now plays the Cappuccino Kid; the discovery of the scheme to start a riot in the Napoli to facilitate redevelopment – for Kim Newman 'a conspiracy theory straight out of *Metropolis*'[74] – evokes the ends if not the means of David Farrar in *Beat Girl*. Temple's musical adaptation differs from *Expresso Bongo*, however, in dispensing with the source novel's 'New Wave' psychology and naturalism. Attempting instead a brash paean to a time when, as Charms' latest teen-idol Baby Boom sings 'You've Never Had it so Good', the past is recreated through an 'abstract expresso-ism', a scatter-gun soundtrack and a saturated mise-en-scène where every frame is overabundant (in Tashlin style The Director Can't Help It), as much a patchwork quilt fashion parade as an MTV musical compendium piece. This is the pop music film as postmodernism.

A pluralist concept roughly equating to 'all is permitted', postmodernism manifests itself through mannerism and stylisation, culling from existing objects/images and repeating or realigning them, erasing distinctions between high art and popular culture and imitating the past through pastiche – or ironising it through parody. For Fredric Jameson it was less a theoretical than a periodising concept firmly aligned to the 1980s and 1990s, its function 'to correlate the emergence of new formal features in culture with the emergence of a new type of social life and a new economic order'.[75] Taking issue with modernism's melorist belief in science and technology (cf. Harold Wilson in the 'mature' 1960s), postmodernism produced new artefacts within a new moment in capitalism, variously termed the post-industrial, consumer or media society. For Jean Baudrillard this was the society of spectacle, a society of recycling that, rather than producing the 'real', reproduced that which was already a reproduction, a simulation or the hyper-real. With no original invoked as a point of comparison, no distinction remained between the real and the copy.[76] Hence in *Absolute Beginners* the replacement of MacInnes' precisely observed musical references (Billie Holiday, Count Basie, modern against trad jazz, even Gilbert and Sullivan) with a mulch of ersatz eighties revival jazz rubbing up against Gil Evans' mambos and Slim Gaillard's be-bop; hence also the pastiche doo-wop of Bowie's title track. 'Authenticity' does not matter since nothing is 'real': the one musical example supposedly 'placed' in its era, Baby Boom's kiddy rock ballad, references instead a trend emerging in the early 1960s (see Helen Shapiro and Craig Douglas in *It's Trad, Dad!*).

Though postmodernism is retrospective, as Susan Hayward notes, 'in its lack of history (defined only in relation to the past), it rejects history, and because it has none of its own – only that of others – the postmodern stands eternally fixed in a series of presents'.[77] *Absolute Beginners'* lack of historical realism clearly disappointed contemporary critics like Marjorie Bilbow who bemoaned 'a prettied-up image of that lusty period of uncouth vitality which preceded the more self-conscious freedom of the so-called Swinging Sixties'.[78] For K.J. Donnelly, this return to the

1950s, bypassing the cultural heritage of the Beatles, 'pointedly parallels Margaret Thatcher's attempt at a renewal of Britain and desire to erase the effects of the 1960s, or at least her desire to blame the decade for the problems faced in the 1980s'.[79] The film thus remains judged as 'neutered' and ideologically conservative. However, I would argue that the 'uncouth vitality', the sixties liberation, plus punk's oppositional orientation, *are* all (eternally) present in *Absolute Beginners* – conveyed via its visual and auditory representational regimes.

The sixties are seen in the casting of matriarchs Sandie Shaw and, with a postmodern mischievousness, Profumo scandal ingénue Mandy Rice-Davies. They are heard – alongside Baby Boom – with Colin's put-upon father, played by the Kinks' Ray Davies. His number, singing about his desire for a 'Quiet Life' in his busy boarding house, is considered an achieved but 'detached' piece: 'It's one of the film's euphoric moments, but stylistically it belongs in another movie.'[80] Donnelly describes the song's elaborate 'Berkeley-referencing cut away family house set'[81] but the movie it belongs in is not a Hollywood spectacular, nor a rebuilt coffee bar musical, but rather its East End music-hall inflected 'bruvver' *What a Crazy World*, a film which Andy Medhurst placed 'in a tradition that has sought to avoid second-hand Americanisms in favour of a pop that addressed more pertinently English structures of feeling'.[82] This music-hall/pop hybrid idiom, if upstaged in the early 1960s by the screams ringing out from Merseyside, remained with groups like the Kinks and the Small Faces and would continue through to Ian Dury, Madness and Blur. Here the Kinks' style both matches Davies' character, a retread of Harry H. Corbett's irascible father figure from *What a Crazy World*, and suits the seaside-postcard slapstick scrambling all around him.

When discussing this space for 'a pop based on Englishness', Medhurst entered the necessary caveats about the term's 'nationalistic and ethnocentric connotations'[83] and *Absolute Beginners*' 'nostalgia' is tempered by recognition of the social tensions gripping 1958 as much as they were 1985. MacInnes loomed large over the primitive pop music film, specifically for his views on the new teenage preference for identification with a style and product, and though first-phase pop films exploited rather than investigated this phenomenon, its exploration arrived when *Privilege*'s concluding concert testified that, whether selling records, fruit or religious fascism, passive acceptance was the most dangerous aspect of youth culture. *Absolute Beginners* reaffirms the trope when Steven Berkoff, portraying a latter-day Oswald Mosley, puffs out his black-shirted chest to sing 'Give Me Your Hate'. His reductive slogans such as 'give me your hands to make us free' uncomfortably parallel

Steve Shorter's simplistic politics of love, while his postures evoke Pink's pop demagogy from *The Wall*. The tie-in *Beginners' Guide* justified the addition of the Fanatic by quoting from 'Pop Songs and Teenagers' (1962), where MacInnes noted that it would be 'possible to see, in the teenage neutralism and indifference to politics, and self-sufficiency, and instinct for enjoyment – in short their kind of happy mindlessness – the raw material for crypto-fascisms of the worst kind'.[84] Berkoff's number may simplify, but it does not skew – or 'prettify' – the novel's outlook. If initially the young just seem out for a good time, all the rest, the propaganda, works only too well and working-class Napoli buys into the seductive rhetoric of late-1950s neo-Nazism. The 'real' 1958 race riots, which MacInnes saw growing out of teenage anomie and restlessness, paradoxically demonstrated youth's attraction to conformity. As cool – not trad – jazz aficionado Dean Swift noted, 'These teenagers are ceasing to be rational, thinking human beings. They're turning into mindless butterflies all of the same size and colour, that have to flutter round exactly the same flowers, in exactly the same gardens.'[85] They also flutter the same across the decades: their heat-driven irrationality in *Absolute Beginners* places the National Front uprisings, less back in rainy 1958, but with Temple's punk-filming apprenticeship in the long hot summer of 1976 – and again, in a series of presents, with their topical mid-1980s Thatcherite revival.

The 'appropriateness' of this riotous ending also exemplifies postmodernism's openness to double – or contradictory – readings. If the race-riot conclusion is adjudged tonally disjointed from the film, it perhaps reanimates the source novel's problem. It could also be argued that its lack of credible 'rooting' in the film's hinterland repeats the video aesthetic that implies narrative rather than creates 'realist' causal connections; further still, the film could be argued to replicate the polysemic nature of MTV where the form's liberating physical pleasures ultimately render signification redundant. A counter-argument would contend that the consistent expressionistic camerawork in *Absolute Beginners* here fulfils the menace sensed throughout in Colin's world. An equivalent effect is created by the choreography: when characters perform kick steps against a backdrop of burning buildings, this does not trivialise the riots any more than *West Side Story* renders gang violence banal. Instead it *mediates* them. It does this explicitly through Call-Me-Cobber's running televised commentary of the riot: for James Hoberman, 'in keeping with the genially postmodern ambience, even this is shown being shown over tv'.[86] It also offers a formal mediation: when Colin's black friend Cool decides to drop the broken bottle and not slice the neck of the Wiz, the white racist who instigated the violence, Crepe Suzette applauds, just as she would a song or dance. All of life is a performance, the film cynically concludes, even as, aware of its teen-film obligations, it sends its titular couple off into each other's arms over a reprise of the title song.

Such a reading places postmodernist culture as ahistorical, signalling a sceptical end to ideology and allowing only form, not content, to fill the void. Without cultural, epistemological or historical divisions, postmodernism allows for no rebellion, certainly no rebel rock. All is reappropriated, but nothing new said, no fresh (subcultural) identity formulated. For instance, the Pet Shop Boys' narrative-free elongated promo *It Couldn't Happen Here* (Jack Bond, 1987) – working title *A Hard Day's Shopping* – so knowingly (and annoyingly) references *inter alia* *Catch Us If You Can* and *Magical Mystery Tour* (Adam Barker saw it as 'outtakes from the worst of Ken Russell'[87]) that Andy Medhurst (politely) terms it 'typically postmodern in the way it invites comparisons with and offers pastiches of other, older texts'.[88] The new musical discourse predicated by an MTV aesthetic was constantly discussed within these paradigms; it was adjudged as reproducing 'a kind of decentredness' and addressing anxieties created by a mediated capitalist society where 'all the traditional categories are being blurred and all institutions questioned – a characteristic of postmodernism'.[89] Indeed, by the mid-1980s the discursive alliance between pop and its media representation had also been adjudged to have eliminated the music's previous *raison d'être*, generational distinction. As well as targeting age groups before and after the traditional 'youth' market's 15 to 24 demographic, the ubiquity of the visual regime and musical commodity opened inter-generational access, selling everything from back-catalogues to blue jeans, to Goldcrest executives as much as to Crepe Suzettes. As John Mundy observes: '"Youth", as the subject of conflicting historical discourses in specific cultural formations, no longer existed, and the notion of an ideology of "rock", with its connotations of "authenticity" and "opposition", had become meaningless.'[90] Therefore, while a 1960s corporate 'construct' such as the Monkees had been severely criticised for their cynical exploitation of the Beatles' formula, a 1990s group such as the Spice Girls appealed largely *because of* their foregrounded artificiality, their openly constructed ordinariness.

The mature postmodern pop music film: *Spice World* (1997)

Three years after answering an advert in *The Stage* magazine, working up an image of 'Girl Power' and running with a cross-platform campaign

targeted at pre-teen girls that had made them globally the most successful girl group of all time, scoring six consecutive UK number one hits
and breaking the notoriously difficult US market, the Spice Girls starred
in their own musical vehicle *Spice World* (Bob Spiers, 1997). Produced
by PolyGram and shot over 43 days that summer with relatively low-
tech production values and a modest $25 million budget, the film was
programmed for mutual commercial exploitation with a new year world
tour and a pre-released soundtrack LP. *Spice World* the album, released in
November 1997, broke all records in shifting over seven million copies
in its first two weeks: final sales topped ten million. The accompanying film, which went on British general release on Boxing Day, made
over £11 million at the UK box office, $30 million in the US and $75
million worldwide. The film's enraptured prepubescent target audience
meant it was critic-proof, probably an advantage since knowing praise
was mixed with plentiful condemnation. Matthew Sweet thought it
'an uproarious pantomime of ironies' and 'one of the most intriguing
documents of post-modernity that film has yet produced, fusing the
recursively self-referential qualities of Fellini's *8½* with the disposable
peppiness of *Help!* And I say that without a hint of irony.'[91] An equally
unironic Roger Ebert opined that the Spice Girls 'occupy *Spice World* as
if they were watching it: they're so detached they can't even successfully
lip-synch their own songs'.[92] Supporting his view, the film was nominated for nine Golden Raspberry Awards, the girls 'winning' the award
for 'Worst Actresses'.

Both views, in postmodern style, can hold. The first major-studio pop-
group exploitation vehicle since the genre's 1960s heyday, *Spice World*
flaunts its knowing, ironic, 'postmodern' approach to its cinematic and
musical heritage as accompanying parents, unmoved by the Spice Girls'
cartoonish antics, could instead congratulate themselves on picking up
the myriad pop culture references. A backstage musical that replicates
the getting-to-the-concert-on-time plotline of *A Hard Day's Night* while
getting there in a *Summer Holiday* London double-decker bus, the film's
unbridled self-reflexivity allows it both to showcase Spice Girls and
their 17 songs in non-diegetic, ambient diegetic and lavish performance
modes, *and* to parody the nature of the pop packaging and media discourse that both/either fostered and/or followed their celebrity. Much
of the budget paid for the numerous cameo appearances, many with
pop music film baggage: alongside brief appearances by Elton John,
Bob Geldof and Bob Hoskins as themselves, Barry Humphries plays
the Australian newspaper tycoon who hires photojournalist Richard
O'Brien to sabotage the girls' gig, while Roger Moore phones in his

part as the sinister Chief, a Blofeld Bond villain parody reminiscent of *Help!* While much of the remaining casting and intertextual referencing has a hermetic British slant (Jonathan Ross and jokes on Gary Barlow), the mise-en-scène consistently taps into an exportable Cool Britannia packaging with a theme-park presentation of London's landmarks and Union Jacks all over the girls' bus and Geri's bust.

Spice World's main commercial purpose is to showcase the Spice Girls in performance, and this physical pleasure is regularly repeated, from their opening appearance on *Top of the Pops*, through rehearsals and a quick concert in Milan on to their Albert Hall finale. Nonetheless, in (British) self-deprecating mode, the film addresses public concerns on whether the girls really can sing outside of a studio setting ('that was absolutely perfect, without being actually any good' their director tells them); whether the dancing on their videos is up to scratch (military dance-master Michael Barrymore tears apart their choreography); and – bravely – whether they are already last year's model (the Murdoch-style subplot confronting the build-them-up-knock-them-down attitude of the tabloids). *Spice World* similarly plays with its own 'reality': Alan Cumming is a pretentious, accident-prone filmmaker looking to get beyond the 'well-oiled global machine' and make a documentary on the 'real' Posh, Sporty, Ginger, Baby and Scary; their road manager (Richard E. Grant) meets with an American film producer (George Wendt) whose fantastical scenarios for the group – ranging from sci-fi and *Charlie's Angels* to Jackie Kennedy and Mods – are all briefly visualised. Add in the film's ending where the Girls prepare to shoot a scene from a new more 'realistic' pitch that is clearly *Spice World* and the resultant 'decentred' narrative denies an (adult) acceptance of the diegetic world created by the narrative.

Nonetheless, *Spice World* wants it both ways and, playing with its pseudo-biographic format, presents a demo version of 'Wannabe', the Spice Girls' first single/number one, by means of the flashback technique. Fixing on their performance 'a very long time ago' for café proprietor Brian, both setting and function parallel *The Tommy Steele Story* as, though now given a collective, female and introspective focus, the flashback's 'naturalising processes' again create an authenticating subjective truth.[93] Coming when the pressures of their schedule force the group to walk out of a rehearsal and away from each other, the film's flashback scene, as noted by Elizabeth Eva Leach, 'at once projects a natural (authentic) coming together for the Spice Girls through growing up together, and facilitates the fantasy, predicated on inauthenticity, which allows a group of ordinary girls to enjoy fame'.[94] This is again, 'in reality', pure fiction, but the film's polysemy allows different audience groupings to construct the 'reality' they require: here the 'younger' Spice Girls' use of substitute microphones – sauce bottles and sugar cellars – and their freestyle dancing replicate how the vast majority of their audience would have responded to the song at the time of its release, making the Girls the celluloid embodiment of that cinema audience's subjectivity.

Such binary/Byzantine self-reflexivity impacts more widely on character and performance. Early in the film the girls dress as each other at a photo shoot (Figure 5.6). For Cynthia Fuchs the scene 'emphasises the plasticity and transience of identity, the potential for perpetual transformation and self-recreation allowed by faith in the tenets of "Spice World"'.[95] However, the shoot concludes with a quick reversion to type, and later scenes 'naturalise' each Girl's emblematic quality (even Geri's feisty 'Gingerness'). This process is aided by the overplayed star parodies surrounding them and awards for bad acting could thus be interpreted as confirmation of the Girls' core 'reality'. This raises a potential problem with Mel B (Melanie Brown)'s 'Scariness' – though one allowing another of postmodernism's simultaneous readings, here of accepting but also amending 'stereotypical' presentations. The film maintains Scary Spice's arguably racist identity construct with her 'jungle' animal-print costumes, 'wild' hair and frequently displayed tongue piercing, but performances suggest a healthy 'colour blindness' amongst the

Figure 5.6 Photo pomo: Sporty as Posh as Baby as Scary as Ginger as Sporty – *Spice World*

group itself, its entourage and especially its young fan base, refuting accusations that Scary's participation as a Spice Girl is cynically 'token'. All of which is, of course, both true and not true.

Spice World, a one-off generic revival by a group matching the Beatles for popularity, may be seen as a poor woman's *A Hard Day's Night* but it is, finally, the film that Malcolm McLaren dearly wanted to make. Postmodern pop allows for ubiquitous a-ethical exploitation and, as Mark Sinker noted, 'the main running gags second-guess so much of the recent "bad" publicity (ructions with management, tabloid claims that the bubble's burst) that you catch yourself believing that maybe every element in the backlash was generated by and scripted at Spice Central Control'.[96] While film journals and broadsheets rushed to revere *Spice World*'s ludic autotely, one can nonetheless understand the tabloid vitriol: not only did the film diegetically present them as idiots, its prescience demonstrated how even the professional cynic could be fully media manipulated – and then exposed. Add in the soundbite promises of 'Girl Power' that its majority audience would soon realise were empty rhetoric and, as Johnny Rotten said on leaving the Sex Pistols, did you ever get the feeling you've been cheated?

Alternatives for the new millennium

Spice World was produced by the Spice Girls' early manager Simon Fuller. He repeated the tactic, with much diminished box-office results, in the epigonic *Seeing Double* (Nigel Dick, 2003), 'starring' the similarly con-structed S Club. Another sub-Lesteroid race-against-time movie, *Seeing Double* adds in ontological uncertainty as the tired 'guys' are replaced by compliant clones, a plot twist termed by Wally Hammond 'a neat junior league po-mo conceit'.[97] A Fuller 'family tree' of cloning can be traced from S Club, more successful in its various Monkees-style televi-sion manifestations, through to recent teen-oriented music shows such as *High School Musical* and *Glee*. It also led Fuller to world domination through the *Pop Idol* franchise, a televised 'reality' talent-show format that replicates exhibiting the 'rags-to-riches' processes of stardom previ-ously adumbrated in the pop music biopic.

A second cross-media strand has seen the cinematic release of theatri-cally successful 'jukebox musicals'. Initially a term for pop music films *tout court* (as in Andrew Sarris' *Citizen Kane* encomium to *A Hard Day's Night*), a jukebox musical currently signifies the contextualising of a pop artist's songs into a dramatic plot. The $2 billion international stage suc-cess of *Mamma Mia!*, written by British playwright Catherine Johnson and employing the music of ABBA, motivated a film release in 2008.

Directed by Phyllida Lloyd, *Mamma Mia! The Movie* received decidedly mixed reviews – ranging from 'cute, clean, camp fun'[98] to a 'shit' and 'soulless panto'[99] – yet it quickly became the most commercially successful British movie ever, both at home with a gross of £67 million and worldwide where box-office returns reached $600 million. After a history of the British musical's aesthetic, ideological and economic subordination to Hollywood models, these takings also made *Mamma Mia!* the highest-ever-grossing film musical worldwide – before it became Britain's bestselling DVD ever with over five million bought. It strikes as an unparalleled British cinematic success story – but as a pop music film it is devoid of British pop stars (Pierce Brosnan's singing did not launch an Anthony Newley-style parallel career) and features a Swedish group's soundtrack; it also has an American lead in Meryl Streep and (as so often) American Universal's financing. Whichever winner takes it all, it is not the UK.[100]

Several jukebox musicals placed an artist's back-catalogue in a biographical and performance-mode context – 2005 saw *Jersey Boys* (excellent) and *Lennon* (bad) – and this provides a third strand for the historical British pop music film, a return to generic origins with the star biopic. Much as the filmmaking generation of the 1970s had revisited their rock'n'roll youth – Claude Whatham would unwisely replay his David Essex diptych in present-day Slough with *Buddy's Song* (1990) where Roger Daltrey's superannuated Ted (good) tries to promote the pop talents of son Chesney Hawkes (awful) – so the millennium generation adhered to the 20-year rule of revivalism, mostly to depict the careers of post-punk and new wave musicians. Pop biopics had appeared intermittently, notably exploiting the Beatles' apprenticeship in *Birth of the Beatles* (Richard Marquand, 1979), *The Hours and Times* (Christopher Munch, 1991) and *Backbeat* (Iain Softley, 1993) through to *Nowhere Boy* (Sam Taylor-Wood, 2009). Now, after Alex Cox's flamboyant outrider *Sid and Nancy* (1986) came a new wave of pop music nostalgia films, back-catalogue biopics that form part of what Simon Reynolds has identified as an age of 'retromania' where the increased accessibility of music creates a poverty of abundance: 'Instead of being about itself, the 2000s has been about every other previous decade happening again all at once: a simultaneity of pop time that abolishes history while nibbling away at the present's own sense of itself as an era with a distinct identity and feel.'[101]

Contrasting approaches to this ahistorical biopic can be seen from film treatments of Manchester post-punk band Joy Division. They feature in Michael Winterbottom's *24 Hour Party People* (2002), a faux-drama-doc/bricolaged biopic shot on digital video and centred on record producer Tony Wilson and the rise and fall of his Factory Records empire. This first (and best) new millennium pop biopic is the most explicitly postmodern, commenting on its own appropriation of the past through relentless self-reflexivity. As with *The Great Rock'n'Roll Swindle*, Winterbottom works to contextualise the music scene, intercutting news links, documentary footage – including the Sex Pistols at the Manchester Free Trade Hall, Wilson's Damascene moment – and interviews with performers. However, this is problematised as the film foregrounds the interrogation of its own performance, its deconstructing of the myth-making process a self-reflexive critiquing of the new 'pop nostalgia' industry to which it contributes. When Wilson (Steve Coogan) complains that 'I'm a minor character in my own story' it echoes back to John Lennon on the set of *Help!* Lest anyone miss the point, he points out that he is 'being postmodern, before it's fashionable'.

Control (2007) narrows the focus to the story of Joy Division's lead-singer Ian Curtis from meeting his future wife Deborah (on whose memoir the film is based) up to his suicide in 1980. It was directed by Dutch photographer Anton Corbijn, whose 1979 photos of the trench-coated group members had helped to establish their (fascist/collectivist connoting) image and mythology: thus, rather than contextualising, Corbijn here works to re-create his own previous imagery. Though shot in extreme high-contrast black-and-white Cinemascope, John Orr favours a comparison with a Bressonian cinema of 'concrete abstractions', dealing with the physiology before the psychology of existence.[102] Such a reading may be applicable to the band's musical style, which simply appears fully formed, without any examination of the processes of its sonic development. However, *Control* is visually more 'obviously' a 1960s New Wave pastiche, and it replays the misogynistic narrative drive of much of that cinema – and earlier pop 'biopics' like *That'll Be the Day* – as Curtis (Sam Riley) seeks to escape less from his class environment than from 'feminine' domesticity, his wife and daughter functioning primarily as obstacles to the male freedoms offered by a band on the road. In contrast to Winterbottom, and more comparable to Mat Whitecross' music-hall-inflected treatment of proto-punk 'geezer' Ian Dury in *Sex & Drugs & Rock & Roll* (2010), the film roots and 'explains' the music in the tortured genius of the artist and not in any socio-historical specificities. In *Control* the liberating 'masculine' music is depicted via a highly skilled recreation of Joy Division performing live,

their on-stage numbers re-recorded and Riley precisely impersonat-
ing Curtis' stage moves – notably his infamous 'epileptic dance'.
By contrast, the film's most stilted performance is the careful but
mimed representation of the 'Love Will Tear Us Apart' video. As Noel
McLaughlin has discussed, this powerful rearticulation of the band's
original power on-stage complicates issues of musical authenticity
and 'presents a partial challenge to the notion of performative origi-
nality'.[103] It again fits the pop biopic into a postmodern aesthetic,
eliding distinctions between the real and the reproduction as we (un)
happily sing along to the minimalist simulacra.

These star biographies are either disparately raucous or reductively
psychological, but both result in a postmodern skein of competing
discourses as resistant to a utopian project as the bullet in the brain
of *Performance*. What of the pop music film with a clear social intent,
focused back on the music's consumers? Cultural commentators
bemoaned the lack of musical responses to the Occupy London activists and summer riots of 2011, but a saving exception was found in hip
hop artist/soul singer Plan B, aka Ben Drew, whose widely hailed 'Ill
Manors' – for Dorian Lynskey 'the first great mainstream protest song
in years'[104] – explored the causes and consequences of the riots, and
offered a voice for the urban disenfranchised, demonised as 'council
estate kids – scum of the earth'. Plan B had called his previous albums
'films for the blind'[105] and made this song of teenage alienation –
which (unironically) referenced estate kids as 'just another brick in
the wall' – the basis of his feature-film directing and writing debut
Ill Manors (2012). Shot with a cast of largely untrained local actors,
the film was produced for roughly £100,000 (half funded by Drew)
under the auspices of the Film London/BBC Microwave scheme and
distributed by Revolver Entertainment. The punning title references
the sink estates of London's Forest Gate and the aggressive attitude of
its blighted residents, while the film itself tells six interlinked stories
of the estate's pervasive gang-culture, with Drew off-screen rapping
each new character's backstory over busy montage sequences, spliced
together from cameraphone and CCTV footage. *Ill Manors'* heritage
of dissent, its desire to counter the jingoism of the 2012 'Jubilympics'
much as punk had punctured the Silver Jubilee back in 1977, is displayed by the presence of Mancunian punk poet John Cooper Clarke,
reading his work in the East End pub where the intersecting narratives finally conflagrate. While taking close to £500,000 at the UK
box office, *Ill Manors* was intended as a rebooted exploration of the
'youth-as-trouble' trope rather than its exploitation, and not least of

its achievements was the rekindling of long-lost generational discord: Cooper Clarke's plea to 'Pity the plight of young fellows' was not met by the right-wing press' Christopher Tookey for whom Drew had made 'a film so awful he should now be contemplating Plan C',[106] nor by Tim Riley for whom '*Ill Manors* is hard-hitting in all the worst ways, like being repeatedly thumped by a randomly furious street hawker'.[107] The film received its share of positive press reviews, though many felt its early dynamism dissipated until, for Peter Bradshaw, 'it turns out to be disappointingly and determinedly apolitical'.[108] The title track, in hypothesising that 'politics, ain't it all smoke and mirrors?', illustrated the lack of interest shown by many young people in political solutions, while simultaneously engaging in a powerful polemic. The film does not retain that commentary on social disorder as the evidence of its cinematic influences creates a 'critical' distance to replace the song's creative duality. *Ill Manors* begins with television footage that alludes to the riots and the finale reworks a news photo of burning buildings, but in between it displays most fully the narrative influence of Nicolas Winding Refn's 1996 *Pusher* trilogy. The fledgling director also draws on Quentin Tarantino's template from *Pulp Fiction* (1994) for *Ill Manors'* multi-narrative strands and temporal trickery, but whereas Tarantino often seems in thrall to the criminal ethic, *Ill Manors*, like Revolver stablemate *Adulthood* (Noel Clarke, 2008) in which Drew appeared, strives to explain if not exculpate its young characters as victims of an environment that creates the conditions for inevitable violence. While *Ill Manors* may dilute the title song's impact – for Matthew Taylor 'one suspects that Drew has said more on record in five minutes than he has in nearly two hours here'[109] – the generically innovative choric rap soundtrack binds together what otherwise remains an atomised set of stories: as Anna Smith notes, this both gives the film 'a hip-hop musical feel' and 'makes it easier to accept the contrived coincidences and melodramatic staging'.[110]

Thus, in the early years of a new decade, the pop music film, endlessly recycling its generic tropes, finds itself reworking the dichotomy of its first phase 'coffee bar films'. The majority are impersonated biopics that focus on the creation of celebrity, though favouring the biographical imperative before an economic/industrial examination; Plan B has revived the social (melo)drama with added musical numbers (absent for 30 years), exploring environment and ideology, and focusing on the (perceived) practices of criminality. If a pattern emerged from those 1950s pop film vehicles, this study contends that it was not so much of rebellion instantly tamed, but of 'delayed disruption': the initial foregrounding of a contained world of teenagers with 'clean' pop star aspirations ceding only later to a confrontational world of teenagers with more insidious, socially delinquent motivations, as in *Serious Charge* and *Beat Girl*. The genre quickly reasserted its unifying power in the Cliff Richard Technicolor musicals, but those confrontations would return, through *Privilege* and punk and *Pink Floyd: The Wall*. 'Rebel Rock' has found a new questioning voice for a new generation in the debut work of Plan B.

6
Conclusion: Music Matters

An affective genre

This book has undertaken a comprehensive genre study, examining the complete life-cycle of the British pop music film, plus its ensuing sporadic twitches of reanimation. The approach has been both historicist and formalist, since genre is a two-faced entity, its internal elements inseparable from historical processes, and it has worked to foreground its selected films as both culturally and cinematically important. Often essentially opportunistic, exploitative ventures, the British pop music film has frequently undercut the hegemonic formal invisibility and exposed the ideological meanings embodied by such conventions. A 'coming-of-age' genre concerning young people and new musical forms, the British pop music film is shown to be heavily negotiated, doubly defining the relation of a 'minor' to 'parental' culture. This can be seen as both formal, working with and against the omnipresent models of the American musical, and technological, fighting the upstart medium of television until it usurped the pop music film's primary financial function. Using the genre to explore social history, this study reveals a further, recurring duality which, especially at times of profound social change, saw its principal players, the young, both celebrated as the harbingers of an exciting and prosperous future and, from Margaret Hinxman with *Beat Girl* to Christopher Tookey with *Ill Manors*, condemned as exemplifying a new moral and cultural bankruptcy.

Within the historiography of British cinema, the book contributes a further, revisionist exploration of what Julian Petley once termed its 'lost continent'. Employing and extrapolating the tripartite structure of a generic life-cycle to the British pop music film, it shows a lively opening 'primitive' phase before its articulate 'maturity' held the twin youth tropes in equilibrium before merging them in its politicised, polemical 'decadence'. Thereafter the genre staggered on, briefly reviving with new subcultural movements or technological platforms, hitting occasional aesthetic or commercial highs, but always lacking a sustained ideological or financial momentum. The later film works of the Beatles, Rolling Stones and punk have received prior critical attention from both auteurist and generic approaches, but less so the 'primitive' cinematic efforts of Gerard Bryant and Terry Dene. The chronological duration of that first phase of pop music film, running parallel to the privileged category of social realist cinema, allows the reappraisal of a set of generic texts marginalised or omitted from academic study, seemingly for their explicit commercial intentions: there was, to put it bluntly, more to the period than the British New Wave. Chronology, though, is a permeable container: here, as later, 'residual' and 'emergent' paradigms co-exist as issues of identity, autonomy and difference are played out in storylines, soundtracks and generic structure.

Central to these films' generic identity, indeed to their very existence, is the capital importance of their headlining pop performers. Alongside the varying degrees of success in developing synergistic cross-media alliances with the wider 'family' of the entertainment industry, this study shows how the pop star also signifies, at times contradictorily or, particularly in gender depictions, unwittingly, as a condenser of social and ideological values. Whether portraying a clean-living Variety artist in the making, a Swinging Sixties icon or an advocate of Girl Power, or else a leather-jacketed pseudo Teddy boy, a fascist demagogue or a spokesman for council-estate hoodies, the pop star vehicle allows re-presentations of issues as broad as urban development, educational philosophy, gender fixity and subcultural affiliations. Nonetheless, while these films merit and sustain intense textual and contextual analysis, with narrative and direction yielding both social and cinematic discovery, their defining feature must ultimately reside in the presence of these 'authentic' (extra-diegetically existent) singers on-screen, the placing of an element of fact amongst the fiction making, since *music* is at their heart and, however manipulated from its origins, a music that matters because it remains a genuine expression of a desire to change, to transcend existing cultural modes – if only through the ecstasy of rhythm.

At the genre's outset changing demographics and economics created a distinctive cultural space where young people could, to an unprecedented degree, locate a sense of their own identity and power. For cultural theorist Lawrence Grossberg this commitment to musical expression is explained through the idea of 'authenticity'. Firstly, there is the way the valued music articulates 'private but common desires, feelings and experiences into a shared public language' thus constructing or expressing that enduring utopian concept of a 'community'. Secondly, authenticity is located in the 'construction of a rhythmic and sexual body' – a particular and perennial concern to parental society.[1] Grossberg's work is valuable in offering an account of how certain forms of music matter to us – through the production of *affect* – and how we try to legitimate such affects via rational argument. This book attempts such a balancing act for music's cinematic manifestations. 'Brit beat', prog rock, punk and hip hop have all created visceral and critical responses in Britain: as a music of and aimed at a particular age and social group, all have signified a challenge to the bourgeois hegemony, and all have been allowed a negotiated cinematic treatment.

Like so much pop product of the past 40 years, let us return to origins, back to the Soho coffee bar where reporter Pat O'Brien bought his child's safety while Tommy Steele advocated filial ingratitude. Perhaps more than any subsequent musical movement, the arrival of rock'n'roll offers this *foundational* myth, and the first exponents of the new music are 'captured' in Britain's earliest pop music films working at a culture in need of and, however formally contained, enjoying the first sights and sounds of liberation. This (admittedly retrospective) *symbolic* importance has been pragmatically recognised since, with the wiping of so much early television fare, the musical performances contained in the first British pop music films are now valued for providing a record of an important contribution to a strand of popular *musical* culture no longer seen as valueless, and the celluloid preservations of these 1950s artists, pioneers, pastichers or parodists, have been extracted for television documentaries and 'democratised' on file-sharing sites such as YouTube. This study contends that the films in which these musical performances are embedded, long considered of minimal cultural worth, are themselves important sites of cultural negotiation and historical record. They and their own 'offspring', developing from their first uncertain steps to the sophisticated intertexuality of their postmodern afterlife, merit not only conservation or academic consideration, but also celebration.

Notes

1 Introduction

1. Anonymous, 'Tommy Steele for Anglo Rock'n'Roll Film', *Kinematograph Weekly*, 24 January 1957.
2. It is merely listed amongst 'nineteen support films' in Peter Hutchings' monograph, *Terence Fisher* (Manchester University Press, 2002), p. 57.
3. 'While the use of the word "popular" in relation to the lighter forms of music goes back to the mid-19th century, the abbreviation "pop" was not in use as a generic term until the 1950s when it was adopted as the umbrella name for a special kind of musical product aimed at a teenage market.' Peter Gammond, *The Oxford Companion to Popular Music* (Oxford University Press, 1991), p. 457.
4. Arthur Marwick, *The Sixties: Cultural Revolution in Britain, France, Italy and the United States, c. 1958–1974* (Oxford University Press, 1998), p. 7.
5. Arthur Marwick, *British Society since 1945*, 4th edn (Harmondsworth: Penguin, 2003), p. 13.
6. Ibid., pp. 131–2.
7. Dick Hebdige, *Hiding in the Light: On Images and Things* (London: Routledge, 1988), p. 19.
8. Christine Gledhill, 'Genre', in Pam Cook (ed.), *The Cinema Book*, 3rd edn (London: British Film Institute, 2008), pp. 254, 259.
9. The book will not treat (those rare) British productions or co-productions where the star is not British, such as Frank Zappa's *200 Motels* (Frank Zappa, Tony Palmer, 1971), nor (those numerous) films where British pop artists make brief cameo appearances but do not star, such as the Searchers in *Saturday Night Out* (Robert Hartford-Davis, 1963).
10. Eric Barnouw, *Documentary: History of the Non-Fiction Film*, 2nd edn (Oxford University Press, 1993), pp. 231–53; Michael Renov (ed.), *Theorising Documentary* (London: Routledge, 1993), pp. 37–57. For studies of the 'rockumentary', see Jonathan Romney and Adrian Wootton (eds), *Celluloid Jukebox: Popular Music and the Movies since the 50s* (London: British Film Institute, 1995), pp. 82–105; Thomas F. Cohen, *Playing to the Camera: Musicians and Musical Performance in Documentary Cinema* (London: Wallflower, 2012).
11. Romney and Wootton, *Celluloid Jukebox*, p. 7.
12. André Bazin, *What Is Cinema, Vol. 2* (Berkeley: University of California Press, 2005); Robert Warshow, *The Immediate Experience: Movies, Comics, Theatre and Other Aspects of Popular Culture* (Cambridge, MA: Harvard University Press, 2002). While Bazin accesses a very limited archive, Warshow deduces generic shape from a reading of just three films.
13. Barry Langford, *Film Genre: Hollywood and Beyond* (Edinburgh University Press, 2005), p. 135.
14. For informative surveys of 'the king' on celluloid, see Eric Braun, *The Elvis Film Encyclopedia* (London: Batsford, 1997) and Douglas Brode, *Elvis, Cinema and Popular Culture* (New York: McFarland, 2006).

15. Steve Neale, *Genre and Hollywood* (London: Routledge, 1999), p. 51.
16. Andrew Caine, *Interpreting Rock Movies: The Pop Film and its Critics in Britain* (Manchester University Press, 2004), p. 8.
17. Rick Altman, *Film / Genre* (London: British Film Institute, 1999), p. 14.
18. Steve Neale, *Genre* (London: British Film Institute, 1980), p. 19.
19. Gregory Lukow and Steven Ricci, 'The "Audience" goes "Public": Inter-Textuality, Genre and the Responsibilities of Film Literacy', *On Film*, 12, 1984, pp. 29–36.
20. Susan Hayward, *Key Concepts in Cinema Studies* (London: Routledge, 1996), p. 160.
21. Caine, *Interpreting Rock Movies*, pp. 15–33.
22. Ibid., p. 8.
23. Franco Moretti, *Graphs, Maps, Trees: Abstract Models for a Literary Theory* (London: Verso, 2005), p. 14.
24. Andrew Dix, *Beginning Film Studies* (Manchester University Press, 2008), p. 178.
25. Ibid.
26. David Buckingham, *Children Talking Television: The Making of Television Literacy* (London: Falmer Press, 1993), p. 137.
27. Thomas Schatz, *Hollywood Genres: Formulas, Filmmaking and the Studio System* (New York: Random House, 1981).
28. Richard Dyer, *The Movie*, no. 75 (1981), p. 1484.
29. Jane Feuer, *The Hollywood Musical* (London: Macmillan, 1982), p. 88.
30. John G. Cawelti, '*Chinatown* and Generic Transformation in Recent American Films', in Barry Keith Grant (ed.), *Film Genre Reader* (Austin: University of Texas Press, 1986), p. 200.
31. Brian Taves, *The Romance of Adventure: The Genre of Historical Adventure Movies* (Jackson: Mississippi University Press, 1993), p. 22.
32. Dyer, *The Movie*, p. 1484.
33. James Leggott, 'Nothing to Do Around Here: British Realist Cinema in the 1970s', in Robert Shail (ed.), *Seventies British Cinema* (London: Palgrave Macmillan, 2008), p. 98.
34. Terry Threadgold, 'Talking about Genre: Ideologies and Incompatible Discourses', *Cultural Studies*, vol. 3, no. 1, January 1989, p. 109.
35. John Fiske, *Television Culture* (London: Routledge, 1987), p. 110.
36. Will Wright, *Six Guns and Society: A Structural Study of the Western* (Berkeley: University of California Press, 1975).
37. Tim O'Sullivan et al., *Key Concepts in Communication* (London: Methuen, 1983), p. 128.
38. Hayward, *Key Concepts in Cinema Studies*, p. 161.
39. Neale, *Genre*, p. 62.
40. Hayward, *Key Concepts in Cinema Studies*, p. 165.
41. Christine Gledhill (ed.), *Stardom: The Industry of Desire* (London: Routledge, 1991), p. 215.
42. Margaret Hinxman, *Daily Herald*, 29 October 1960.
43. Additional Beatles' histories include Bill Harry's illustrated filmography, *Beatlemania: The History of the Beatles on Film* (London: Virgin, 1984) and Edward Gross' anecdotal *The Fab Films of the Beatles* (Las Vegas: Pioneer Books, 1990). Even Bob Neaverson's academic study *The Beatles Movies* (London: Cassell, 1997) is predominantly contextual and 'leaves plenty of

room for further analysis and debate'. Rowana Agajanian, 'Nothing Like any Previous Musical, British or American', in Anthony Aldgate et al. (eds), *Windows on the Sixties* (London: I.B. Tauris, 2000), p. 110.

44. See also Fred Dellar, *NME Guide to Rock Cinema* (London: Hamlyn, 1981) and David Ehrenstein and Bill Reed, *Rock on Film* (London: Virgin, 1982).

45. Danny Graydon, *Empire*, no. 150, December 2001, p. 164.

46. Julian Petley, 'The Lost Continent', in Charles Barr (ed.), *All Our Yesterdays: 90 Years of British Cinema* (London: British Film Institute, 1986), p. 98. For the transformation from 'scarcity to abundance', see Alan Lovell, 'The British Cinema: The Known Cinema', in Robert Murphy (ed.), *The British Cinema Book*, 2nd edn (London: British Film Institute, 2002), p. 200.

47. One could cite *inter alia* Pam Cook (ed.), *Gainsborough Pictures* (London: Cassell, 1997); Steve Chibnall and Robert Murphy (eds), *British Crime Cinema* (London: Routledge, 1999); I.Q. Hunter (ed.), *British Science Fiction Cinema* (London: Routledge, 1999); Steve Chibnall and Julian Petley (eds), *British Horror Cinema* (London: Routledge, 2001); I.Q. Hunter and Laraine Porter (eds), *British Comedy Cinema* (London: Routledge, 2012). Peter Hutchings' ground-breaking *Hammer and Beyond: The British Horror Film* (Manchester University Press, 1993) influences the subtitle of this study.

48. John Mundy, *The British Musical Film* (Manchester University Press, 2007), p. 9.

49. Steve Chibnall, Review of K.J. Donnelly and John Mundy, *Music, Sound and the Moving Image*, vol. 3, no. 2, 2009, p. 256.

2   The Primitive Pop Music Film

1. Fred Dellar, *NME Guide to Rock Cinema* (London: Hamlyn, 1981), p. 10; David Ehrenstein and Bill Reed, *Rock on Film* (London: Virgin, 1982), p. 14.

2. Sue Harper and Vincent Porter, *British Cinema of the 1950s: The Decline of Deference* (Oxford University Press, 2003), p. 1.

3. Jeffrey Richards, 'New Waves and Old Myths: British Cinema in the Sixties', in B. Moore-Gilbert and J. Seed (eds), *Cultural Revolution? The Challenge of the Arts in the 1960s* (London: Routledge, 1992), p. 218.

4. Anthony Bicat, 'Fifties Children: Sixties People', in V. Bogdanor and R. Skidelsky (eds), *The Age of Affluence 1951–1964* (London: Macmillan, 1970), p. 324.

5. Nik Cohn, *AwopBopALooBopAWopBamBoom: Pop from the Beginning* (London: Weidenfeld and Nicolson, 1969), p. 21.

6. Anonymous, *Kinematograph Weekly*, 23 May 1957. 'B' features rarely figured in the national press and there are no extant reviews in the BFI archive.

7. Matthew Sweet, *British B-movies: Truly Madly Cheaply*, BBC4, broadcast 21 June 2008.

8. George Melly, *Revolt into Style* (Harmondsworth: Penguin, 1972), p. 4.

9. Trevor Philpott, 'Bermondsey Miracle', *Picture Post*, 25 February 1957.

10. Anonymous, *Sunday Times*, 9 July 1957.

11. David Robinson, *Sight and Sound*, vol. 27, no. 1, Summer 1957, p. 43.

12. Harper and Porter, *British Cinema of the 1950s*, p. 308.

13. For the 'real' story of Steele's apprenticeship, see Pete Frame, *The Restless Generation: How Rock Music Changed the Face of 1950s Britain* (London: Rogan

House, 2007), pp. 138–50; Vickie Holt, 'Tommy Steele: Before the Invasion', *Blue Suede News*, vol. 69, Winter 2004, pp. 5–9.

14. Melly, *Revolt into Style*, p. 39.
15. Ibid., p. 47.
16. Colin MacInnes, 'Pop Songs and Teenagers', *The Twentieth Century*, February 1958, reprinted in Hanif Kureishi and Jon Savage (eds), *The Faber Book of Pop* (London: Faber and Faber, 1995), p. 85.
17. Press release of Anglo-Amalgamated Film Distributors Ltd – BFI microfiche.
18. Maureen Turim, *Flashbacks in Film: Memory and History* (London: Routledge, 1989), p. 17.
19. Susan Hayward, *Key Concepts in Cinema Studies* (London: Routledge, 1996), p. 124.
20. Turim, *Flashbacks in Film*, p. 17.
21. Melly, *Revolt into Style*, p. 48; Andrew Caine, *Interpreting Rock Movies: The Pop Film and its Critics in Britain* (Manchester University Press, 2004), p. 115.
22. Richard Dyer, *Stars* (London: British Film Institute, 1980), p. 35.
23. Advertisement, *Kinematograph Weekly*, 23 May 1957, p. 12.
24. Caine, *Interpreting Rock Movies*, p. 122.
25. MacInnes, 'Pop Songs and Teenagers', p. 89.
26. Harper and Porter, *British Cinema of the 1950s*, p. 192.
27. Turim, *Flashbacks in Film*, p. 171.
28. Philpott, 'Bermondsey Miracle', p. 66. Steele himself recalled how, in his first Variety performance, at the Sunderland Empire, 'a mass scream started in the darkness of the auditorium and rolled over the footlights towards me like a giant killer wave'. Tommy Steele, *Bermondsey Boy* (London: Michael Joseph, 2006), p. 253.
29. Jane Feuer, *The Hollywood Musical* (London: Macmillan, 1982), p. 27.
30. See Charlie Gillett, *The Sound of the City* (London: Sphere, 1971), pp. 25–6.
31. David Bordwell and Kristin Thompson, *Film Art: An Introduction*, 4th edn (New York: McGraw Hill, 1993), p. 159.
32. This reading predicts Steele's own feelings two years later: 'How many records had I sold today and how many would I sell tomorrow? I didn't want the mathematics of pop. I wanted the majesty of the theatre and I wanted the thrill of it forever.' Steele, *Bermondsey Boy*, p. 305.
33. Colin MacCabe, *Performance* (London: British Film Institute, 1998), pp. 78, 24.
34. *Kinematograph Weekly*, 19 September 1957. For a fuller treatment of Dene's career, see Frame, *The Restless Generation*, pp. 258–67.
35. Donald Zec, *Daily Mirror*, 14 March 1958.
36. Nina Hibbin, *Daily Worker*, 15 March 1958.
37. Sue Harper, *Women in British Cinema* (London: Continuum, 2000), p. 81.
38. Frank Jackson, *Reynolds News*, 16 March 1958.
39. Feuer, *The Hollywood Musical*, p. 45.
40. Jon Savage, 'The Simple Things You See Are All Complicated', in Kureishi and Savage (eds), *The Faber Book of Pop*, p. xxiii.
41. Colin Larkin (ed.), *Encyclopedia of Stage and Film Musicals* (London: Virgin, 1999), p. 198.
42. For full changes, see Ian Bevan and Kurt Ganzl, *The British Musical Theatre, Vol. II: 1915–1984* (London: Palgrave Macmillan, 1986), pp. 715–19.

43. Val Guest, *So You Want to Be in Pictures* (London: Reynolds and Hearn, 2001), p. 136.
44. Ibid.
45. Josh Billings, *Kinematograph Weekly*, 28 January 1960.
46. William Whitebait, *New Statesman*, 5 December 1959.
47. Paul Dehn, *News Chronicle*, 27 November 1959.
48. Hollis Albert, *Saturday Review*, 12 March 1960.
49. David Robinson, *The Times*, 30 November 1959.
50. Fred Majdalany, *Daily Mail*, 27 November 1959.
51. Isabel Quigly, *Spectator*, 4 December 1959.
52. Ben Thompson, 'Pop and Film: The Charisma Crossover', in Jonathan Romney and Adrian Wootton (eds), *Celluloid Jukebox: Popular Music and the Movies since the 50s* (London: British Film Institute, 1995), p. 40.
53. Geoff Brown in John Pym (ed.), *Time Out Film Guide 17* (London: Time Out Guides, 2007), p. 330.
54. Bruce Eder in Marshall Crenshaw, *Hollywood Rock* (London: Plexus, 1994), p. 78.
55. Angela Dalle Vacche, *Cinema and Painting: How Art is Used in Film* (Austin: University of Texas Press, 1996), p. 114.
56. Charles Barr, 'Broadcasting and Cinema', in Charles Barr (ed.), *All Our Yesterdays: 90 Years of British Cinema* (London: British Film Institute, 1986), p. 216.
57. See John Hill, *Sex, Class and Realism: British Cinema 1956–1963* (London: British Film Institute, 1986), p. 174.
58. Arthur Marwick, '*Room at the Top, Saturday Night and Sunday Morning* and the "Cultural Revolution" in Britain', *Journal of Contemporary History*, vol. 19, no. 1, January 1984, p. 129.
59. Arthur Marwick, *British Society since 1945*, 4th edn (Harmondsworth: Penguin, 2003), p. 134.
60. Hill, *Sex, Class and Realism*, p. 132.
61. John Mundy, *Popular Music on Screen: From Hollywood Musical to Musical Video* (Manchester University Press, 1999), p. 167.
62. Stuart Hall and Tony Jefferson (eds), *Resistance through Rituals: Youth Sub-Cultures in Post-War Britain*, 2nd edn (London: Routledge, 2006), p. 71.
63. See Tony Aldgate, 'From Script to Screen: *Serious Charge* and Film Censorship', in Ian MacKillop and Neil Sinyard (eds), *British Cinema of the 1950s: A Celebration* (Manchester University Press, 2003) and Anthony Aldgate and James C. Robertson, *Censorship in Theatre and Cinema* (Edinburgh University Press, 2005), pp. 86–101.
64. Steve Turner, *Cliff Richard: The Biography* (Oxford: Lion Publishing, 1993), p. 140.
65. BBFC File, *Serious Charge*, Examiner's Report by John Trevelyan, 14 September 1958.
66. David Robinson, *The Times*, 20 May 1959.
67. William Whitebait, *New Statesman*, 23 May 1959.
68. Anonymous, *Sunday Express*, 17 May 1959.
69. Dilys Powell, *Sunday Times*, 17 May 1959.
70. George Sterling, *Sunday Dispatch*, 17 May 1959.
71. Josh Billings, *Kinematograph Weekly*, 17 December 1959, p. 3.
72. Melly, *Revolt into Style*, p. 55.

73. Cohn, *Pop from the Beginning*, p. 70.
74. Patrick Doncaster and Tony Jasper, *Cliff* (London: Octopus Books, 1983), p. 619.
75. Thomas Elsaesser, 'Tales of Sound and Fury: Observations on the Family Melodrama', in Christine Gledhill (ed.), *Home is Where the Heart is: Studies in Melodrama and the Woman's Film* (London: British Film Institute, 1987), p. 51.
76. Hayward, *Key Concepts in Cinema Studies*, p. 205.
77. Ibid.
78. For 'the male weepie', see Thomas Schatz, *Hollywood Genres: Formulas, Filmmaking and the Studio System* (New York: Random House, 1981), pp. 239–43. For film's deployment of Freud's Oedipus complex theories, see Stella Bruzzi, *Bringing Up Daddy: Fatherhood and Masculinity in Postwar Hollywood* (London: British Film Institute, 2005).
79. Geoffrey Nowell-Smith, 'Minnelli and Melodrama', in Gledhill (ed.), *Home is Where the Heart is*, p. 73.
80. Stephen Bourne, *Brief Encounters: Lesbians and Gays in British Cinema 1930–1971* (London: Cassell, 1996), p. 138.
81. Marcia Landy, *British Genres: Cinema and Society, 1930–60* (Princeton University Press, 1991), p. 480.
82. Andy Medhurst, '*Victim*: Text as Context', in Andrew Higson (ed.), *Dissolving Views: Key Writings on British Cinema* (London: Cassell, 1996), p. 128.
83. Ibid.
84. For a survey of Faith's career, see Frame, *The Restless Generation*, pp. 412–19.
85. Adam Faith, *Poor Me* (London: Four Square, 1961), p. 48.
86. Anonymous, *Monthly Film Bulletin*, vol. 15, no. 172, April 1948, p. 47.
87. For an assessment of her crime fiction, see Steve Holland, 'The Lady Holds a Gun: On the Trail of Dail Ambler', in Steve Holland, *Mean Streetmaps: Essays into Crime* (Colchester: Bear Alley Books, 2011).
88. BBFC file, *Beat Girl*, Reader's Report by Frank Crofts, 7 March 1959.
89. BBFC file, letter from John Trevelyan to George Willoughby, 7 April 1959.
90. BBFC file, Exception Form by Frank Crofts, 30 November 1959.
91. See Anthony Aldgate, *Censorship and the Permissive Society: British Cinema and Theatre 1955–65* (Oxford: Clarendon Press, 1995), p. 98.
92. Donald Gomery, *Daily Express*, 28 October 1960.
93. Anonymous, *Kinematograph Weekly*, 6 October 1960.
94. Faith, *Poor Me*, p. 51.
95. Ehrenstein and Reed, *Rock on Film*, p. 267.
96. Lez Cooke, 'British Cinema: A Struggle for Identity', in Clive Bloom and Gary Day (eds), *Literature and Culture in Modern Britain, Vol. 3: 1956–1999* (London: Longman, 2000), pp. 151, 150, 149.
97. Peter Hutchings, 'Beyond the New Wave: Realism in British Cinema, 1959–63', in Robert Murphy (ed.), *The British Cinema Book*, 2nd edn (London: British Film Institute, 2002), p. 149.
98. Hill sees 'exploitation' films like *Beat Girl* as 'looking back less to documentary and Ealing than to the more melodramatic offerings of Gainsborough, such as *Good Time Girl* (1947) and *The Boys in Brown* (1949)'. Hill, *Sex, Class and Realism*, p. 117.
99. Hayward, *Key Concepts in Cinema Studies*, p. 202.

100. The scene is glimpsed in Val Guest's tale of apocalyptic angst *The Day the Earth Caught Fire* (1961) and Guy Hamilton's exploitative/elegiac *The Party's Over* (1963).
101. Nowell-Smith, 'Minnelli and Melodrama', p. 73.
102. This became the eponymous phrase for Max Décharné's *Straight from the Fridge, Dad: A Dictionary of Hipster Slang* (Harpenden: No Exit Press, 2000).
103. Andy Medhurst, 'It Sort of Happened Here: The Strange, Brief Life of the British Pop Film', in Romney and Wootton (eds), *Celluloid Jukebox*, p. 65.
104. Laura Mulvey, 'Notes on Sirk and Melodrama', in Gledhill (ed.), *Home is Where the Heart is*, p. 77.
105. Hill, *Sex, Class and Realism*, p. 119.
106. John Mundy, *The British Musical Film* (Manchester University Press, 2007), p. 185.
107. Mulvey, 'Notes on Sirk and Melodrama', p. 77.
108. Nowell-Smith, 'Minnelli and Melodrama', pp. 73–4.
109. Pam Cook, 'Melodrama and the Women's Picture', in Sue Aspinall and Robert Murphy (eds), *BFI Dossier No. 18: Gainsborough Melodrama* (London: British Film Institute, 1983), p. 18.
110. Caine, *Interpreting Rock Movies*, p. 149.
111. Gillett, *The Sound of the City*, p. 256.
112. Cohn, *Pop from the Beginning*, p. 75.
113. Turner, *Cliff Richard*, p. 143.
114. Hayward, *Key Concepts in Cinema Studies*, p. 241.
115. Rick Altman, *The American Film Musical* (Bloomington: Indiana University Press, 1989), p. 127.
116. Cliff Richard, *Which One's Cliff?* (London: Hodder and Stoughton, 1977), pp. 59–60.
117. The Shadows comprised Hank Marvin on lead guitar, Bruce Welch on rhythm guitar and Brian Bennett on drums. Jet Harris was then on bass.
118. Josh Billings, *Kinematograph Weekly*, 11 January 1962.
119. Paul Dehn, *Daily Herald*, 16 December 1961.
120. Nina Hibbin, *Daily Worker*, 16 December 1961.
121. Anonymous, *Monthly Film Bulletin*, January 1962, p. 15.
122. David Robinson, *Financial Times*, 15 December 1961.
123. Patrick Gibbs, *Daily Telegraph*, 16 December 1961.
124. Altman, *The American Film Musical*, p. 57.
125. Richard Dyer, 'Entertainment and Utopia', in Bill Nichols (ed.), *Movies and Methods, Vol. 2* (Berkeley: University of California Press, 1985), pp. 224–5.
126. Ibid., pp. 225–8.
127. Feuer, *The Hollywood Musical*, p. 17.
128. Ibid., p. 228.
129. Dyer, 'Entertainment and Utopia', p. 228.
130. Harper, *Women in British Cinema*, p. 135.
131. Rick Altman, *Film / Genre* (London: British Film Institute, 1999), pp. 190–1.
132. Dyer, 'Entertainment and Utopia', pp. 225–8.
133. Harper, *Women in British Cinema*, p. 135.
134. Dyer, 'Entertainment and Utopia', p. 228.
135. Ibid.
136. Feuer, *The Hollywood Musical*, p. 94.

137. Dyer, 'Entertainment and Utopia', p. 228.
138. Altman, *The American Film Musical*, p. 223.
139. Feuer, *The Hollywood Musical*, p. 30 (my italics).
140. Altman, *The American Film Musical*, p. 25.
141. Richard, *Which One's Cliff?*, p. 61.
142. John Huntley, *Back Row*, Radio 4, 21 October 2000.
143. Turner, *Cliff Richard*, p. 205.
144. Anonymous, *Kinematograph Weekly*, 10 January 1963.
145. Richard, *Which One's Cliff?*, p. 61.
146. Margaret Hinxman, *Daily Herald*, 9 January 1963.
147. Penelope Gilliatt, *Observer*, 13 January 1963.
148. Anonymous, *Daily Mail*, 9 January 1963.
149. Felix Barker, *Evening News*, 10 January 1963.
150. Between 1951 and 1961 travel abroad had doubled to four million annually. Marwick, *British Society since 1945*, p. 248.
151. Feuer, *The Hollywood Musical*, p. 67.
152. Altman, *The American Film Musical*, p. 108.
153. Ibid., p. 24.
154. Ibid., p. 176.
155. Ibid., p. 109.
156. Nina Hibbin, *Daily Worker*, 9 January 1963.
157. Altman, *The American Film Musical*, p. 109.
158. Ibid.
159. Ibid., p. 158.
160. Ibid., p. 177.
161. Ibid., p. 180.
162. Ibid., p. 183.
163. Laura Mulvey, 'Visual Pleasure and Narrative Cinema', *Screen*, vol. 16, no. 3, Autumn 1975.
164. M.A. Doane, 'The Woman's Film: Possession and Address', in M.A. Doane, P. Mellencamp and L. Williams (eds), *Re-Vision: Essays in Feminist Film Criticism* (Frederick, MD: American Film Institute, 1984).
165. Altman, *The American Film Musical*, pp. 190–1.
166. Ibid., p. 109.
167. K.J. Donnelly, *British Film Music and Film Musicals* (Basingstoke: Palgrave Macmillan, 2007), p. 147.
168. Altman, *The American Film Musical*, p. 163.
169. Ibid., p. 109.
170. Mike Read, *The Story of the Shadows* (London: Elm Tree Books, 1983), p. 132.
171. Richard Dyer, *Heavenly Bodies: Film Stars and Society* (London: Macmillan, 1987), p. 182.
172. Richard, *Which One's Cliff?*, p. 63.
173. P.G.B., *Films and Filming*, vol. 10, no. 11, August 1964, p. 26.
174. Leonard Mosley, *Daily Express*, 1 July 1964.
175. John Coleman, *New Statesman*, 3 July 1964.
176. Dilys Powell, *Sunday Times*, 5 July 1964.
177. Michael Thornton, *Sunday Express*, 5 July 1964.
178. Feuer, *The Hollywood Musical*, p. 68.

179. Peter Wollen, 'Godard and Counter Cinema: *Vent d'Est* (1972)', *Afterimage*, Autumn 1972, p. 11.
180. Feuer, *The Hollywood Musical*, p. 90.
181. Ibid.
182. Ibid.

3 The Mature Pop Music Film

1. Harold Wilson, *Purpose in Politics: Selected Speeches of Harold Wilson* (London: Riverside, 1964), p. 10.
2. Philip Norman, *Shout! The True Story of the Beatles* (London: Elm Tree Books, 1981), p. 257.
3. Robert Murphy, *Sixties British Cinema* (London: British Film Institute, 1992), p. 307.
4. There are no extant reviews from national newspapers in the BFI Library files. In the sole study to date of Winner's films, *Play It Cool* is curtly dismissed: 'a detailed description would be futile, a critical discussion almost impossible'. Bill Harding, *The Films of Michael Winner* (London: Frederick Muller, 1978), p. 17.
5. Andrew Caine, *Interpreting Rock Movies: The Pop Film and its Critics in Britain* (Manchester University Press, 2004), p. 175.
6. Bruce Eder in Marshall Crenshaw, *Hollywood Rock* (London: Plexus, 1994), p. 173.
7. Michel Ciment, *John Boorman* (London: Faber and Faber, 1986), p. 10.
8. John Mundy, *The British Musical Film* (Manchester University Press, 2007), p. 200.
9. Phil Hardy and Dave Laing, *The Faber Companion to 20th-Century Popular Music* (London: Faber and Faber, 1990), p. 96.
10. Caine, *Interpreting Rock Movies*, p. 158.
11. Anonymous, *Monthly Film Bulletin*, vol. 30, no. 359, December 1963, p. 175. The film was consigned to the lowest III rating.
12. Alexander Walker, *Evening Standard*, 5 December 1963.
13. Simon Frith and Angela McRobbie, 'Rock and Sexuality', in Simon Frith and Andrew Goodwin (eds), *On Record: Rock, Pop and the Written Word* (London: Routledge, 1990), p. 371.
14. Susan Hayward, *Key Concepts in Cinema Studies* (London: Routledge, 1996), p. 153.
15. For 'the crisis of masculinity' in *The Full Monty*, see John Hill, 'Failure and Utopianism: Representations of the Working Class in British Cinema of the 1990s', in Robert Murphy (ed.), *British Cinema of the 90s* (London: British Film Institute, 2000).
16. Hayward, *Key Concepts in Cinema Studies*, p. 246.
17. Dilys Powell, *Sunday Times*, 1 April 1962.
18. Felix Barker, *Evening News*, 29 March 1962.
19. Anonymous, *Kinematograph Weekly*, 14 April 1960.
20. Anonymous, *Kinematograph Weekly*, 5 December 1963.
21. Alexander Walker, *Hollywood, England: The British Film Industry in the Sixties* (London: Michael Joseph, 1974), p. 222.
22. Neil Sinyard, *The Films of Richard Lester* (Beckenham: Croom Hill, 1985), p. 6.

23. Philip French, 'Richard Lester', *Movie*, no. 14, Autumn 1965, p. 10.
24. Robert Hughes, *The Shock of the New*, 2nd edn (London: Thames and Hudson, 1991), p. 351.
25. Roy Armes, *A Critical History of British Cinema* (London: Secker and Warburg, 1978), p. 259.
26. Murphy, *Sixties British Cinema*, p. 135.
27. Walker, *Hollywood, England*, p. 222.
28. Jeff Nuttall, *Bomb Culture* (London: MacGibbon and Kee, 1968), p. 49.
29. Nigel Young, *An Infantile Disorder? The Crisis and Decline of the New Left* (London: Routledge, 1977), p. 28.
30. Sinyard, *The Films of Richard Lester*, p. 11.
31. Nuttall, *Bomb Culture*, p. 51.
32. George Melly, *Revolt into Style* (Harmondsworth: Penguin, 1972), p. 60.
33. David Robinson, *The Times*, 29 March 1962.
34. *You Can't Do That: The Making of A Hard Day's Night*, MPI Home Video, 1994.
35. Roy Carr, *Beatles at the Movies: Scenes from a Career* (London: HarperCollins, 1996), p. 30.
36. Bill Harry, *The Ultimate Beatles Encyclopedia* (London: Virgin, 1992), p. 506.
37. Carr, *Beatles at the Movies*, p. 47.
38. Michael Thornton, *Sunday Express*, 13 July 1964.
39. Dick Richards, *Daily Mirror*, 8 July 1964.
40. Cecil Wilson, *Daily Mail*, 7 July 1964.
41. Isabel Quigly, *Spectator*, 10 July 1964.
42. Geoffrey Nowell-Smith, *Sight and Sound*, vol. 33, no. 4, Autumn 1964, pp. 196–7.
43. Anonymous, *Monthly Film Bulletin*, August 1964.
44. Andrew Sarris, *Village Voice*, 27 August 1964.
45. Hunter Davies, *The Beatles* (London: Heinemann, 1968), p. 212.
46. Alongside Rowana Agajanian, 'Nothing Like any Previous Musical, British or American', in Anthony Aldgate, James Chapman and Arthur Marwick (eds), *Windows on the Sixties* (London: I.B. Tauris, 2000) and Bob Neaverson, *The Beatles Movies* (London: Cassell, 1997), see Stephen Glynn, *A Hard Day's Night* (London: I.B. Tauris, 2004) and Melanie Williams, '*A Hard Day's Night*', in Sarah Barrow and John White (eds), *Fifty Key British Films* (London: Routledge, 2008).
47. Ian MacDonald, *Revolution in the Head* (London: Fourth Estate, 1994), p. 102.
48. Quoted in Joseph Gelmis (ed.), *The Film Director as Superstar* (London: Secker and Warburg, 1971), p. 316.
49. Eric Shanes, *Warhol: The Masterworks* (London: Studio Editions, 1991), p. 100.
50. Klaus Honnof, *Andy Warhol* (Berlin: Taschen, 1990), p. 68.
51. Neaverson, *The Beatles Movies*, p. 17.
52. Michael Braun, *'Love Me Do!' – The Beatles' Progress* (London: Penguin, 1964), p. 74.
53. Jane Feuer, *The Hollywood Musical* (London: Macmillan, 1982), p. 107.
54. Francis Wheen, *The Sixties* (London: Century/Channel 4, 1982), p. 23.
55. Jann Wenner, *Lennon Remembers* (London: Verso, 2000), p. 84.
56. Richard Lester, *Hollywood UK*, BBC, broadcast 1993.
57. Michael Thornton, *Sunday Express*, 1 August 1965.
58. Penelope Houston, *Financial Times*, 30 July 1965.

59. Patrick Gibbs, *Daily Telegraph*, 30 July 1965.
60. Alexander Walker, *Evening Standard*, 27 July 1965.
61. Hollis Alpert, *Saturday Review*, 28 August 1965.
62. Pauline Kael, *For Keeps: 30 years at the Movies* (New York: E.P. Dutton, 1994), p. 221.
63. Sinyard, *The Films of Richard Lester*, p. 34.
64. Steven Soderbergh, *Getting Away with It* (London: Faber and Faber, 1999), p. 56.
65. French, 'Richard Lester', p. 10.
66. Hughes, *The Shock of the New*, p. 340.
67. Ibid.
68. Soderbergh, *Getting Away with It*, p. 49.
69. Hughes, *The Shock of the New*, p. 341.
70. Walker, *Hollywood, England*, p. 268.
71. Neaverson, *The Beatles Movies*, p. 38.
72. For a fuller elaboration of this argument, see Stephen Glynn, 'The Beatles' *Help!*: Pop Art and the Perils of Parody', *Journal of British Cinema and Television*, vol. 8, no. 1, 2011.
73. Tony Bennett, 'James Bond as Popular Hero', *Politics, Ideology and Popular Culture 2, Unit 21* (Milton Keynes: Open University Press, 1982), p. 13.
74. Melly, *Revolt into Style*, p. 168.
75. Ella Shohat and Robert Stam, *Unthinking Eurocentrism: Multiculturalism and the Media* (London: Routledge, 1994), p. 140.
76. Raymond Durgnat, *A Mirror for England: British Movies from Austerity to Affluence* (London: Faber and Faber, 1970), p. 151.
77. Shohat and Stam, *Unthinking Eurocentrism*, p. 2.
78. Jim Pines, 'British Cinema and Black Representation', in Robert Murphy (ed.), *The British Cinema Book*, 2nd edn (London: British Film Institute, 2002), p. 211.
79. *The Beatles Anthology* (London: Weidenfeld and Nicolson, 2000), p. 171.
80. Norman, *Shout!*, p. 259.
81. Demitri Coryton and Joseph Murrells, *Hits of the Sixties* (London: B.T. Batsford, 1990), p. 76.
82. Walker, *Hollywood, England*, p. 384.
83. Ciment, *John Boorman*, p. 236.
84. Ibid., p. 56.
85. Kenneth Tynan, *Observer*, 7 July 1965.
86. Anonymous, *The Times*, 8 July 1965.
87. Cecil Wilson, *Daily Mail*, 7 July 1965.
88. Margaret Hinxman, *Sunday Telegraph*, 11 July 1965.
89. Anonymous, *Kinematograph Weekly*, 8 July 1965.
90. Pauline Kael, *5001 Nights at the Movies*, rev. edn (New York: Henry Holt, 1991), p. 244.
91. David Ehrenstein and Bill Reed, *Rock on Film* (London: Virgin, 1982), p. 172.
92. James Monaco, *Alain Resnais* (London: Secker and Warburg, 1978), p. 85.
93. Andy Medhurst, 'It Sort of Happened Here: The Strange, Brief Life of the British Pop Film', in Jonathan Romney and Adrian Wootton (eds), *Celluloid Jukebox: Popular Music and the Movies since the 50s* (London: British Film Institute, 1995), p. 68.

94. Ibid.
95. Peter Conrad, *Modern Art, Modern Places: Life and Art in the Twentieth Century* (London: Thames and Hudson, 1999), p. 289.
96. Marco Livingstone, *Pop Art: A Continuing History* (London: Thames and Hudson, 2000), p. 148.
97. Ciment, *John Boorman*, p. 55.
98. Richard Hamilton, 'Letter to Peter and Alison Smithson', in *Collected Words* (London: Thames and Hudson, 1982), p. 28.
99. Hughes, *The Shock of the New*, p. 344.
100. Jon Savage, 'Snapshots of the Sixties: Swinging London in Pop Films', in *Time Travel: Pop, Media and Sexuality 1977–96* (London: Chatto and Windus, 1996), p. 306.
101. Ciment, *John Boorman*, p. 56.
102. Ibid., p. 14.
103. Ibid., p. 47.
104. Ibid., p. 14.
105. Ibid., pp. 28–9.
106. Carl Jung, *Symbols of Transformation*, in *Collected Works, Vol. 5* (Princeton University Press, 1967), p. 375.
107. Ciment, *John Boorman*, p. 20.
108. Murphy, *Sixties British Cinema*, p. 139.
109. Ciment, *John Boorman*, p. 56.
110. Savage, 'Snapshots of the Sixties', p. 306.
111. Anonymous, *Monthly Film Bulletin*, vol. 33, no. 385, February 1966, p. 22.
112. Medhurst, 'It Sort of Happened Here', pp. 68–9.
113. For the period's popular music on British television, see John Hill, 'Television and Pop: The Case of the 1950s', in John Corner (ed.), *Popular Television in Britain: Studies in Cultural History* (London: British Film Institute, 1991) and John Mundy, *Popular Music on Screen: From Hollywood Musical to Musical Video* (Manchester University Press, 1999), pp. 193–208.

4 The Decadent Pop Music Film

1. Anonymous, *Monthly Film Bulletin*, vol. 34, no. 405, October 1967, p. 157.
2. Mark Kermode, *Celluloid Jukebox*, Radio 2, August 1999.
3. Steve Turner, *Cliff Richard: The Biography* (Oxford: Lion Publishing, 1993), p. 234.
4. Ian MacDonald, *Revolution in the Head* (London: Fourth Estate, 1994), p. 166.
5. Brian McFarlane, *Lance Comfort* (Manchester University Press, 1999), p. 122.
6. Jim Pines, *Blacks in Films* (London: Studio Vista, 1977), p. 117.
7. John Russell Taylor, *The Times*, 7 September 1967.
8. Robert Robinson, *Sunday Telegraph*, 10 September 1967.
9. Robert Murphy, *Sixties British Cinema* (London: British Film Institute, 1992), p. 149.
10. Paul Jones, 'On *Privilege*', *Sight and Sound*, vol. 3, no. 5, May 1993, p. 18. Burdon would finally land the lead as a self-destructive rock star in *Comeback* (Christel Buschmann, 1982).
11. Robin Bean, *Films and Filming*, vol. 13, no. 9, June 1967, p. 27.

12. Anonymous, *Daily Express*, 19 April 1967.
13. Alexander Walker, *Hollywood, England: The British Film Industry in the Sixties* (London: Michael Joseph, 1974), p. 350.
14. Alexander Walker, *Evening Standard*, 27 April 1967.
15. Dilys Powell, *Sunday Times*, 30 April 1967.
16. Nina Hibbin, *Morning Star*, 26 April 1967.
17. Penelope Gilliatt, *Observer*, 30 April 1967.
18. Joseph A. Gomez, *Peter Watkins* (Boston: Twayne Publishers, 1979), p. 74.
19. Jean Shrimpton, *An Autobiography* (London: Ebury Press, 1990), pp. 156–7.
20. Lester Friedman, 'The Necessity of Confrontation Cinema – Peter Watkins Interviewed', *Literature/Film Quarterly*, vol. 11, no. 4, 1983, p. 241.
21. Patrick Doncaster and Tony Jasper, *Cliff* (London: Octopus Books, 1983), p. 683.
22. Cliff Richard, *Which One's Cliff?* (London: Hodder and Stoughton, 1977), p. 80.
23. Anonymous, *Monthly Film Bulletin*, vol. 35, no. 415, August 1968, p. 123.
24. Jones, 'On *Privilege*', p. 18.
25. Gilliatt, *Observer*.
26. Quoted in J. Philip di Franco, *The Beatles in Richard Lester's A Hard Day's Night – a Complete Pictorial Record of the Movie* (Harmondsworth: Penguin, 1977), p. 5.
27. Garry Mulholland, *Popcorn: Fifty Years of Rock'n'Roll Movies* (London: Orion, 2010), p. 70.
28. Bean, *Films and Filming*, p. 27.
29. Anonymous, *Time*, 11 August 1967.
30. Andrew Sarris, *Village Voice*, 3 August 1967.
31. Turner, *Cliff Richard*, p. 242.
32. S.M.J. Arrowsmith, 'Peter Watkins', in George W. Brandt (ed.), *British Television Drama* (Cambridge University Press, 1981), p. 231.
33. Gilliatt, *Observer*.
34. Guy Debord, *Society of the Spectacle*, trans. Donald Nicholson-Smith (London: Zone Books, 1994 [1967]), paragraph 218.
35. Watkins later admitted that the film's conclusion demonstrated 'a certain dismissal of the public which I very much regret now'. Gomez, *Peter Watkins*, p. 84.
36. Roy Carr, *Beatles at the Movies: Scenes from a Career* (London: HarperCollins, 1996), p. 148.
37. For the film's troubled production, see Robert R. Hieronimus' *Inside the Yellow Submarine* (Iola: Krause, 2002) and Al Brodax's own, more partial memoir, *Up Periscope Yellow: The Making of the Beatles Yellow Submarine* (New York: Limelight Editions, 2004).
38. Bill Harry, *Beatlemania: The History of the Beatles on Film* (London: Virgin, 1984), p. 37.
39. John Coleman, *New Statesman*, 28 July 1968.
40. Anonymous, *Time*, 27 December 1968.
41. Anonymous, *Time*, 22 November 1968.
42. John Russell Taylor, *The Times*, 18 July 1968.
43. David Robinson, *Financial Times*, 19 July 1968.
44. Tom Milne, *Observer*, 21 July 1968.
45. Alexander Walker, *Evening Standard*, 18 July 1968.

46. Coleman, *New Statesman*.
47. Tim Riley, *Tell Me Why: A Beatles Commentary* (London: Bodley Head, 1988), p. 234.
48. For the wealth of accompanying merchandise, including alarm clocks, snow-domes, watches and 'the world's first ever full colour paperback', see Richard Buskin, *Beatle Crazy!: Memories and Memorabilia* (London: Salamander, 1994), p. 84.
49. Nina Hibbin, *Morning Star*, 17 July 1968.
50. Ian Christie, *Daily Express*, 17 July 1968.
51. Walker, *Evening Standard*.
52. Nigel Gosling, *Observer*, 28 July 1968.
53. Cecil Wilson, *Daily Mail*, 17 July 1968.
54. For example, Ray Connolly, *Evening Standard*, 6 August 1968; Judith Simons, *Daily Express*, 6 August 1968.
55. Harry, *Beatlemania*, p. 712.
56. Bob Neaverson, *The Beatles Movies* (London: Cassell, 1997), p. 88.
57. MacDonald, *Revolution in the Head*, p. 220.
58. Quoted in Hieronimus, *Inside the Yellow Submarine*, p. 166.
59. Quoted in Gavin Martin, 'Yellow Fever', *The Times* – Guide, 28 August–3 September 1999.
60. Dilys Powell, *Sunday Times*, 21 July 1968.
61. David Bowman, 'Scenarios for the Revolution in Pepperland', *Journal of Popular Film*, vol. 1, no. 3, Summer 1972, p. 178.
62. Anonymous, *Time*, 27 December 1968.
63. George Orwell, *Nineteen Eighty-Four* (London: Penguin Books, 1989 [1948]), p. 230.
64. Robinson, *Financial Times*.
65. Wilfrid Mellers, *Twilight of the Gods: The Beatles in Retrospect* (London: Faber and Faber, 1976 [1973]), p. 89.
66. Neaverson, *The Beatles Movies*, p. 90.
67. MacDonald, *Revolution in the Head*, p. 203.
68. For a more detailed comparison, see Stephen Glynn, 'From Pepperland to *The Prisoner*: *Yellow Submarine* and Social Change', in Jorg Helbig and Simon Warner (eds), *Summer of Love: The Beatles, Art and Culture in the Sixties* (Trier: WVT, 2008).
69. Daniel O'Brien, *SF:UK: How British Science Fiction Changed the World* (London: Reynolds and Hearn, 2000), p. 98.
70. Leslie Halliwell, *Halliwell's Television Companion*, 3rd edn (London: Grafton, 1986), p. 499.
71. Matthew de Abaitua, *SF:UK*, Channel Four, broadcast March 2001.
72. Greg Rowland, ibid.
73. MacDonald, *Revolution in the Head*, p. 243.
74. de Abaitua, *SF:UK*.
75. Russell Taylor, *The Times*, 1968.
76. Simon Frith and Angela McRobbie, 'Rock and Sexuality', in Simon Frith and Andrew Goodwin (eds), *On Record: Rock, Pop and the Written Word* (London: Routledge, 1990), p. 375.
77. Andrew Loog Oldham, *Stoned* (London: Secker and Warburg, 2000), p. 30.
78. Ibid., p. 31.

79. William Rees-Mogg, *The Times*, 1 July 1967.
80. Tom Milne (ed.), *Godard on Godard* (New York: Da Capo, 1986), p. 182.
81. Anonymous, *Monthly Film Bulletin*, vol. 32, no. 376, May 1965, p. 79.
82. David Ehrenstein and Bill Reed, *Rock on Film* (London: Virgin, 1982), p. 77.
83. Anonymous, 'Thump ... Then Exit Godard', *Guardian*, 30 November 1968.
84. Alexander Walker, *Evening Standard*, 2 December 1968.
85. Quoted in Demitri Coryton and Joseph Murrells, *Hits of the Sixties* (London: B.T. Batsford, 1990), p. 219.
86. Philip Strick, *Films and Filming*, vol. 15, no. 5, February 1969, p. 67.
87. Jonathan Cott and Sue Cox, 'An Interview with Mick Jagger', in David Dalton (ed.), *The Rolling Stones: An Unauthorised Biography in Words, Photographs and Music* (New York: AMSCO Music, 1972), p. 100.
88. Philip Norman, *The Stones* (London: Hamish Hamilton, 1984), p. 283.
89. Raymond Durgnat, 'One Plus One', in Ian Cameron (ed.), *The Films of Jean-Luc Godard* (London: Studio Vista, 1967), p. 183.
90. David Sterritt, *The Films of Jean-Luc Godard: Seeing the Invisible* (Cambridge University Press, 1999), p. 112.
91. Durgnat, 'One Plus One', p. 178.
92. Richard Roud, *Sight and Sound*, vol. 37, no. 4, Autumn 1968, p. 182.
93. Jan Dawson, *Sight and Sound*, vol. 39, no. 2, Spring 1970, p. 91.
94. Ginette Vincendeau, *The Companion to French Cinema* (London: British Film Institute, 1996), p. 84.
95. Jill Forbes, *The Cinema in France after the New Wave* (London: Palgrave Macmillan, 1992), p. 26.
96. Kent E. Carroll, 'Film and Revolution', in Royal S. Brown (ed.), *Focus on Godard* (Englewood Cliffs, NJ: Prentice-Hall, 1972), p. 62.
97. Vincendeau, *The Companion to French Cinema*, p. 84.
98. Eric Rhode, *Listener*, 12 December 1968.
99. Nick Dagger, *Uncut*, no. 56, January 2002, p. 72.
100. Carey Schofield, *Jagger* (London: Methuen, 1983), p. 161.
101. Walker, *Hollywood, England*, p. 417.
102. For a full production history, see Paul Buck, *Performance: A Biography of the 60s Masterpiece* (London: Omnibus Press, 2012).
103. Peter Schjeldahl, *New York Times*, 16 August 1970.
104. John Simon, *New York Times*, 23 August 1970.
105. Andrew Sarris, *Village Voice*, 30 July 1970.
106. Michael Goodwin, *Rolling Stone*, 17 September 1970.
107. Derek Malcolm, *Guardian*, 8 January 1971.
108. Michael Wood, *New Society*, 21 January 1971.
109. Alexander Walker, *Evening Standard*, 7 January 1971.
110. Nina Hibbin, *Morning Star*, 1 January 1971.
111. John Coleman, *New Statesman*, 8 January 1971.
112. John Russell Taylor, *The Times*, 8 January 1971.
113. Gavin Millar, *The Listener*, 14 January 1971.
114. David Robinson, *Financial Times*, 8 January 1971.
115. Cecil Wilson, *Daily Mail*, 8 January 1971.
116. Ann Pacey, *Sun*, 2 January 1971.
117. Colin MacCabe, *Performance* (London: British Film Institute, 1998), p. 24.

118. For example, Jon Savage, '*Performance*: Interview with Donald Cammell', in Steve Chibnall and Robert Murphy (eds), *British Crime Cinema* (London: Routledge, 1999), pp. 110–16.
119. K.J. Donnelly, '*Performance* and the Composite Film Score', in K.J. Donnelly (ed.), *Film Music: Critical Approaches* (Edinburgh University Press, 2001), p. 153.
120. Gordon Gow, *Films and Filming*, vol. 17, no. 7, April 1971, p. 48.
121. Coleman, *New Statesman*.
122. John Izod, *The Films of Nicolas Roeg: Myth and Mind* (London: Palgrave Macmillan, 1992), p. 20.
123. Jon Savage, 'Snapshots of the Sixties: Swinging London in Pop Films', in *Time Travel: Pop, Media and Sexuality 1977–96* (London: Chatto and Windus, 1996), p. 309.
124. Walker, *Evening Standard*.
125. Gow, *Films and Filming*.
126. Mick Brown, *Performance* (London: Bloomsbury, 1999), p. 181.
127. Tony Sanchez, *Up and Down with the Rolling Stones* (New York: Da Capo Press, 1996), p. 182. Faithfull broadly concurs with this reading: Marianne Faithfull, *Faithfull* (London: Michael Joseph, 1994), p. 213.
128. Norman, *The Stones*, p. 203.
129. John Walker, *The Once and Future Film: British Cinema in the Seventies and Eighties* (London: Methuen, 1985), p. 95.
130. Simon Reynolds and Joy Press, *The Sex Revolts: Gender, Rebellion and Rock'n'Roll* (London: Serpent's Tail, 1995), p. 145.
131. Marjorie Bilbow, *Today's Cinema*, 7 May 1971.
132. Michael Goodwin, *Rolling Stone*, 3 September 1970.

5 Afterlife

1. Steve Turner, *Cliff Richard: The Biography* (Oxford: Lion Publishing, 1993), p. 263.
2. John Mundy, *The British Musical Film* (Manchester University Press, 2007), p. 226.
3. Andrew Yule, *Enigma: David Puttnam, the Story So Far* (Edinburgh: Mainstream, 1988), p. 86.
4. Anonymous, *Sight and Sound*, vol. 43, no. 4, Autumn 1974, p. 254.
5. Alexander Walker, *National Heroes: British Cinema in the Seventies and Eighties* (London: Harrap, 1985), p. 71.
6. Ben Thompson, 'Pop and Film: The Charisma Crossover', in Jonathan Romney and Adrian Wootton (eds), *Celluloid Jukebox: Popular Music and the Movies since the 50s* (London: British Film Institute, 1995), p. 40.
7. Tony Rayns, *Monthly Film Bulletin*, vol. 42, no. 494, March 1975, p. 54.
8. Thompson, 'Pop and Film', p. 40.
9. Geoff Brown, *Monthly Film Bulletin*, vol. 42, no. 497, June 1975, p. 143.
10. Justin Smith, *Withnail and Us: Cult Films and Film Cults in British Cinema* (London: I.B. Tauris, 2010), p. 137.
11. Alexander Walker, *Evening Standard*, Friday 28 March 1975.
12. Dilys Powell, *Sunday Times*, Sunday 30 March 1975.
13. David Wilson, *Sight and Sound*, vol. 44, no. 3, Autumn 1975, p. 193.

14. Ken Russell, *Tommy* DVD interview, 2004.
15. Jon Lewis, *The Road to Romance and Ruin: Teen Films and Youth Culture* (London: Routledge, 1992), p. 162.
16. Andrew Sarris, *Village Voice*, 31 March 1975.
17. Wilson, *Sight and Sound*.
18. Jonathan Rosenbaum, *Monthly Film Bulletin*, vol. 42, no. 495, April 1975, p. 88.
19. Smith, *Withnail and Us*, p. 137.
20. Jon Landau, *Rolling Stone*, 24 April 1975.
21. Ali Catterall and Simon Wells, *Your Face Here: British Cult Movies since the Sixties* (London: Fourth Estate, 2001), p. 147.
22. Richard Barkley, *Sunday Express*, 19 August 1979.
23. Felix Barker, *Evening News*, 16 August 1979.
24. Anonymous, *Films and Filming*, January 1980, p. 29.
25. Pierre Sorlin, *The Film in History: Restaging the Past* (Oxford: Basil Blackwell, 1980), p. 83.
26. Notable are Kevin J. Donnelly, 'British Punk Films: Rebellion into Money, Nihilism into Innovation', *Journal of Popular British Cinema*, no. 1, 1988; Stacy Thompson, 'Punk Cinema', *Cinema Journal*, vol. 43, no. 2, 2004, pp. 47–66; Claire Monk, '*Jubilee*, Punk and British Film in the Late 1970s', in Robert Shail (ed.), *Seventies British Cinema* (London: Palgrave Macmillan, 2008); David Laderman, *Punk Slash Musicals* (Austin: University of Texas Press, 2010).
27. Steve Jenkins, *Monthly Film Bulletin*, vol. 48, no. 574, November 1981, p. 225.
28. Jon Savage, *England's Dreaming: Sex Pistols and Punk Rock* (London: Faber and Faber, 1991), p. 377.
29. Quoted in Julie Birchill, 'The Kid Who Wouldn't Wear Clarke's Sandals', *New Musical Express*, 18 April 1978.
30. Vivienne Westwood, 'Open T-shirt to Derek Jarman' http://collections.vam.ac.uk/item/O68609/top/ (accessed 23 May 2012).
31. Monk, '*Jubilee*, Punk and British Film in the Late 1970s', p. 91.
32. Derek Jarman, *Dancing Ledge* (London: Quartet Books, 1984), p. 172.
33. Robert Rosenstone, *Visions of the Past: The Challenge of Film to our Idea of History* (London and Cambridge, MA: Harvard University Press, 1980), p. 149.
34. Joel McIver, *The Sex Pistols: The Making of The Great Rock'n'Roll Swindle* (London: Unanimous, 2005), pp. 116–17.
35. Donnelly, 'British Punk Films', p. 108.
36. John Pym, *Monthly Film Bulletin*, vol. 47, no. 555, April 1980, p. 75.
37. Whitehead's full footage of Pink Floyd was released in 2005 as *London '66–'67*.
38. Mark Blake (ed.), *Pink Floyd: Q Special Edition* (London: EMAP Metro, 2004), p. 93.
39. Alan Parker, *Rolling Stone*, 16 September 1982.
40. Quoted in Jeff Bench and Daniel O'Brien, *Pink Floyd's The Wall: In the Studio, on Stage and on Screen* (London: Reynolds and Hearn, 2004), p. 118.
41. Roger Ebert, *Chicago Sun-Times*, 24 February 2010.
42. Steve Jenkins, *Monthly Film Bulletin*, vol. 49, no. 583, August 1982, p. 173.
43. Paul Taylor, *Time Out*, 29 July 1982. The punning put-down earned itself an entry in Colin Jarman (ed.), *The Book of Poisonous Quotes* (London: Guinness Books, 1992), p. 186.

44. Marjorie Bilbow, *Screen International*, 24 July 1982, p. 20.
45. Ibid.
46. Andy Mabbett, *The Complete Guide to the Music of Pink Floyd* (London: Omnibus Press, 1995), p. 85.
47. Bench and O'Brien, *Pink Floyd's The Wall*, p. 119.
48. Susan Sontag, 'Fascinating Fascism', in *Under the Sign of Saturn* (London: Penguin, 2009), p. 91.
49. Ibid.
50. 'The tastes for the monumental and for mass obeisance to the hero are common to both fascist and communist art, reflecting the view of all totalitarian regimes that art has the function of "immortalizing" its leaders and doctrines.' Ibid.
51. Bench and O'Brien, *Pink Floyd's The Wall*, p. 124.
52. I do not include here the Joan Collins MILF vehicle *The Stud* (Quentin Masters, 1978) which, as K.J. Donnelly points out, could also be considered 'a backstage disco film'. *Pop Music in British Cinema* (London: British Film Institute, 2001), p. 58.
53. Marjorie Bilbow, *Screen International*, 5 August 1978.
54. Ian Birch, *Time Out*, 7 November 1980.
55. Paul Taylor, *Monthly Film Bulletin*, vol. 46, no. 544, May 1979, p. 100.
56. Steve Jenkins, *Monthly Film Bulletin*, vol. 47, no. 562, November 1980, p. 209.
57. Richard Dyer, 'Feeling English', *Sight and Sound*, vol. 4, no 3, March 1994, pp. 16–19.
58. Julie Birchill, *Time Out*, 12 September 1985, p. 8.
59. Jake Eberts and John Ilott, *My Indecision is Final: The Rise and Fall of Goldcrest Films* (London: Faber and Faber, 1990), pp. 633–4.
60. Alexander Walker, *Icons in the Fire: The Decline and Fall of Almost Everybody in the British Film Industry* (London: Orion, 2004), p. 29.
61. Anonymous, *Sun*, 5 April 1986.
62. Kim Newman, *Monthly Film Bulletin*, vol. 53, no. 627, April 1986, p. 103.
63. Marjorie Bilbow, *Screen International*, 5 April 1986.
64. Todd McCarthy, *Variety*, 26 March 1986.
65. Walker, *Icons in the Fire*, pp. 52–3.
66. Marco Calavito, 'MTV Aesthetics at the Movies: Interrogating a Film Criticism Fallacy', *Journal of Film and Video*, vol. 59, no. 3, Fall 2007, pp. 15–31.
67. Chris Peacock, *Time Out*, 2 April 1986.
68. Andrew Goodwin, *Dancing in the Distraction Factory: Music Television and Postmodern Culture* (London: Routledge, 1993), p. 33.
69. Caryn James, *New York Times*, 18 April 1986.
70. Lewis, *The Road to Romance and Ruin*, p. 82.
71. Mundy, *The British Musical Film*, p. 238.
72. Newman, *Monthly Film Bulletin*.
73. Todd McCarthy, *Variety*, 26 March 1986.
74. Newman, *Monthly Film Bulletin*.
75. Fredric Jameson, 'Postmodernism and Consumer Society', in Hal Foster (ed.), *Postmodern Culture* (London: Pluto Press, 1983), p. 113.
76. For an application of Baudrillard to film, see Giuliana Bruno, 'Ramble City: Postmodernism and *Blade Runner*', *October*, 41, 1987.

77. Susan Hayward, *Key Concepts in Cinema Studies* (London: Routledge, 1996), p. 301.
78. Bilbow, *Screen International*.
79. Donnelly, *Pop Music in British Cinema*, p. 106.
80. James, *New York Times*.
81. K.J. Donnelly, *British Film Music and Film Musicals* (Basingstoke: Palgrave Macmillan, 2007), p. 169.
82. Andy Medhurst, 'It Sort of Happened Here: The Strange, Brief Life of the British Pop Film', in Jonathan Romney and Adrian Wootton (eds), *Celluloid Jukebox: Popular Music and the Movies since the 50s* (London: British Film Institute, 1995), pp. 65–7.
83. Ibid.
84. Vicky Hayward (ed.), *The Beginners' Guide to Absolute Beginners The Musical* (London: Corgi, 1986), p. 83.
85. Colin MacInnes, *Absolute Beginners* (London: Allison and Busby, 2011 [1959]), p. 64.
86. James Hoberman, *Village Voice*, 29 April 1986.
87. Adam Barker, *Monthly Film Bulletin*, vol. 55, no. 655, August 1988, p. 234.
88. Medhurst, 'It Sort of Happened Here', p. 70.
89. E. Ann Kaplan, *Rocking Around the Clock: Music Television, Postmodernism, and Consumer Society* (London: Methuen, 1987), p. 3.
90. John Mundy, *Popular Music on Screen: From Hollywood Musical to Musical Video* (Manchester University Press, 1999), p. 232.
91. Matthew Sweet, *Independent on Sunday*, 28 December 1997.
92. Roger Ebert, *Chicago Sun-Times*, 23 January 1998.
93. Maureen Turim, *Flashbacks in Film: Memory and History* (London: Routledge, 1989), p. 17.
94. Elizabeth Eva Leach, 'Vicars of "Wannabe": Authenticity and the Spice Girls', *Popular Music*, vol. 20, no. 2, May 2001, p. 161.
95. Cynthia Fuchs, 'Too Much of Something is Bad Enough: Success and Excess in Spice World', in Frances K. Gateward and Murray Pomerance (eds), *Sugar, Spice and Everything Nice: Cinemas of Girlhood* (Detroit: Wayne State University Press, 2002), p. 348.
96. Mark Sinker, *Sight and Sound*, vol. 8, no. 2, February 1998, p. 49.
97. Wally Hammond in John Pym (ed.), *Time Out Film Guide 17* (London: Time Out Guides, 2007), p. 945.
98. Angie Errigo, *Empire*, 11 July 2008.
99. Peter Bradshaw, *Guardian*, 10 July 2008.
100. For a fuller exploration, see Louise FitzGerald and Melanie Williams (eds), *Mamma Mia! The Movie: Exploring a Cultural Phenomenon* (London: I.B. Tauris, 2012).
101. Simon Reynolds, *Retromania: Pop Culture's Addiction to its own Past* (London: Faber and Faber, 2012), pp. x–xi.
102. John Orr, '*Control* and British Cinema', *Film International*, vol. 6, no. 1, February 2008, p. 19.
103. Noel McLaughlin, 'Rattling Out of Control: A Comparison of U2 and Joy Division on Film', *Film, Fashion and Consumption*, vol. 1, no. 1, 2012, p. 108.
104. Dorian Lynskey, *Guardian*, 15 March 2012.
105. Decca Aitkenhead, *Guardian*, 7 June 2012.

106. Christopher Tookey, *Daily Mail*, 7 June 2012.
107. Tim Riley, *Daily Telegraph*, 7 June 2012.
108. Peter Bradshaw, *Guardian*, 7 June 2012.
109. Matthew Taylor, *Sight and Sound*, vol, 22, no. 6, June 2012, p. 67.
110. Anna Smith, *Empire*, 3 June 2012.

6   Conclusion

1. Lawrence Grossberg, 'Is There a Fan in the House? The Affective Sensibility of Fandom', in Lisa A. Lewis (ed.), *The Adoring Audience: Fan Culture and Popular Media* (London and New York: Routledge, 1992), pp. 62–3.

Select Bibliography

Newspapers and periodicals

Chapter notes indicate the newspapers and periodicals used for film reviews. These were mostly taken from the British Film Institute's microfiche film collection. Quotations come from reviews and articles in the following British newspapers and periodicals: *Daily Express, Daily Herald, Daily Mail, Daily Mirror, Daily Telegraph, Daily Worker, Evening News, Evening Standard, Financial Times, Guardian, Independent on Sunday, Listener, Morning Star, New Society, New Statesman, News Chronicle, Observer, Picture Post, Reynolds News, Saturday Review, Spectator, Sun, Sunday Dispatch, Sunday Express, Sunday Telegraph, Sunday Times, Time Out* and *The Times*. These illustrate a range of opinion from both quality and popular press and across the political spectrum. American reviews are cited from *Chicago Sun-Times, New York Times, Time* and *Village Voice*.

Film journals and trade papers

Again chapter notes indicate sources. For reviews *Empire* represents the popular and *Films and Filming* the middle-brow film journalism of Britain, while its quasi-intellectual film culture is evidenced in the pages of the *Monthly Film Bulletin* and *Sight and Sound*. *Kinematograph Weekly, Today's Cinema* and *Screen International* provide background from and the views of Britain's trade press, while *Variety* has been occasionally cited for American trade reviews. Music press perspectives come from *Uncut* in the UK and *Rolling Stone* in the US.

Unpublished sources

British Board of Film Censors (BBFC), files on *Beat Girl* (7 March 1959 to 5 October 1960) and *Serious Charge* (16 March 1955 to 26 March 1962).

Biographies, autobiographies and diaries

Beatles, *The Beatles Anthology* (London: Weidenfeld and Nicolson, 2000).
Braun, Michael, *'Love Me Do!' – The Beatles' Progress* (London: Penguin, 1964).
Brodax, Al, *Up Periscope Yellow: The Making of the Beatles Yellow Submarine* (New York: Limelight Editions, 2004).
Dalton, David, ed., *The Rolling Stones: An Unauthorised Biography in Words, Photographs and Music* (New York: AMSCO Music, 1972).
Davies, Hunter, *The Beatles* (London: Heinemann, 1968).
Doncaster, Patrick and Tony Jasper, *Cliff* (London: Octopus Books, 1983).
Eberts, Jake and John Ilott, *My Indecision is Final: The Rise and Fall of Goldcrest Films* (London: Faber and Faber, 1990).

Faith, Adam, *Poor Me* (London: Four Square, 1961).

Faithfull, Marianne, *Faithfull* (London: Michael Joseph, 1994).

Frame, Pete, *The Restless Generation: How Rock Music Changed the Face of 1950s Britain* (London: Rogan House, 2007).

Guest, Val, *So You Want to Be in Pictures* (London: Reynolds and Hearn, 2001).

Hamilton, Richard, *Collected Words* (London: Thames and Hudson, 1982).

Jarman, Derek, *Dancing Ledge* (London: Quartet Books, 1984).

Norman, Philip, *Shout! The True Story of the Beatles* (London: Elm Tree Books, 1981).

—— *The Stones* (London: Hamish Hamilton, 1984).

Oldham, Andrew Loog, *Stoned* (London: Secker and Warburg, 2000).

Read, Mike, *The Story of the Shadows* (London: Elm Tree Books, 1983).

Richard, Cliff, *Which One's Cliff?* (London: Hodder and Stoughton, 1977).

Sanchez, Tony, *Up and Down with the Rolling Stones* (New York: Da Capo Press, 1996).

Schofield, Carey, *Jagger* (London: Methuen, 1983).

Shrimpton, Jean, *An Autobiography* (London: Ebury Press, 1990).

Soderbergh, Steven, *Getting Away with It* (London: Faber and Faber, 1999).

Steele, Tommy, *Bermondsey Boy* (London: Michael Joseph, 2006).

Turner, Steve, *Cliff Richard: The Biography* (Oxford: Lion Publishing, 1993).

Wenner, Jann, *Lennon Remembers* (London: Verso, 2000).

Yule, Andrew, *Enigma: David Puttnam, the Story So Far* (Edinburgh: Mainstream, 1988).

Books and monographs

Aldgate, Anthony, *Censorship and the Permissive Society: British Cinema and Theatre 1955–65* (Oxford: Clarendon Press, 1995).

Aldgate, Anthony, James Chapman and Arthur Marwick, eds, *Windows on the Sixties* (London: I.B. Tauris, 2000).

Aldgate, Anthony and James C. Robertson, *Censorship in Theatre and Cinema* (Edinburgh University Press, 2005).

Altman, Rick, *The American Film Musical* (Bloomington: Indiana University Press, 1989).

—— *Film / Genre* (London: British Film Institute, 1999).

Armes, Roy, *A Critical History of British Cinema* (London: Secker and Warburg, 1978).

Barnouw, Eric, *Documentary: History of the Non-Fiction Film*, 2nd edn (Oxford University Press, 1993).

Barr, Charles, ed., *All Our Yesterdays: 90 Years of British Cinema* (London: British Film Institute, 1986).

Barrow, Sarah and John White, eds, *Fifty Key British Films* (London: Routledge, 2008).

Bazin, André, *What is Cinema, Vol. 2* (Berkeley: University of California Press, 2005).

Bench, Jeff and Daniel O'Brien, *Pink Floyd's The Wall: In the Studio, on Stage and on Screen* (London: Reynolds and Hearn, 2004).

Bevan, Ian and Kurt Ganzl, *The British Musical Theatre, Vol. II: 1915–1984* (London: Palgrave Macmillan, 1986).

Blake, Mark, ed., *Pink Floyd: Q Special Edition* (London: EMAP Metro, 2004).

Bloom, Clive and Gary Day, eds, *Literature and Culture in Modern Britain, Vol. 3: 1956–1999* (London: Longman, 2000).

Bordwell, David and Kristin Thompson, *Film Art: An Introduction*, 4th edn (New York: McGraw Hill, 1993).

Bourne, Stephen, *Brief Encounters: Lesbians and Gays in British Cinema 1930–1971* (London: Cassell, 1996).

Brandt, George W., ed., *British Television Drama* (Cambridge University Press, 1981).

Braun, Eric, *The Elvis Film Encyclopedia* (London: Batsford, 1997).

Brode, Douglas, *Elvis, Cinema and Popular Culture* (New York: McFarland, 2006).

Brown, Mick, *Performance* (London: Bloomsbury, 1999).

Brown, Royal S., ed., *Focus on Godard* (Englewood Cliffs, NJ: Prentice-Hall, 1972).

Bruzzi, Stella, *Bringing Up Daddy: Fatherhood and Masculinity in Postwar Hollywood* (London: British Film Institute, 2005).

Buck, Paul, *Performance: A Biography of the 60s Masterpiece* (London: Omnibus Press, 2012).

Buckingham, David, *Children Talking Television: The Making of Television Literacy* (London: Falmer Press, 1993).

Buskin, Richard, *Beatle Crazy!: Memories and Memorabilia* (London: Salamander, 1994).

Caine, Andrew, *Interpreting Rock Movies: The Pop Film and its Critics in Britain* (Manchester University Press, 2004).

Cameron, Ian, ed., *The Films of Jean-Luc Godard* (London: Studio Vista, 1967).

Carr, Roy, *Beatles at the Movies: Scenes from a Career* (London: HarperCollins, 1996).

Catterall, Ali and Simon Wells, *Your Face Here: British Cult Movies since the Sixties* (London: Fourth Estate, 2001).

Chapman, James, *Licence To Thrill: A Cultural History of the James Bond Films* (London: I.B. Tauris, 1999).

Chibnall, Steve and Robert Murphy, eds, *British Crime Cinema* (London: Routledge, 1999).

Ciment, Michel, *John Boorman* (London: Faber and Faber, 1986).

Cohen, Thomas F., *Playing to the Camera: Musicians and Musical Performance in Documentary Cinema* (London: Wallflower, 2012).

Cohn, Nik, *AwopBopALooBopAWopBamBoom: Pop from the Beginning* (London: Weidenfeld and Nicolson, 1969).

Conrad, Peter, *Modern Art, Modern Places: Life and Art in the Twentieth Century* (London: Thames and Hudson, 1999).

Cook, Pam, ed., *The Cinema Book*, 3rd edn (London: British Film Institute, 2008).

Corner, John, ed., *Popular Television in Britain: Studies in Cultural History* (London: British Film Institute, 1991).

Coryton, Demitri and Joseph Murrells, *Hits of the Sixties* (London: B.T. Batsford, 1990).

Crenshaw, Marshall, *Hollywood Rock* (London: Plexus, 1994).

Dalle Vacche, Angela, *Cinema and Painting: How Art is Used in Film* (Austin: University of Texas Press, 1996).

Debord, Guy, *Society of the Spectacle*, trans. Donald Nicholson-Smith (London: Zone Books, 1994 [1967]).

Décharné, Max, *Straight from the Fridge, Dad: A Dictionary of Hipster Slang* (Harpenden: No Exit Press, 2000).

Dellar, Fred, *NME Guide to Rock Cinema* (London: Hamlyn, 1981).

di Franco, J. Philip, *The Beatles in Richard Lester's A Hard Day's Night – a Complete Pictorial Record of the Movie* (Harmondsworth: Penguin, 1977).

Dix, Andrew, *Beginning Film Studies* (Manchester University Press, 2008).

Doane, M.A., P. Mellencamp and L. Williams, eds, *Re-Vision: Essays in Feminist Film Criticism* (Frederick, MD: American Film Institute, 1984).

Donnelly, K.J., *Pop Music in British Cinema* (London: British Film Institute, 2001).

—— ed., *Film Music: Critical Approaches* (Edinburgh University Press, 2001).

—— *British Film Music and Film Musicals* (Basingstoke: Palgrave Macmillan, 2007).

Durgnat, Raymond, *A Mirror for England: British Movies from Austerity to Affluence* (London: Faber and Faber, 1970).

Dyer, Richard, *Stars* (London: British Film Institute, 1980).

—— *Heavenly Bodies: Film Stars and Society* (London: Macmillan, 1987).

Ehrenstein, David and Bill Reed, *Rock on Film* (London: Virgin, 1982).

Feuer, Jane, *The Hollywood Musical* (London: Macmillan, 1982).

Fiske, John, *Television Culture* (London: Routledge, 1987).

FitzGerald, Louise and Melanie Williams, eds, *Mamma Mia! The Movie: Exploring a Cultural Phenomenon* (London: I.B. Tauris, 2012).

Forbes, Jill, *The Cinema in France after the New Wave* (London: Palgrave Macmillan, 1992).

Foster, Hal, ed., *Postmodern Culture* (London: Pluto Press, 1983).

Frith, Simon and Andrew Goodwin, eds, *On Record: Rock, Pop and the Written Word* (London: Routledge, 1990).

Gammond, Peter, *The Oxford Companion to Popular Music* (Oxford University Press, 1991).

Gateward, Frances K. and Murray Pomerance, eds, *Sugar, Spice and Everything Nice: Cinemas of Girlhood* (Detroit: Wayne State University Press, 2002).

Gelmis, Joseph, ed., *The Film Director as Superstar* (London: Secker and Warburg, 1971).

Gillett, Charlie, *The Sound of the City* (London: Sphere, 1971).

Gledhill, Christine, ed., *Home is Where the Heart is: Studies in Melodrama and the Woman's Film* (London: British Film Institute, 1987).

—— ed., *Stardom: The Industry of Desire* (London: Routledge, 1991).

Glynn, Stephen, *A Hard Day's Night* (London: I.B. Tauris, 2004).

Gomez, Joseph A., *Peter Watkins* (Boston: Twayne Publishers, 1979).

Goodwin, Andrew, *Dancing in the Distraction Factory: Music Television and Postmodern Culture* (London: Routledge, 1993).

Grant, Barry Keith, ed., *Film Genre Reader* (Austin: University of Texas Press, 1986).

Gross, Edward, *The Fab Films of the Beatles* (Las Vegas: Pioneer Books, 1990).

Hall, Stuart and Tony Jefferson, eds, *Resistance through Rituals: Youth Sub-Cultures in Post-War Britain*, 2nd edn (London: Routledge, 2006).

Halliwell, Leslie, *Halliwell's Television Companion*, 3rd edn (London: Grafton, 1986).

Hardy, Phil and Dave Laing, *The Faber Companion to 20th-Century Popular Music* (London: Faber and Faber, 1990).

Harper, Sue, *Women in British Cinema* (London: Continuum, 2000).

Harper, Sue and Vincent Porter, *British Cinema of the 1950s: The Decline of Deference* (Oxford University Press, 2003).

Harry, Bill, *Beatlemania: The History of the Beatles on Film* (London: Virgin, 1984).

—— *The Ultimate Beatles Encyclopedia* (London: Virgin, 1992).

Hayward, Susan, *Key Concepts in Cinema Studies* (London: Routledge, 1996).

Hayward, Vicky, ed., *The Beginners' Guide to Absolute Beginners The Musical* (London: Corgi, 1986).

Hebdige, Dick, *Hiding in the Light: On Images and Things* (London: Routledge, 1988).

Helbig, Jorg and Simon Warner, eds, *Summer of Love: The Beatles, Art and Culture in the Sixties* (Trier: WVT, 2008).

Hieronimus, Robert R., *Inside the Yellow Submarine* (Iola: Krause, 2002).

Higson, Andrew, ed., *Dissolving Views: Key Writings on British Cinema* (London: Cassell, 1996).

Hill, John, *Sex, Class and Realism: British Cinema 1956–1963* (London: British Film Institute, 1986).

Honnef, Klaus, *Andy Warhol* (Berlin: Taschen, 1990).

Hughes, Robert, *The Shock of the New*, 2nd edn (London: Thames and Hudson, 1991).

Hutchings, Peter, *Hammer and Beyond: The British Horror Film* (Manchester University Press, 1993).

—— *Terence Fisher* (Manchester University Press, 2002).

Izod, John, *The Films of Nicolas Roeg: Myth and Mind* (London: Palgrave Macmillan, 1992).

Jung, Carl, *Symbols of Transformation*, in *Collected Works, Vol. 5* (Princeton University Press, 1967).

Kael, Pauline, *5001 Nights at the Movies*, rev. edn (New York: Henry Holt, 1991).

—— *For Keeps: 30 years at the Movies* (New York: E.P. Dutton, 1994).

Kaplan, E. Ann, *Rocking Around the Clock: Music Television, Postmodernism, and Consumer Society* (London: Methuen, 1987).

Kureishi, Hanif and Jon Savage, eds, *The Faber Book of Pop* (London: Faber and Faber, 1995).

Laderman, David, *Punk Slash Musicals* (Austin: University of Texas Press, 2010).

Landy, Marcia, *British Genres: Cinema and Society, 1930–60* (Princeton University Press, 1991).

Langford, Barry, *Film Genre: Hollywood and Beyond* (Edinburgh University Press, 2005).

Larkin, Colin, ed., *Encyclopedia of Stage and Film Musicals* (London: Virgin, 1999).

Lewis, Jon, *The Road to Romance and Ruin: Teen Films and Youth Culture* (London: Routledge, 1992).

Lewis, Lisa A., ed., *The Adoring Audience: Fan Culture and Popular Media* (London and New York: Routledge, 1992).

Livingstone, Marco, *Pop Art: A Continuing History* (London: Thames and Hudson, 2000).

Mabbett, Andy, *The Complete Guide to the Music of Pink Floyd* (London: Omnibus Press, 1995).

MacCabe, Colin, *Performance* (London: British Film Institute, 1998).

MacDonald, Ian, *Revolution in the Head* (London: Fourth Estate, 1994).

MacInnes, Colin, *Absolute Beginners* (London: Allison and Busby, 2011 [1959]).

MacKillop, Ian and Neil Sinyard, eds, *British Cinema of the 1950s: A Celebration* (Manchester University Press, 2003).

Marwick, Arthur, *British Society since 1945*, 4th edn (Harmondsworth: Penguin, 2003).

—— *The Sixties: Cultural Revolution in Britain, France, Italy and the United States c. 1958–1974* (Oxford University Press, 1998).

McFarlane, Brian, *Lance Comfort* (Manchester University Press, 1999).

McIver, Joel, *The Sex Pistols: The Making of The Great Rock'n'Roll Swindle* (London: Unanimous, 2005).

Mellers, Wilfrid, *Twilight of the Gods: The Beatles in Retrospect* (London: Faber and Faber, 1976 [1973]).

Melly, George, *Revolt into Style* (Harmondsworth: Penguin, 1972).

Milne, Tom, ed., *Godard on Godard* (New York: Da Capo, 1986).

Monaco, James, *Alain Resnais* (London: Secker and Warburg, 1978).

Moretti, Franco, *Graphs, Maps, Trees: Abstract Models for a Literary Theory* (London: Verso, 2005).

Mulholland, Garry, *Popcorn: Fifty Years of Rock'n'Roll Movies* (London: Orion, 2010).

Mundy, John, *Popular Music on Screen: From Hollywood Musical to Musical Video* (Manchester University Press, 1999).

—— *The British Musical Film* (Manchester University Press, 2007).

Murphy, Robert, *Sixties British Cinema* (London: British Film Institute, 1992).

—— ed., *British Cinema of the 90s* (London: British Film Institute, 2000).

—— ed., *The British Cinema Book*, 2nd edn (London: British Film Institute, 2002).

Neale, Steve, *Genre* (London: British Film Institute, 1980).

—— *Genre and Hollywood* (London: Routledge, 1999).

Neaverson, Bob, *The Beatles Movies* (London: Cassell, 1997).

Nichols, Bill, ed., *Movies and Methods, Vol. 2* (Berkeley: University of California Press, 1985).

Nuttall, Jeff, *Bomb Culture* (London: MacGibbon and Kee, 1968).

O'Brien, Daniel, *SF:UK: How British Science Fiction Changed the World* (London: Reynolds and Hearn, 2000).

O'Sullivan, Tim, John Hartley, Danny Saunders and Martin Montgomery, *Key Concepts in Communication* (London: Methuen, 1983).

Park, James, *British Cinema: The Lights that Failed* (London: B.T. Batsford, 1990).

Pines, Jim, *Blacks in Films* (London: Studio Vista, 1977).

Pym, John, ed., *Time Out Film Guide 17* (London: Time Out Guides, 2007).

Renov, Michael, ed., *Theorising Documentary* (London: Routledge, 1993).

Reynolds, Simon, *Retromania: Pop Culture's Addiction to its own Past* (London: Faber and Faber, 2012).

Reynolds, Simon and Joy Press, *The Sex Revolts: Gender, Rebellion and Rock'n'Roll* (London: Serpent's Tail, 1995).

Riley, Tim, *Tell Me Why: A Beatles Commentary* (London: Bodley Head, 1988).

Romney, Jonathan and Adrian Wootton, eds, *Celluloid Jukebox: Popular Music and the Movies since the 50s* (London: British Film Institute, 1995).

Rosenstone, Robert, *Visions of the Past: The Challenge of Film to our Idea of History* (London and Cambridge, MA: Harvard University Press, 1980).

Savage, Jon, *England's Dreaming: Sex Pistols and Punk Rock* (London: Faber and Faber, 1991).

—— *Time Travel: Pop, Media and Sexuality 1977–96* (London: Chatto and Windus, 1996).

Schatz, Thomas, *Hollywood Genres: Formulas, Filmmaking and the Studio System* (New York: Random House, 1981).

Shail, Robert, ed., *Seventies British Cinema* (London: Palgrave Macmillan, 2008).

Shanes, Eric, *Warhol: The Masterworks* (London: Studio Editions, 1991).

Shohat, Ella and Robert Stam, *Unthinking Eurocentrism: Multiculturalism and the Media* (London: Routledge, 1994).

Sinyard, Neil, *The Films of Richard Lester* (Beckenham: Croom Helm, 1985).

Smith, Justin, *Withnail and Us: Cult Films and Film Cults in British Cinema* (London: I.B. Tauris, 2010).

Sontag, Susan, *Under the Sign of Saturn* (London: Penguin, 2009).

Sorlin, Pierre, *The Film in History: Restaging the Past* (Oxford: Basil Blackwell, 1980).

Sterritt, David, *The Films of Jean-Luc Godard: Seeing the Invisible* (Cambridge University Press, 1999).

Taves, Brian, *The Romance of Adventure: The Genre of Historical Adventure Movies* (Jackson: Mississippi University Press, 1993).

Turim, Maureen, *Flashbacks in Film: Memory and History* (London: Routledge, 1989).

Vincendeau, Ginette, *The Companion to French Cinema* (London: British Film Institute, 1996).

Walker, Alexander, *Hollywood, England: The British Film Industry in the Sixties* (London: Michael Joseph, 1974).

—— *National Heroes: British Cinema in the Seventies and Eighties* (London: Harrap, 1985).

—— *Icons in the Fire: The Decline and Fall of Almost Everybody in the British Film Industry* (London: Orion, 2004).

Walker, John, *The Once and Future Film: British Cinema in the Seventies and Eighties* (London: Methuen, 1985).

Warshow, Robert, *The Immediate Experience: Movies, Comics, Theatre and Other Aspects of Popular Culture* (Cambridge, MA: Harvard University Press, 2002).

Wheen, Francis, *The Sixties* (London: Century/Channel 4, 1982).

Wilson, Harold, *Purpose in Politics: Selected Speeches of Harold Wilson* (London: Riverside, 1964).

Wright, Will, *Six Guns and Society: A Structural Study of the Western* (Berkeley: University of California Press, 1975).

Young, Nigel, *An Infantile Disorder? The Crisis and Decline of the New Left* (London: Routledge, 1977).

Filmography

Fiction film vehicles for British pop music stars

1957

Rock You Sinners – director Denis Kavanagh
These Dangerous Years [USA title: *Dangerous Youth*] – director Herbert Wilcox
The Tommy Steele Story [USA title: *Rock Around the World*] – director Gerard Bryant

1958

The Duke Wore Jeans – director Gerald Thomas.
The Golden Disc [USA title: *The In-Between Age*] – director Don Sharp
Six-Five Special [USA title: *Calling the Cats*] – director Alfred Shaughnessy

1959

Expresso Bongo – director Val Guest
The Heart of a Man – director Herbert Wilcox
Idle on Parade [USA title: *Idol on Parade*] – director John Gilling
The Lady is a Square – director Herbert Wilcox
Serious Charge [USA title: *A Touch of Hell*] – director Terence Young
Sweet Beat [USA title: *The Amorous Sex*] – director Ronnie Albert
Tommy the Toreador [USA title: *Tommy Toreador*] – director John Paddy Carstairs

1960

Beat Girl [USA title: *Wild for Kicks*] – director Edmond T. Gréville
Climb Up the Wall – director Michael Winner

1961

The Young Ones [USA title: *It's Wonderful to be Young*] – director Sidney J. Furie

1962

It's Trad, Dad! [USA title: *Ring-A-Ding Rhythm*] – director Dick Lester
Play It Cool – director Michael Winner

1963

It's All Happening [USA title: *The Dream Maker*] – director Don Sharp
It's All Over Town – director Douglas Hickox
Just for Fun – director Gordon Flemyng
Just for You [USA title: *Disk-O-Tek Holiday*] – director Douglas Hickox
Live It Up [USA title: *Sing and Swing*] – director Lance Comfort
Summer Holiday – director Peter Yates
What a Crazy World – director Michael Carreras

1964

A Hard Day's Night – director Richard Lester
Every Day's a Holiday [USA title: *Seaside Swingers*] – director James Hill
Ferry 'Cross the Mersey – director Jeremy Summers
Wonderful Life [USA title: *Swingers' Paradise*] – director Sidney J. Furie

1965

Be My Guest – director Lance Comfort
Catch Us If You Can [USA title: *Having a Wild Weekend*] – director John Boorman
Cuckoo Patrol – director Duncan Wood
Dateline Diamonds – director Jeremy Summers
Gonks Go Beat – director Robert Hartford-Davis
Help! – director Richard Lester
I've Gotta Horse [USA title: *Wonderful Day*] – director Kenneth Hume
Pop Gear [USA title: *Go Go Mania*] – director Frederic Goode
Three Hats for Lisa – director Sidney Hayers

1966

Blow Up – director Michelangelo Antonioni
Finders Keepers – director Sidney Hayers
The Ghost Goes Gear – director Hugh Gladwish

1967

Privilege – director Peter Watkins
To Sir, with Love – director James Clavell

1968

Mrs Brown, You've Got a Lovely Daughter – director Saul Swimmer
One Plus One/Sympathy for the Devil – director Jean-Luc Godard
Popdown – director Fred Marshall
Two a Penny – director James F. Collier
Yellow Submarine – director George Dunning

1970

Performance – directors Donald Cammell, Nicolas Roeg
Permissive – director Lindsay Shonteff

1971

Bread – director Stanley Long

1973

Take Me High – director David Askey
That'll Be the Day – director Claude Whatham

1974

Flame – director Richard Loncraine
Stardust – director Michael Apted

1975

Never Too Young to Rock – director Dennis Abey
Side by Side – director Bruce Beresford
Tommy – director Ken Russell

1976

The Song Remains the Same – directors Peter Clifton, Joe Massot

1978

Jubilee – director Derek Jarman

1979

The Music Machine – director Ian Sharp
Quadrophenia – director Franc Roddam
Radio On – director Chris Petit

1980

Babylon – director Franco Rosso
Breaking Glass – director Brian Gibson
The Great Rock'n'Roll Swindle – director Julien Temple
Rude Boy – directors Jack Hazan, David Mingay

1981

Take It or Leave It – director Dave Robinson

1982

Pink Floyd: The Wall – director Alan Parker

1984

Give My Regards to Broad Street – director Peter Webb

1986

Absolute Beginners – director Julien Temple

1987

It Couldn't Happen Here – director Jack Bond

1990

Buddy's Song – director Claude Whatham

1997

Spice World – director Bob Spiers

2003

Seeing Double [USA title: *S Club: Seeing Double*] – director Nigel Dick

2012

Ill Manors – director Ben Drew

Biopics of British pop music stars

1979: *Birth of the Beatles* – director Richard Marquand
1986: *Sid and Nancy* – director Alex Cox
1991: *The Hours and Times* – director Christopher Munch
1993: *Backbeat* – director Iain Softley
2002: *24 Hour Party People* – director Michael Winterbottom
2005: *Stoned* – director Stephen Woolley
2007: *Control* – director Anton Corbijn
2008: *Telstar* – director Nick Moran
2009: *Nowhere Boy* – director Sam Taylor-Wood
2010: *Sex & Drugs & Rock & Roll* – director Mat Whitecross

Index

244

Milton Keynes UK
Ingram Content Group UK Ltd.
UKHW020053191223
434640UK00004B/103